Olive Oil

by Amy Riolo and Simon Poole, MD

for dummies®
A Wiley Brand

Olive Oil For Dummies®

Published by: **John Wiley & Sons, Inc.**, 111 River Street, Hoboken, NJ 07030-5774,
www.wiley.com

For general information on our other products and services, please contact our Customer
Care Department within the U.S. at 877-762-2974, outside the U.S. at 317-572-3993, or
fax 317-572-4002. For technical support, please visit https://hub.wiley.com/community/
support/dummies.

Wiley publishes in a variety of print and electronic formats and by print-on-demand. Some
material included with standard print versions of this book may not be included in e-books
or in print-on-demand. If this book refers to media that is not included in the version you
purchased, you may download this material at http://booksupport.wiley.com. For more
information about Wiley products, visit www.wiley.com.

Library of Congress Control Number: 2024946944

ISBN 978-1-394-28286-9 (pbk); ISBN 978-1-394-28288-3 (ebk);
ISBN 978-1-394-28287-6 (ebk)
SKY10085863_092424

Recipes at a Glance

Second Courses

Desserts

Table of Contents

Introduction

O lives are the ingredient most commonly associated with
the Mediterranean diet — and that's for a good reason!
There are more than 950 million olive trees are in the
region, comprising the majority of the world's total. It is said
that 25 to 40 percent of the daily caloric intake of people in the
Mediterranean region has traditionally come from olive oil.

To us, olive oil is much more than a favorite culinary ingredient
to savor and promote, it's truly liquid gold — brimming with
tradition, history, lore, and nutrition. Olive oil is a common bond
that unites the people of the entire Mediterranean region not
only to each other, but also to the world at large. In addition to
being the fat of choice that we use to cook with, good-quality
extra-virgin olive oil is essential in our personal care and health
rituals as well. Our shared passion for the olive fruit has given
olive oil a starring role in both of our careers and led us to begin
working together years ago. We've both written on the topic
extensively in our previous works as well as our trilogy of diabetes books for the *For Dummies* series and are known as worldwide
experts on the topic. (Additionally, Simon is an international
authority, teacher, and medical consultant on olive oil; and Amy
has her own brand of private label olive oil and co-leads cuisine
and culture tours to olive-producing countries.)

Olive trees are an especially important form of cultural heritage
which ties us to the land, our ancestors, and future generations
while providing shade, beauty, industry, and good health. While
giving a joint presentation on the role of extra-virgin olive oil

and the Mediterranean Diet in preventing and treating diabetes, we laid the foundation for a professional partnership that would allow us to discuss not only a favorite topic, but also the keys to cooking and living with both pleasure and health in mind.

About This Book

People all over the world are beginning to value olive oil's unique and extraordinary place in the Mediterranean diet and embrace its exquisite flavors and powerful health benefits. According to data from the European Commission, the United States Department of Agriculture, and the International Olive Council, olive oil is one of the fastest growing global industries, and the United States is the second largest consumer in the world.

The key to getting the most from the juice of the fruit of this ancient tree is through understanding its past and learning about the extraordinary gifts of the most precious extra-virgin olive oils. Unfortunately, there are still a lot of myths and a shroud of mystery surrounding the consumption of olive oil and the industry at large. In *Olive Oil For Dummies*, we demystify recent clinical research about the nutritional properties of olive oil *and* clearly explain its ingredient-specific terminology as well as how to incorporate more of it into our daily meals and get the most nutritional value from it as possible.

Researchers are concluding that the most important and exciting health-giving constituents, found only in extra-virgin olive oil, are the unique and abundant antioxidant polyphenols of the olive fruit. These fascinating compounds, produced by the tree as defense in its challenging environment, also have profound protective effects on our health. In Chapter 6, we explore the story of polyphenols in depth, helping you to understand how to recognize and taste the power of polyphenols.

A few of the potential health benefits of consuming extra-virgin olive oil, as we explain in Part 2, include its association with:

>> Reducing the risk of heart attacks, strokes, diabetes, osteoporosis, rheumatoid arthritis; breast, colon, and

bowel cancer; and the incidence of melanoma, memory loss, and dementia in old age

>> Boosting the immune system against the negative effects of toxins, microorganisms, parasites, and other foreign substances

>> Increasing healthful gut bacteria and nutrient absorption in food

Nowadays, most people have a difficult time choosing which olive oil they should use. Complicated labelling terms, high prices, country of origin information, and lack of knowledge make it really difficult for consumers to make educated decisions. In Part 4, we discuss everything that you need to know to understand the labels, ensure proper packaging and storage, and make the best purchasing decisions for your health and wallet.

In *Olive Oil For Dummies*, you'll discover how to recreate crave-worthy olive oil–based dishes from morning to noon to night. Whether you're in the mood for breakfast, lunch, an appetizer, or a dessert, you'll enjoy delicious, time-honored tastes that are perfectly suited to the modern palate. Each of Amy's recipes offer pairings of delicious dishes with specific types of olive oil and wine. You'll also find wholesome and tasty base recipes that are rich in olive oil to elevate your daily cooking. With increasing amounts of great olive oils available around the world, it's the perfect time to share the tips that will enhance flavor, nutrition, and variety in our diets. We'll also show you how to properly taste and test olive oil to ensure quality, freshness, and flavor.

Ever wondered how quality olive oil is produced? We take you behind the scenes of the world's artisan producers so that you can learn classifications and definitions while appreciating the production process. *Olive Oil For Dummies* also demystifies how to decipher the appearance and taste of the most widely available types while explaining the importance of their *terroir* (the soil, environment, and climate where the olives are grown). Finally, you'll witness the life-affirming role that olive oil plays in the livelihood of its producers and native regions while being inspired to take full advantage of its bounty yourself.

Foolish Assumptions

This book assumes that you know nothing about olive oil, nutrition, and cooking with it, so you won't have to face a term that you've never heard of before and that isn't explained. For those who already know a lot about olive oil, you can find more in-depth explanations in this book as well. You can pick and choose how much you want to know about a subject, but the key points are clearly marked. You may also assume that it will never be an easy task to select the best olive oil, get the most value for your money, and cook all sorts of new recipes with it. Each chapter will help you to find everything that you need to know in order to enjoy olive oil, prepare better tasting food, and discover optimal health.

Icons Used in This Book

The icons alert you to information you must know, information you should know, and information you may find interesting but can live without.

REMEMBER

When you see this icon, it means the information is essential and you should be aware of it.

TIP

This icon marks important information that can save you time and energy.

FROM THE AUTHORS

We use this icon whenever we tell a story based on our personal experience.

FROM THE DOCTOR

This icon is used to help you with medical advice about the choices you have to optimize your treatment.

TECHNICAL
STUFF

This icon gives you technical information or terminology that may be helpful, but not necessary, to your understanding of the topic.

WARNING

This icon warns against potential problems (for example, things to avoid when buying, purchasing, storing, or cooking with extra-virgin olive oil).

Finally, a little tomato icon (🍅) is used to highlight vegetarian recipes in the Recipes in This Chapter lists, as well as in the Recipes at a Glance at the front of this book.

Beyond the Book

In addition to the content of this book, you can access some related material online. We've posted the Cheat Sheet at www. dummies.com. It contains important information that you may want to refer to on a regular basis. To find the Cheat Sheet, simply visit www.dummies.com and search for **Olive Oil For Dummies cheat sheet**.

Where to Go from Here

Where you go from here depends on your level of interest and passion. Personally speaking, we never tire of learning more about olive oil. If you already have basic knowledge of olive oil and want to know more about labeling regulations, go to Chapter 13. If you're a novice, start at Chapter 1. If you want to know more about how to cook with extra-virgin olive oil, go to Chapters 17 through 22. Chapter 14 helps you determine how to get the most value for your money. You may have specific interests at different times, so check the Table of Contents to find what you need rapidly.

REMEMBER

The wonderful world of olive oil is steeped in history, tradition, and lore as well as science, modern industry, and technology trends. Go at your own pace and enjoy the process. Remember that like extra-virgin olive oil, learning new information also helps to keep us healthy.

1

Introduction to Olive Oil

Chapter **1**

Exploring the Story of Olive Oil

To understand what the olive tree and olive oil means to people who have grown up in its shade, it's important to know how the tree and its fruit have shaped the lives and cultural heritage of their ancestors. The olive tree is deeply rooted in the landscape and the traditions of the Mediterranean regions where it has flourished for millennia, and its history is deeply intertwined with the development of human civilization.

Throughout history, olive oil as a culinary ingredient was of great importance in cooking, and its health benefits were very much valued. In addition to olive oil, other olive products are also found in the entire region. Olives, olive wood, and olive pomace are used to make everything from food and furniture to fuel and soap.

This chapter journeys across time and continents to explore the history and significance of olive oil. It explains how olive oil has been used in food, medicine, and culture historically and in modern times.

Defining the Olive Tree throughout its History

The history of the relationship between humankind and the olive tree stretches back many millennia. There is archaeological evidence suggesting that people in the countries of the Eastern Mediterranean consumed olives in neolithic times, as well as using the wood for fire. It's likely that curing or fermenting techniques to reduce the natural bitterness of olives would have been known to communities during this time. Though these processes would be refined and improved particularly in the Roman period, the use of wood ash with brine to cure the fruit to make them more palatable was widespread. By the fourth millennium BCE, there is evidence to show the systematic harvesting and crushing of olives for oil. And by the Bronze Age, this was a well-established technique to produce oil for food, cosmetics, and lamp fuel.

From wilderness to farm

When humans started to farm rather than moving to hunt and gather food about 10,000 years ago, the wild olive tree, probably originating from Persia and Mesopotamia, was among the earliest plant species to be domesticated and planted in the so-called *fertile crescent*. The fertile crescent included lands that now span from Iran and Iraq to Syria, Jordan, Lebanon, Israel, and Palestine. Archeologists have found olive pits suggesting that that the olive trees in those areas were first domesticated 8,000 years ago. Selective breeding ensured that the hardiest and most productive trees — *Olea europaea* — survived. Known as the common olive, it's a variety of an evergreen tree native to the Mediterranean region that is still growing today with its various subspecies and regional varieties.

Farming also allowed people to experiment with new agricultural techniques and improve milling to get the most oil from the olives. Olive presses were larger and became valued and protected resources near to the communities they served. Stone wheels often moved in circles by harnessed donkeys or mules became the most efficient way of crushing the olives ahead of "pressing" them and separating juice (or oil) from the flesh, pit, and skin. Evidence of this method being used dates from 6,000 years ago and widely practiced until the early part of the last century. (An ancient press is shown in Figure 1-1.) Traditionally, each community had its own mill. Locals brought their recently harvested olives to their local mills for pressing. For this reason, there is a deep desire among people in the Mediterranean region to use "their own oil," even today. People who live in olive-producing areas have long-lasting ties with a local, "trustworthy" mill. They bring their olives to that mill — often watching the oil being extracted — and later with their families enjoy the oil throughout the year. This way they ensure the best quality, flavors of choice, and freshest oil possible.

FIGURE 1-1:
An ancient press in Volubilis, Morocco.

TIP

There are some olive oils that are still produced using ancient milling techniques. This can produce some good quality oils, but greater care needs to be taken to ensure that it is not spoiled. When visiting olive oil — producing countries, it can be a fun and informative experience to visit both modern and ancient mills. Modern methods of milling are generally much more efficient, protecting and preserving the flavor and health benefits of extra-virgin olive oil. This is discussed in greater detail in Chapter 3.

Olive trees can live for hundreds, and sometimes thousands of years. In each Mediterranean culture, the ancient trees are viewed with more prestige and importance. There are names in each language specifically dedicated to the trees that are hundreds of years and thousands of years old. Oil that comes from those trees is extremely valuable culturally and commands higher prices when sold. In Italy, for example, *secolari* is the term used to describe trees that are hundreds of years old and *millenari* is the word used to describe trees that are thousands of years old. Olive trees are extraordinarily resilient, having adapted to thrive in harsh environments and can produce new shoots even after devastating droughts or fires. It's extraordinary to think that some trees are so ancient that they date back perhaps three thousand years. Their gnarled massive, beautiful forms are imposing and often are a symbol to local people of their own history and survival.

From ship to shore

In the late Bronze Age, from around 1200 BCE, Phoenician sailors and traders from what is now Lebanon established colonies and trading posts throughout the Mediterranean to North Africa, Sicily, and the Iberian Peninsula. Historians believe they played an important role in expanding olive cultivation and milling across the Mediterranean. Archeologists often find evidence of olive oil production and typical storage jars called *amphorae* at sites and in cities that were founded by these masterful merchants and explorers. One of the recipes found in the jars was the now trendy aioli sauce, which Chef Amy teaches you how to make in Chapter 17.

Although they aren't talked about very often on a daily basis, the Phoenicians' legacy in spreading the olive tree and its cultivation practices is a testament to their role as key players in the agricultural and economic history of the Mediterranean. Many of the similarities in Mediterranean cuisine are a result of their commercial efforts.

Shaping ancient empires

In cultures such as Ancient Persia, Egypt, Greece, and Magna Grecia in the fourth millennium BCE, olive oil played a vital role as a food and important source of nutrition. It was fundamental to the economy of the expanding empire and was not only a cornerstone of everyday life but also had profound religious and symbolic meaning.

Ancient Egypt

By the fourth millennium BCE, the ancient Egyptians were using olive oil not only for culinary purposes, but also for cosmetics and perfumes. Since perfume making was so important to Mediterranean trade at that time, the role of olive oil in its production made olives an even more significant crop, surpassing even the grape in importance. According to the Egyptians it was the goddess Isis, sister and wife of Osiris, who taught humans how to grow olive trees and extract their oil. The ancient Egyptians cultivated many olive orchards. An inscription on a temple dedicated to the god Ra dating from the twelfth century BCE during the rule of Ramses II describes the olive orchards around the city of Heliopolis producing pure oil, the best quality in all of Egypt, for lighting the lamps in sacred places.

Ancient Greece

During this time, the olive became a more important crop than the grape. Mycenaean tablets mentioning olive trees dating 3,500 years ago were found on the Greek island of Crete along with amphoras at the Palace of Knossos. An example of a Greek amphora is shown in Figure 1-2.

FIGURE 1-2: An Ancient Greek amphora depicting olive harvesting.

© CPA Media Pte Ltd/Alamy Stock Photo

In the traditional diet of Crete, where scientists first described the Mediterranean diet, it is said that 70 percent of total fat consumption comes from olive oil. Mediterranean cuisine "swims" in olive oil. The culinary term *lathera*, translated as "the ones with oil," is a traditional Greek cooking method and category of dishes. The dishes are integral to the Mediterranean diet and particularly the Cretan diet, being rich in olive oil, often with tomatoes, onions, beans, other vegetables, various herbs and spices, and bread for soaking up the oil. The olive oil not only serves as the cooking medium but also adds significant flavor and nutritional value to the dishes.

Athens was the birthplace for Greek olive oil. Olive tree depictions also decorated the walls of ancient Egyptian and Greek palaces. Olive oil during this time was used as fuel for lamps, to clean and moisturize the body, as well as for a balsam for wounds and in perfumes. Aristotle himself promoted the divine powers of olive oil, using it to anoint himself before he met with his disciples, believing that it would give him increased knowledge and confidence during debates. In Athens, the revered goddess Athena gave the founders of the city the fruit and oil of the olive tree to nourish and sustain them (see Figure 1-3), leading to the creation of an empire as well as the naming of the city.

Ever since, the olive tree was central to the genesis mythology of Athens and also featured large in other legends and tales. In 480 BCE following the battle of Salamis, the general Themistocles recaptured the Acropolis, which had been burned to the ground by the invading Persian army. A sacred tree atop the hill was said to have immediately grown healthy, fresh buds from its charred remains that represented fresh hope and the promise of a bright future to those who rebuilt the city. To the Greek poet Homer, olive oil was nothing less than "liquid gold."

After thousands of years of promotion by philosophers, gods, goddesses, and demigods alike, olive oil continued to be highly valued and prized throughout the Mediterranean and Asia Minor. In its purest form, it was used as a medicine and food. It also provided health and cleansing of the skin, including bathing rituals of athletes, and could be used as oil for handheld clay lamps, a lubricant and even a base for paints. It was offered to the gods and was central to many religious ceremonies. Victorious Olympic athletes would be adorned with olive leaf wreaths and perhaps even more welcome was the prize of

14   PART 1 Introduction to Olive Oil

quantities of olive oil worth a small fortune. Olive groves were a common sight in the Greek countryside, and laws were even enacted to protect these valuable trees. The olive branch remains a symbol of peace and prosperity, a legacy that can be traced back to its revered status in ancient Greece. It is extraordinary to think that the oldest living olive tree in Crete is estimated to predate the first ancient games.

FIGURE 1-3: Amy with "the sacred trees of Athena," Acropolis, Athens.

Physicians and philosophers, including the "father of medicine" Hippocrates, knew of the contribution of olive oil to good nutrition and health, referring to it as "the great healer," and it was regularly included in recipes and medicines used to cure ailments. Olive oil was also considered to sooth the spirit and calm the mind as well as treat earaches, hemorrhoids, and sunburn; reverse baldness; alleviate the bites of mythical or real sea creatures; and ward off evil spirits.

Aristotle contemporary and philosopher Theophrastus, born in Lesbos, was the first Greek author to write a treatise on the

"Maintenance of One's Body" and in particular on the use of ointments and perfumes. He was the first to coin the term "botany" and understood it as a science that studies plants and their healing power. According to Theophrastus, the *unguentum*, an ancient Latin word for perfumed ointment, must be composed as follows: a fatty base of animal origin and one of vegetal origin (olive oil); the resin as a fixative; salts; and essences extracted from flower petals with the so-called "Enfleurage."

Modern medicinal uses of olive oil are considered in Chapter 7.

The Roman Empire

The Ancient Greeks were efficient at producing and using olive oil, but the Romans took it to the next level by increasing production and expanding its use to a much wider area. Feeding the vast empire relied on sophisticated logistics of production and transportation of important staples like grain, wine, and olive oil. In fact, those three items became the pantry staples of what would later become known as the Mediterranean diet. By combining freshly harvested local produce and dairy with grains, wine, and olive oil, the ancients laid the foundation for the world's healthiest eating plan.

Following Julius Caesar's return to Rome after defeating his enemies in modern-day Tunisia, the Greek philosopher Plutarch observed that Caesar's first reaction was to make a speech to the people in order to impress them with his victory. Caesar claimed that he had conquered a country large enough to supply the public every year with 200,000 Attic bushels (an old measurement) of grain and three million pounds of olive oil. Olive oil production on a large scale could generate great wealth and political leverage in Roman times. There were significant advances in the technology of oil production with the emergence of screw presses, the mechanism of which increased pressure and improved yield.

During the latter half of the first century CE, Pedanius Dioscorides, a military physician under the Roman Emperor Nero, known as the "father of pharmacognosy," (the study of medicines from natural sources), advocated the use of the early harvest, bitterest, "greenest" olive oil for conditions that may have had an inflammatory basis. This ancient doctor did not apply modern medical methods to prove his beliefs, but it can be observed that his oil was likely to be richest in anti-inflammatory compounds, which is discussed in detail on Chapter 6.

The Romans were experts in agriculture and the writer Pliny the Elder in his book *Natural History* described the way in which olives should be grown and even categorized olive oil according to quality in a classification, which is quite similar to modern chemical and sensory grading. Coincidentally, the oldest preserved olive oil in the world, now in a museum on Naples, was discovered close to where the author met his death in the devastating eruption of Vesuvius at Pompeii in 79 CE.

At the time, the city of Naples was heavily influenced by Greek culture. Nero used to recite in Greek, not Latin, in Rome's amphitheaters, and writers of the time dubbed it as a city in which "one could live and die in the manner of the Greeks."

Religious and culinary influences

In the Mediterranean, the ancient traditions of using olive oil as a healthy food continued alongside the symbolic and cultural importance of the olive tree in religion and culture. Olive oil and the olive tree had an important place in ceremonies and mythology, including giving the strength to Hercules, not least in his fearsome club of olive wood. The olive leaf and branch continued to have symbolic meaning, including signifying peace and hope.

The topic of the historical religious appreciation of olive oil deserves a book of its own, as olive oil has a revered position in three monotheistic faiths — Christianity, Judaism, and Islam — as well as in ancient worshipping traditions. The Bible refers to the olive tree as "the key of trees" and the "tree of life." It is mentioned on numerous occasions in the Qur'an and the Bible. From an olive branch brought by a dove as a sign of peace to Noah in the Old Testament, to events on the Mount of Olives in the New Testament, and the description of the olive representing the gifts of variety and abundance in the Qur'an, the olive tree has a special and sacred status to many people of faith.

The reason why olive branches were used as symbols of peace in the Mediterranean since antiquity is because it took 20 years for them to bear fruit. Olive trees weren't planted in areas where people couldn't establish long-term settlements (meaning areas of conflict). For this reason, olive trees became associated with peace from a practical sense as well as a spiritual one. Hanukah commemorates the miracle of one day's worth of olive oil lasting eight nights as recorded in the Talmud. Christians use olive oil to consecrate crowned rulers and church dignitaries. According to Islamic tradition, the Prophet Muhammad is said to have proclaimed, "Take oil of olive and massage with it. It is a blessed tree." In antiquity, olive oil was coveted as an ointment, fragrance, and an essential element of religious ceremonies in addition to its flavor and nutritional uses.

PROTECTING A CENTRAL MILL BEHIND STONEWALLS

The value of olive oil in antiquity can't be overstated. A few years ago, a local farmer in a remote part of Jordan was expanding his olive grove on a high plateau when he came across stonework, which was obviously of great historical importance. Archeologists from the capital Amman, in partnership with the British Museum, soon established this site to be a significant, heavily defended and protected structure dating back to the Bronze Age — 4,500 years ago. This seemed odd because it was known that at that point in history, raids by the Egyptians had decimated large settlements in the area, the result of which was "urban collapse" and the retreat of populations to rural areas.

Living in smaller, scattered locations reduced the likelihood of attack, so there was less need to build thick walls for defense. The walls here seemed to be different, and as the soil was carefully removed, it became apparent that this was an ancient olive press for the area. No doubt, bringing large quantities of harvested olives over the space of a few weeks to a central mill for the production of valuable olive oil made it a very real target for attack. It's easy to imagine people in those ancient times bringing their precious fruit to a place of safety for the production of olive oil, reassured as they made their way up the hill past heavily armed guards and the solid walls of the olive mill.

Northern and Central European writers and artists began documenting olive trees in their famous works during the nineteenth and twentieth centuries. Featured in the poetry of Wilde and Yeats and the paintings of leading artists, the allure of olive trees could not be ignored. Vincent van Gogh, the Dutch post-impressionist painter, held a deep fascination and reverence for olive trees, for whom they held a sense of history and awe (see Figure 1-4). He struggled to capture their intricateness and beauty, especially the shimmering silver of the underside of the leaf.

FIGURE 1-4:
Olive groves painting by Vincent van Gogh.

© dbrnjhrj/Adobe Stock

Much of what we know about olive oil and the deepening of its usage is due to the many Muslim Caliphates and empires that ruled in the Mediterranean.

There are many surviving Medieval Arabic culinary texts that provide a wealth of knowledge into this much overlooked area of Mediterranean culinary history by the West. During the Medieval period it is the reign of the Abbasid Caliphate, which set trends from Baghdad to modern Spain. In fact, the palace meals were so lavish during the time that the Muslim prince Abd al-Rahman hired his chief cook and trendsetter, nicknamed Ziryab, to bring his knowledge and insights to the courts of Andalusia in the ninth century CE. Thanks to Ziryab, whose real name was Abu al-Hasan, Andalusia gained music (he was credited for inventing the lute), fashion styles, rich garden architecture, numerous elevated recipes, and "new" ingredients such as rice, saffron, spices, and hibiscus procured from Egypt.

When combined with the olives and olive oil tradition already deeply rooted in Spain thanks to the Romans, Medieval Spanish and practices introduced from Iraq, as well as the cuisine of the lands under their empire, gained many layers of flavor and intricacy. Marinated olives in herbs were served on the table of Ibrāhīm ibn al-Mahdī, an eighth century CE Abbasid prince, singer, composer and poet, just as they are served across the Mediterranean today. The Abassid caliphate based much of their cuisine on the Persian tradition. Vegetables sautéed in olive oil and then finished off with vinegar were very popular at the time. The Bedouin method of roasting lamb in olive oil also continued to flourish. Simple recipes for items such as bulgur with lentils, garlic sauce, chicken with olives, and meat and stuffed olive stew used at least ¼ cup of olive oil for a recipe that serves four. Original Moroccan recipes for tajines with vegetables such as cardoons (similar flavor to artichokes) were created to test the quality of the new olive harvest.

In the tenth century, for example when Fatimid rulers from modern-day Tunisia ruled from Sicily and Tunisia and as far East as Mecca, they used to promote cross-cultural religious festivities. They would encourage people of all faiths to come out and partake in the merrymaking of religious festivities of their neighbors. Because of the multi-religious populations of the Mediterranean region, which were ruled by different groups, cooking with olive oil continued to be a way in which to create cuisine that could be enjoyed by all. During Orthodox fasting periods, for example, animal fat is prohibited and meals that were once cooked with meat or animal fat were now replaced with olive oil. The Jewish community also embraced these dishes because they were meat-free options, ensuring that no non-kosher animal products were part of the dishes.

Court rulers who held dinners for large multi-national organizations needed to ensure that all of their guests could partake in the lavish foods that they were serving, despite their religious origins. By the end of the Ottoman Empire (fifteenth through nineteenth centuries CE) an entire category of olive oil–based dishes called *Zeytinyağlı* emerged and is still popular in modern Turkiye today. In fact, internationally acclaimed chef, humanitarian, and restaurateur José Andrés named one of his restaurant concepts Zaytinia in Washington, DC, after it.

The most popular of these olive oil–laden dishes that graced the tables of Ottoman palaces included artichokes and string beans braised in olive oil. While the ingredients are few, it is the manner of cooking the vegetables that makes them "sing." And modern Turkish cooks follow strict guidelines in order to make the recipes live up to their legacy. Sometimes rice and tomatoes are added to the dishes, and they are usually served at room temperature. Garnished with dill or parsley, these recipes are still a testament to Medieval cooking and the capacity for food to be both delicious and nutritious. Vegetables, legumes, grains, cheese, and extra-virgin olive oil continued to nourish and entice palates and feed the masses in the Mediterranean during the Middle Ages as in ancient times.

Recognizing the New World of Olive Oil

With the "discovery" of the Americas by ships launched from Spain and Portugal came a new chapter in the expansion of the olive tree. Those who love the olive tree and olive oil and who inhabit parts of the world with a climate similar to the Mediterranean have for centuries experimented with growing and harvesting its fruit in new regions. In general, this hardy tree can survive and flourish where summers are hot and dry, with mild and often wet winters. Although there will always be localized variations in climate, these conditions are often found between 30- and 45-degree latitudes both north and south of the equator as shown in Figure 1-5.

Groves going west

In the sixteenth century the great powers of Spain and Portugal began to explore and colonize the Americas. Early settlers in Argentina, Chile and Peru found the climate in the Southern

Hemisphere conducive to agriculture they were familiar with at home and brought with them vines for wine cultivation and olive trees for olives and olive oil. The first olive cuttings were brought to California in the late eighteenth century by Franciscan missionaries. More recently, olive oil production has expanded to other regions including Florida and Texas in the United States, and countries like Uruguay, Brazil, and Mexico in Central and South America.

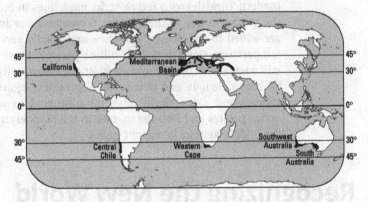

Thomas Jefferson, the third President of the United States, encountered olive oil during his time as a diplomat in Southern France and considered the olive tree to be "surely the greatest gift of heaven." He was also an advocate of excellence in nutrition. Unfortunately, the climate thwarted his attempts to establish a working olive grove at his Monticello estate in Virginia.

Nowadays the California olive oil industry has emerged as a major player in the global marketplace. Olive oil is one of the most important of the state's 350 agricultural products. According to the California Olive Council, the modern industry includes 75 different varieties of olives. Known for having a great variety, creative blends, and tasty flavor profiles, the unique *terroir* (soil, environment, and climate) of Californian olive oils distinguishes them from oils made of the same varieties in other places. Despite the large amount of olive oil that California produces, American demand is still far greater than the supply, making it necessary to import olive oil from the Mediterranean region and from other areas of the world.

Expansion into Asia and beyond

The expansion from traditional growing areas in the Mediterranean to South and East Asia is a more recent phenomenon, mainly occurring in the twentieth and twenty-first centuries.

India has seen experimental and commercial planting of olive trees, especially in the states of Rajasthan and Gujarat. The initiative, often supported by collaboration with experts from established areas of production, aims to tap into the growing domestic demand for olive oil in India and explore export possibilities. China has also embraced olive cultivation, with regions like Sichuan province becoming centers for olive production.

The Japanese consume more olive oil per person than other Asian countries. This is mainly imported. However, there is some local production which began in 1908 on the island of Shodoshima in the Seto Inland Sea, which enjoys a moderate climate that allows olive cultivation.

Regions with a climate similar to the Mediterranean are often suitable for wine production, and so it is no coincidence that the cultivation of vines and olive trees often goes hand in hand. Australia and New Zealand, with vast areas of land potentially available, are now not only famous for large scale production of wines, but also production of high-quality olive oil. Olive oil production on this scale has been introduced relatively recently in comparison to winemaking, but the 1990s saw significant planting and investment in large scale facilities for olive oil production.

Olive oil in Africa

Countries on the North Coast of Africa bordering the Mediterranean Sea, including Tunisia, Algeria, Morocco and Libya were central to the early story of olive oil cultivation and production and its story is included in our narrative above.

In the Southern Hemisphere, African olive oil production is a more recent development.

The first recorded attempt at olive oil production in South Africa dates back to the sixteenth century, when Jan van Riebeeck, commander and founder of Cape Town, in 1655 attempted to produce foods that would sustain Dutch trading ships sailing around the Cape of Good Hope to the Dutch East Indies. However, it wasn't until much later, in the nineteenth century, that olive cultivation became more established in South Africa, with several farms in the Paarl and Stellenbosch regions planting olive trees, resulting in the wine and olive route journeys possible today (see Figure 1-6).

FIGURE 1-6: An olive grove in the Cape area of South Africa.

Chapter **2**

Understanding Olive Oil Classifications

D etermining quality olive oil is one of the most difficult tasks for consumers. One of the first questions people usually ask about olive oil is the difference between olive oil and extra-virgin olive oil. This chapter will help you understand the distinctions between the categories of olive oil and to appreciate the difference this makes to the taste and health benefits. The criteria for each category are explored in this chapter, with more details on testing and regulation in Chapter 4.

It is not known when the term *virgin* was first used to describe olive oil, but it refers to an uncontaminated and unadulterated quality, with *extra virgin* suggesting even more purity. Other standards are applied in certain growing regions to denote the origin of an olive oil or its organic credentials, which may not directly affect the taste of an oil. However, the standards may reflect a commitment to authenticity and responsible farming practices.

Other than *aged balsamic vinegar of Modena* (the highest grade of balsamic vinegar), extra-virgin olive oil is perhaps one of the longest terms to describe a single food. For reason of convenience, it is often referred to as *EVOO*.

Recognizing the classifications of olive oil

In any supermarket or delicatessen, you are likely to see rows with several different bottles of olive oils. There may be lots of information on the label, the details of which are considered in more detail in Chapter 12. The largest letters will usually tell you that the product is "olive oil" or "extra-virgin olive oil." Most producers aim for the higher standard of extra-virgin oil, which means "virgin olive oil" is less commonly produced. It turns out that there is a very big difference between these terms when it comes to what is in the bottle.

Olive oil categories

The classifications of olive oil are a formal series of definitions, which have been globally established by the International Olive Council (IOC) and by the Codex Alimentarius. The IOC is responsible for promoting olive oil industries worldwide, and its membership consists of major olive-producing countries.

It sets standards for quality, facilitates international trade, and ensures the authenticity of olive products. The Codex Alimentarius, or "Food Code," is a collection of international food standards, guidelines, and codes of practice adopted by the Codex Alimentarius Commission (CAC). The CAC is the central part of the "Joint FAO/WHO Food Standards Programme" — established by the Food and Agriculture Organization of the United Nations (FAO) and World Health Organization (WHO) — to protect consumer health and promote fair practices in food trade.

Each of the categories are different due to their production methods, which are explored in more detail in Chapter 3. But the most important criteria relate to chemistry and flavor, the latter of which is known as its sensory or *organoleptic* profile (appearance, flavor, mouthfeel, or aroma). The categories for olive oil are the following:

>> **Extra-virgin olive oil (EVOO):** Extra-virgin olive oil is the oil obtained from the fruit of the olive tree solely by mechanical or other physical means under specific conditions — particularly temperature conditions — that do not lead to alterations in the oil. The olive oil doesn't undergo any treatment other than washing, crushing, *malaxing* (kneading and mixing the olives), centrifugation, decantation, and/or filtration. Among other analytical requirements, extra-virgin olive oil must have an acidity level of no more than 0.8 percent and no *organoleptic* defects (detected through taste or smell). People in the Mediterranean region prefer high-quality olive oils, containing much lower levels of acidity at 0.3 percent or less, for themselves and their families to consume.

>> **Virgin olive oil (VOO):** Similar to extra-virgin olive oil, virgin olive oil is produced by mechanical means without the use of heat or chemicals. However, it has a slightly higher tolerance for many analytical requirements including an acidity level, up to 2 percent, and may not meet the same sensory standards as extra-virgin olive oil.

>> **Olive oil (OO):** Sometimes described as "extra light" or "pure" olive oil, this product is often available in many shops at a cheaper price than extra-virgin olive oil. It combines the relatively cheap and more available low-quality refined olive oil (described in the next paragraph) with a small percentage of extra-virgin or virgin olive oil. In practice, the content of extra-virgin or virgin olive oil in these blends may range from 1 to 20 percent, but this is highly variable and not often disclosed on product labels. Manufacturers may adjust the blend based on the availability and cost of extra-virgin olive oil or virgin olive oil and the desired characteristics of the final product. There is no sound analytical method to determine this percentage, leaving a grey area for producers and consumers.

>> **Refined olive oil:** When oil is produced at an olive mill and it is not of sufficient quality to be sold as an extra-virgin or virgin olive oil, it can be taken away for "refining." This is an

industrial process involving chemical operations and high temperature procedures that remove much of the defective oil's flavor and aroma. At the same time, the process reduces the acidity and destroys almost all the naturally occurring antioxidant polyphenols.

The result is an odorless and colorless fat that has lost many or all of the other naturally occurring compounds, which are crucially important in the health benefits of extra-virgin olive oil. The low acidity oil has no taste defect. However, this is no longer of relevance because once the oil has undergone the refining process, it cannot by definition be considered virgin or extra virgin but can be sold as olive oil.

>> **Olive pomace oil:** This oil is produced from the pulpy, solid residue left after the mechanical extraction of olive oil from olives. Solvents and heat are used to extract the last remaining oil from the olive pomace. This type of oil is further refined and may be blended with virgin olive oils for flavor for use in commercial kitchens or industrial food production. If not fit for consumption, any remaining oil can be used for soap or other products.

>> **Lampante olive oil:** This olive oil fails to meet the standards of virgin olive oils. They are not fit for human consumption and are likely to have acidity levels of greater than 2 percent and/or fail other analytical requirements as well as having stronger organoleptic defects. The word *lampante* is from a time before electricity when this oil was not considered good enough to eat, but could be used as fuel for lamps. Lampante oil cannot be consumed without further processing (or the refining process).

Manufacturers may describe their olive oils using different terms that are not part of the official IOC classification, and therefore can be meaningless or even potentially misleading. For example, "light or extra-light olive oil" is a description that is not part of any regulation system. It may imply that the oil is lower in calories, but its real meaning is usually that it is light in flavor. This oil is a refined olive oil and will contain a very low percentage (if any) of extra-virgin olive oil or virgin olive oil to achieve the light (or extra light) color and flavor.

The title of this book may be *Olive Oil For Dummies,* but the health and flavor qualities of olive oil are mostly found in extra-virgin olive oil. We recommend enjoying extra-virgin olive every day and for all the recipes and other uses described in this book.

Classification standards

The classification standards of olive oil are based on chemical and sensory (flavor) analysis. It is possible for an olive oil to pass one part of the standard and not the other, but this is unusual because the chemistry and sensory go hand in hand as measures of quality.

Chemistry of olive oil

The chemical classification of oils is not only defined by the acidity, but also by other measurements that indicate the quality and authenticity of an extra-virgin olive oil.

Olive oil largely consists of chains of carbon, hydrogen, and oxygen atoms called *fatty acids.* Three fatty acids are held together by a smaller molecule called *glycerol,* which creates a stable compound called a *triglyceride,* into which the fatty acids are bound. The atoms of the fatty acids are held together by chemical links or bonds; there may be single bonds or double bonds between atoms in a fatty acid, normally called "fat." The arrangements of single and double bonds determine whether a fatty acid is a saturated or unsaturated fat. If the oil has degraded because of damage to the olives or through poor processing or storage conditions, the triglycerides will break down and each of the three fatty acids will separate and become *free fatty acids* (or FFAs).

The *acidity level* of an olive oil is a measurement of the proportion of FFAs and not, as you may expect, a measure of pH levels or the "sourness" or acidic taste that may usually be associated with the acidity. A lower level of acidity in an extra-virgin olive oil is therefore a marker of better initial quality and is used in the categorization of olive oils, but it's not something that can be tasted.

Over time, oils will react with the oxygen naturally present in the air in a process that can be accelerated by light and/or heat, leading to their oxidative degradation or rancidity.

Oxygen is a very reactive atom. and will typically break down the fatty acid chain at its double bonds. The oxidation of olive oil isn't measured by its acidity. Other chemical tests are used instead, which are described in Chapter 4. While humans need oxygen to breathe, oxygen in the atmosphere of our beautiful and energetic world causes metal to rust and the exposed flesh of an apple to change color and taste. And oxygen can react with oil to degrade and break down its healthy fats and other elements, leading the oil to develop oxidation defects and becoming rancid.

Fortunately, there are naturally occurring compounds produced by the tree called *polyphenols* that are transferred to the extra-virgin olive oil during the milling process that prevent oxidation. These antioxidant compounds not only preserve the olive and the oil, but also have a profound effect on human health and are discussed in detail in Chapter 6. They can be measured directly but are not included in the classification of extra-virgin olive oils.

Flavor of olive oil

The sensory classification of oils is particularly important when it comes to classifying an olive oil as extra virgin. Extra-virgin olive oil rightly commands a high price and is valued for its significant health properties. To qualify for extra virgin status, an oil must fulfill certain criteria set out by the IOC or Codex and regulated and enforced by regional governments.

First, the olive oil must have *no* defects, which indicates rancidity or other problems. Terms like "musty" or "fusty," "metallic," and "winey," are used to describe different ways in which damage can be tasted by a trained assessor. These terms are explored in more detail in Chapter 4. There must also be degrees of positive features, including fruitiness, bitterness, and pungency (sometimes described as spiciness or pepperiness).

FROM THE AUTHORS

When Simon talks about olive oil to students at sommelier courses in the United Kingdom, some students will suggest that bitterness and pungency seem unattractive as flavors. But after a long day in the classroom, students who eat a meal at an Asian restaurant called the "Spice Palace" and have a pint of bitter beer will change their opinions. Coffee, teas, dark chocolate, herbs, spices and many vegetables have pleasant bitter and pungent flavors that anyone can enjoy and celebrate.

Some of the most beneficial foods for our bodies contain a bitter taste, so acquiring a palate for them is good for us. Infants are dependent on their sweet mothers' milk and can develop a very deep love for sweet tastes at an early age. Bitter foods, however, take some time to appreciate. It is the polyphenols that are so important for health, which contribute to the bitterness and pungency of an extra-virgin olive oil and many green lettuces and herbs as well. You can, quite literally, taste the health in extra-virgin olive oil and in the greens. This is discussed in much more detail in Chapter 6.

And while extra-virgin olive oil is prized for its complex aroma and flavor profile, there's so much more to tasting extra-virgin olive oil than the presence of fruitiness, bitterness, and pungency. The flavor profiles of different olive oils are explored in Chapter 9.

Defining Other Olive Oil Standards

The IOC and Codex classifications form the basis of international quality standards in olive oil, but different regions, countries, and organizations can impose other criteria as well.

For example, the European Union has established laws around the description and labeling of olive oil, including the wording of health claims. The United Kingdom often applies the same rules. In the United States, the Department of Agriculture (USDA) established its own voluntary grading standards for olive oil produced in the country, including extra-virgin olive oil and virgin olive oil.

TIP

Olive oil producers that pass voluntary standards set by regional organizations often have a seal or mark of compliance added to their bottles to show consumers that more stringent standards have been met.

Australia

In 2011, the Australian government, with the support of the Australian Olive Association, introduced a revolutionary voluntary standard, which is largely observed by producers and retailers in Australia. The standards have strict criteria for what constitutes extra-virgin olive oil, incorporating the traditional analytical parameters present in the IOC or Codex standards with additional tests to measure the "freshness" of the extra-virgin olive oils. This more rigorous standard constituted the base of the standard later developed by the Olive Oil Commission of California.

NAOOA

The North American Olive Oil Association (NAOOA) conducts an olive oil testing and certification program for imported olive oils into the United States. Olive oils are tested for adherence to the physico-chemical standards set by the International Olive Council (IOC) for both purity and quality. The seal is shown in Figure 2-1. A list of the companies that bear the seal can be found on their website: www.naooa.org.

FIGURE 2-1: The NAOOA quality seal.

Courtesy of NAOOA

OOCC

The Olive Oil Commission of California (OOCC) is a government entity of the State of California that supports California olive farmers by: developing and enforcing standards for the purity and quality of California olive oil; verifying California olive oil quality through mandatory government sampling and third-party analysis; promoting simple, clear accurate labels for California olive oil; and conducting research to assist farmers in successfully growing a healthy, sustainable crop.

The OOCC was established and is funded by California olive oil farmers and millers. Producers processing olives into 5,000 gallons of olive oil or more are required by law to participate in the OOCC's mandatory government sampling and testing program. Producers with less than 5,000 gallons may voluntarily participate in the OOCC's government sampling program.

The California Extra-Virgin Olive Oil Standard required under the California Department of Food and Agriculture establishes more stringent parameters for quality tests if compared with IOC or Codex standards. The California Extra-Virgin Olive Oil Standard also includes all the tests and parameters for olive oil purity found in the California Health and Safety Code.

PDO/DOP

The letters "PDO" stand for Protected Designation of Origin. In Italy, this is also known as "DOP," which derives from *Denominazione di Origine Protetta*. It is a European initiative that includes many foods, such as olive oil. These foods should have features, qualities, reputation, and/or characteristics that are essentially attributable to the geographical environment in which they are produced.

In order to bear the mark shown in Figure 2-2, an olive oil may have to be of a typical variety and perhaps from a special *terroir* (the soil, environment, and climate). The process of applying for an olive oil region to have PDO status is rigorous and requires European Union recognition. Producers are required to meet strict government regulations in order to bear the symbol of the PDO/DOP.

The PDO/DOP label on an extra-virgin olive oil bottle guarantees that the oil has been: manufactured in a specific geographic area, produced with the specific varieties of olives harvested in the area, and pressed at a maximum temperature of 28°C (82°F). Furthermore, it reinforces the values of genuine and honest olive oil production.

PONIENTE
de Granada
Denominación de origen protegida

Courtesy of C.R.D.O.P. Poniente de Granada

REMEMBER

An extra-virgin olive oil without a PDO/DOP label doesn't necessarily mean that it's not of the same or superior quality. There are many quality crafted, single-estate olive oils available in the Mediterranean region that meet and exceed the PDO/DOP minimum requirements. Bottles may not have the seal because the producers have not applied for it. The label comes with a hefty price tag for producers. If their sales don't merit the expense, they often forego the certification and specify their quality standards on their websites. If an olive oil made by a larger corporation does not bear the PDO/DOP mark on their label, however, that usually signifies that it does not meet the same quality standards. Chapters 12 through 14 explain the standards in greater detail.

IGP/PGI

Geographic indicators are another way of specifying a type of quality extra-virgin olive oil. IGP, which stands for *Indicazione Geografica Protetta* or PGI (Protected Geographical Indication) in English, is similar to DOP, although less strict. In order for a bottle of extra-virgin olive oil to have the IGP designation, at least one of the stages of production/processing or preparation must take place in the specific area. In many instances, the olives may be grown, harvested, and pressed in the region of origin and then shipped to a headquarters in a larger city for processing and/or preparation. In the PDO/DOP certification mentioned above, everything is done in one defined region place.

Slow Food Presidia

In order to protect biodiversity and quality, the Slow Food organization launched the Extra-Virgin Olive Oil Presidium in 2015. According to this international organization, "The Presidium will promote the environmental, landscape, health and economic value of Italian extra-virgin olive oil, and inform consumers about the qualities of good, clean, and fair oil." This designation ensures that the olive growers who join the Presidium have olive groves with *cultivars* (plant varieties) that are indigenous to the area and managed without the use of synthetic fertilizers or herbicides. Since pruning and harvesting the olives from centuries-old plants is more burdensome compared to harvesting younger plants, the Presidium requires that at least 80 percent of the olive plants used are at least 100 years old in order to protect the older trees and biodiversity, for which Italy is famous, yet at risk of losing.

Organic

Organic standards are designed to increase biodiversity and healthy soil biology through the use of naturally occurring substances for pest control and to aid growth with biologically based farming methods. The idea, established over many decades, is to reduce the use of industrially produced chemical pesticides and fertilizers. Although these substances promote growth and yield, they have the potential to directly or indirectly harm other species and affect human health. Synthetic fertilizers, pesticides, herbicides, and fungicides or genetically modified organisms (GMO) must not be used in the olive grove or contaminate the area from neighboring farms.

The increased need for plants to protect themselves from pests in organic environments may result in higher levels of polyphenol compounds. Some research suggests that organic produce in general is richer in polyphenols. There is some limited evidence so far that this also applies to olive trees and olive oil. A 2019 study published in the journal *Molecules* found a significant increase in polyphenols in organic extra-virgin olive oil produced from the Hojiblanca variety compared with conventional farming techniques.

Olive oils labeled as organic must be certified by an accredited third-party organization that verifies the producer's adherence to organic standards. This certification process involves regular inspections and reviews of farming and processing practices. It requires considerable investment and commitment from a producer.

Certification is usually indicated on the bottle and is regulated by individual countries, although often there are arrangements to ensure that standards are recognized between countries and regions.

Chapter **3**

Appreciating the Production Process

The production of olive oil from the olive fruit has been improved over thousands of years, but the basic principles of extracting the oil are fundamentally the same. Growing, harvesting, and milling techniques have advanced, but it is still possible to visit olive groves where ancient, traditional methods are being kept alive. *Millenary* olive trees are ancient olive trees that are believed to be thousands of years old. These venerable trees are not only agricultural treasures but also cultural and historical landmarks in the regions where they are found, particularly in Mediterranean countries like Greece, Italy, and Spain.

Knowing where our food comes from and the work that goes into its production are truly important when it comes to appreciating and making a valued judgement on what to buy and eat. This chapter explores the ways in which olive oil gets from the grove to your home.

Producing the Best Product

Most olive farmers and olive oil producers are fiercely proud of what they do. Some have inherited groves that have been in their family for generations. Some have returned to locations to plant olives near the villages of their ancestors, while others have introduced olive trees to countries and now harvest many acres of previously barren land or even desert. Many say that it's impossible to really own any of these beautiful trees because they are privileged custodians upholding traditions and looking after the grove for future generations.

FROM THE AUTHORS

Amy and Simon have had the privilege of being guests in numerous olive groves and production facilities in the United States, Europe, North and South Africa, and Australia. They are still amazed by the dedication and passion of those who work so hard to bring the finest extra-virgin olive oils to our kitchen and dining tables. These days it's possible to visit many olive groves and even take part in the harvesting of the olives through *oleo tourism*, which is explored in more detail in Chapter 23.

Tree care and maintenance

Looking after an olive grove involves planning and care throughout the year. Pruning is generally done in late winter or early spring. This helps to shape the trees, remove dead or diseased wood, and encourage air circulation and sunlight penetration, which are vital for fruit development. Soil and biodiversity management, disease prevention, weed control, fertilizing and irrigating when appropriate are all part of the seasonal care necessary to ensure a successful crop of olives. The number of olives developing to maturity and their oil content are dependent on the aforementioned factors, along with natural variables including the weather, pollination, and local conditions. Most olive varieties have a growth pattern known as *alternate bearing* (or biennial bearing.) This pattern involves a cycle where a year of heavy fruit production is followed by a year of lower production yield. Some groves may have trees of a similar age and others may have a mixture of young and older trees, perhaps dating back several hundred years. A seedling may take 10 years or more to first bear fruit and a tree developed from a cutting between 2 and 5 years.

Keeping enemies at bay

The very best extra-virgin olive oils in the world are not created by hoping for the best from the trees, putting some oil in a bottle, and adding a fancy label. The creation of excellence begins in the dormant months in the winter, with care and attention to the development of the olive tree and its fruit — through the annual growing cycle, to the harvest and mill, and beyond.

WARNING

There are a number of threats to the production and supply of olive oil. Climate change is already having a dramatic impact on olive groves. The olive fruit fly is an insect whose larvae feed directly on the fruit, the effects of which can be difficult to combat. *Xylella fastidiosa* is a bacterial infestation that is spread by sap-feeding insects, which can devastate groves by causing severe disease and death in trees. There is no known cure once an olive tree is infected. Containment, control of the insects that are the vectors for the disease, and even the culling of trees are the only current strategies to combat the disease.

Environmental challenges

Olive groves can be, and look, very different in many ways. Traditional groves were often established centuries ago. Trees may have been planted in rows or more haphazardly around boulders or existing vegetation, depending on the topography and soil and may rely only on rainfall for their water supply. These groves are often the home of grazing sheep or goats and adjacent to land where vegetables and other foods are grown. These trees thrive in soils that drain well and can often appear as if they're clinging to the rocky slopes of hillsides that tumble down to the sea.

Accessing and managing these groves can be a challenge in itself with pruning and harvesting often done by hand. A typical traditional farm can have 50 to 100 trees per hectare (around 2½ acres).

Where land is cleared and olive trees are planted for a more mechanized approach to managing and achieving more oil production, an *intensive* grove may support 200 to 500 trees per hectare with efficient irrigation, pest control, and fertilization strategies. In the last 30 years, so-called *super intensive* olive groves have been planted with over 1,500 trees per hectare.

In some parts of the world like Australia, Argentina, California, and Saudi Arabia, intensive and super intensive groves have attracted vast amounts of investment in infrastructure and land purchase, particularly in areas where food production has been difficult in the past. The olive tree, if nurtured, can survive in soils in close to desert conditions. Some of these modern olive groves can be seen from outer space.

Olive trees are very hardy. They can grow on hillsides up to 500 to 600 meters (approximately 1,500–2,000 feet) above sea level. In some exceptional cases with specific *microclimates* (climate conditions in a small area or region), olive trees can grow on mountains at altitudes up to 700 meters (around 2,300 feet) or higher. The increased exposure to ultraviolet (UV) light and the greater variations in temperature make the environment more stressful to plant life, so the tree may respond by limiting its fruit and by increasing production of its protective compounds.

Harvest time

The fruit of the olive tree develops from a proportion of the self- or wind-pollinated white flowers that adorn the olive tree in late spring. The olives grow through the summer, and the central *pit* (or stone) becomes hard. Unlike many fruits, olives grow in fat content rather than sugars. The dense nutritional value of wild olives makes them ideal food for many birds. And despite the bitterness of the fruit, some mammals including rodents and wild boar may also eat them, particularly when the olives are overripe. Seed are dispersed in a little packet of fertilizer when the digested olive is mature. As the days shorten and temperatures start to drop and autumn progresses to winter, olives begin to ripen.

The ripening process involves changes in color from green to purple and finally to black, depending on the variety. Between pit hardening and this color change phase, oil accumulation inside the olive accelerates. At the same time, compounds called *polyphenols* protect the olive from insect infestation and damage from oxygen in the surrounding air during the delicate phase of maturation change in quantity and type. The most bitter and pungent tasting polyphenols, which also protect the olive from being eaten before it is fully ripe, begin to decline as the oil content approaches its peak and colored polyphenols increase to signal to animals and birds that the nutritious olive can provide sustenance. These polyphenols are not only important for plant survival but also have benefits for human health and are explored in greater detail in Chapter 6.

The quality of extra-virgin olive oil depends on many factors including tree maintenance; olive varieties; environmental conditions; and the methods for harvesting, milling, and storing as shown in Figure 3-1. In the Northern Hemisphere, olive harvest usually occurs from October to January, depending on the region and climate. In the Southern Hemisphere, the autumn and winter harvests happen between April and July.

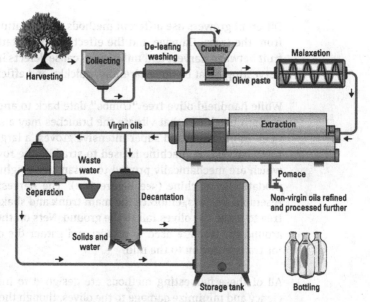

FIGURE 3-1:
The production process.

An early harvest will typically produce less oil for the farmer, but the oil will be higher in polyphenols. The results are a higher intensity of the positive flavor attributes of bitterness and pungency and may be sought after for its health benefits.

As the season and harvest progress, there is greater oil yield, typically with a milder flavor. If the olives are harvested late in the season, the antioxidant polyphenols will diminish as environmental conditions progress, increasing the probability for the olives to be fermented or carry infestations. These conditions can result in failing extra-virgin standards.

The timing of the harvest will vary from year to year, which is based on established customs and practices as well as the variety and cultivation methods. There will always be a tradeoff between taste, quality, and yield. Many premium extra-virgin olive oils being described as "early harvest" are produced in small batches early in the season with a focus on their interesting taste profile and high polyphenol levels. In many high-technology mills, the olive trees chosen for harvest at a particular time may be based on frequent fruit analyses and tasting of small amounts of oil.

Different growers use different methods of separating the olives from the trees. Damage and the effect of fermentations on the fruit between harvest and milling can cause defects in the oil, so harvesting must be done carefully, quickly, and efficiently.

While handheld olive tree "combs" date back to ancient times, modern machines that vibrate the branches may also be handheld. In intensive and super intensive groves, a large "over the row" harvesting machine is used to straddle the rows of trees, which are mechanically pruned to a standard height to accommodate the machine (see Figure 3-2). The harvesters, which resemble tractors, embrace the main trunk and shake the entire tree to make the olives fall to the ground. Nets on the ground or around the tree are used to protect and gather the olives ready for transportation to the mill.

All of these harvesting methods are designed to increase efficiency and minimize damage to the olives, though there is debate about which techniques are the best. In the end, the method used depends on the type of grove, tradition, and available resources, including the number of workers needed to harvest. Waiting for the olives to naturally fall from the tree to be collected at leisure has always been known to be detrimental to the quality of oil.

FIGURE 3-2:
Harvesting
by modern
machine.

Now the race is on to transport the olives to the mill as quickly as possible to produce the freshest, purest, and healthiest juice (or oil).

**FROM THE
AUTHORS**

Simon has had the privilege of helping to harvest olive trees by hand at the UNESCO World Heritage site of Dougga in Tunisia (see Figure 3-3). With the dramatic backdrop of impressive Roman city ruins, it is easy to imagine legionaries supervising this practice 2,000 years ago. The combs and ladders used for harvesting olives depicted on vases and murals of the period were remarkably similar to those used today. At the end of an exhausting but exhilarating day, Simon was able to witness firsthand the commitment and stamina of the local farmers who were able to harvest olives at a remarkable rate.

FIGURE 3-3:
Harvesting
by hand in a
UNESCO
heritage site.

Amy travels to Italy each year during the olive harvest to take part in the most important time in a producer's calendar. She particularly enjoys witnessing the convivial spirit, hard work, and ritualistic attention to detail that goes into harvesting her private label extra-virgin olive oil.

Processing at the Mill

Modern olive mills — though they vary in size, scope and technology — use similar methods to extract the oil from the olives. Most of the old-fashioned stone wheels that moved in circles by harnessed mules to crush the olives are confined to the numerous olive oil museums in the Mediterranean (see Figure 3-4).

FIGURE 3-4:
A model of traditional milling methods.

A single olive grove may have a very small mill that occupies a room of an outbuilding to facilitate sales from the farm. This is an option most farmers cannot afford on their own. Many mills are owned by cooperatives of farmers who invest in the development of the technology and sometimes the branding of the product. Some mills are owned by companies that pay the farmers for the olives and then take care of the production, sales, and supply to other companies who brand the oil.

Most mills in traditional areas produce high-quality premium extra-virgin olive oil at the beginning of the harvest, with lower quality extra-virgin olive oil towards the end of the harvest season. They may sell the lower quality extra-virgin olive oil in larger bottles or cans targeted for use in cooking rather than for dressing. This formula is not always applied, and often it is possible to find high-quality oil in larger quantities. It depends on the marketing and the target consumer.

Juicing the fruit

The production of olive oil can be summarized in five stages:

1. **Receiving, separating and washing the olives.** On arrival at the mill, the olives are separated from any leaves and twigs. Damaged olives will be removed and the remainder will be washed with water. Only clean and healthy olives should be milled to reduce the chances of defective oil.

2. **Crushing and grinding.** The whole olives — the skin, pit, and flesh — are machine ground in stainless-steel containers. This step breaks down the cells of the olives to release the oil droplets, preparing the paste (the solid material) for oil extraction.

3. **Malaxation or kneading.** The paste is slowly mixed in a process called *malaxation*, encouraging the tiny oil droplets to fuse into larger ones that makes them easier to extract. This process is carefully controlled; too little kneading won't allow enough oil to be released, while too much can lead to oxidation and affect the oil's taste and quality. The temperature is also constantly monitored to ensure minimal oxidation.

4. **Extraction or "pressing."** This stage is needed to separate the oil from the paste and water. Screw and hydraulic presses have been largely replaced by modern techniques that rely on a centrifuge to spin the paste at high speeds (see Figure 3-5). This causes the different components, dependent on their specific weight, to separate. The solid material separated from the oil at this step is called *pomace*, consisting of the crushed skin, pit, and flesh.

5. **Clarification and separation.** Additional centrifugation or natural settling is used to *clarify* the oil by removing any remaining water and solids (see Figure 3-5). To produce the more translucid extra-virgin olive oil, further filtration may occur. Some producers do not filter their oil and leave some micro-solids in suspension for a more "authentic" unfiltered appearance of the oil. However, this may impact the quality of the oil over time as those particles settle inside the bottle and decrease the shelf life due to undesirable fermentations of the oil that is in contact with the organic settlings. The oil can be tasted immediately. Although there's nothing quite like that freshly pressed taste, the formal tasting and first bottling is best done a few weeks later.

FIGURE 3-5: Modern milling and production.

Courtesy of Cobram Estate Olives, Australia

Waste not, want not

Good quality, freshly harvested extra-virgin olive oils is a precious product. A mill can choose to release its own label oil for retail outlets, bottle it for a third-party brand, or make it part of a regionally produced line. It may be destined for a supermarket as a *private label* oil — part of the supermarket's brand.

Extra-virgin olive oil also has a commodity price. Very large food companies buy extra-virgin olive oil from virtually anywhere in the world, transport it in bulk by land or sea, and bottle it under a well-recognized international brand, usually with an Italian sounding name. These companies, many of which are not

Italian owned, often have been based in Italy but ship their olive oil from many countries. Current labeling laws demand that it needs to be clear that these oils are the "product of many countries." The extra-virgin olive oils are blended together to create a reproducible taste, which many experts in extra-virgin olive oil describe as bland and uninteresting. These oils undoubtedly have a role to play in the mass market, and may introduce consumers to olive oil and encourage them to explore higher quality and priced extra-virgin olive oils.

Before modern milling techniques were available, it was impossible to extract all the oil from a single inefficient pressing system at low temperatures, so the pomace was often put through a second, or even third pressing to extract more oil. After additional pressings, it would be very unlikely that the oil would pass current extra-virgin quality standards.

This is why the term *first cold pressed* was used to refer to the higher quality oils and as a synonym to extra-virgin olive oil. Although this term is still often used for marketing purposes, it's not accurate to describe the quality of the product.

Any oil that does not pass the standards for "extra virgin" following the "first" pressing, is sold on to refineries to make olive oil. This was described in Chapter 2. The pomace can also be further treated to obtain pomace oil or utilized as an organic amendment, stock feed, or biomass fuel.

Storing at the mill

Most modern olive mills have storage facilities with many huge stainless-steel tanks in spaces protected from sunlight with high ceilings (see Figure 3-6). The oil is stored and sealed at the top with an inert gas like nitrogen to protect the oil from oxidation. When an order for bottles of olive oil is received, the oil can be released from the tanks and bottled on site ready for transportation. Each container will bear a description of the oil variety, quality, and time of harvest. In large milling operations, tanks typically range in size from about 5,000 liters (approximately 1,320 gallons) to over 100,000 liters (approximately 26,400 gallons).

FIGURE 3-6:
Extra-virgin
olive oil
preserved in
storage
tanks.

Maintaining "Green" Groves

There are still some areas in the world where you can see wild olive trees. They exist in environments rich in biodiversity, providing food for animals and birds that in turn nourish the land. Farmers who cultivate olive trees are increasingly interested in developing techniques that encourage their groves to provide a net gain for the environment, like their wild counterparts.

REMEMBER

Olive trees produce antioxidant, bitter-tasting polyphenols that have benefits for health and enhance the flavors in extra-virgin olive oils. Although the quantity of these polyphenols depends on numerous factors, a positive correlation between water stress and polyphenol content in the fruit and subsequent oil in particular has been consistently demonstrated.

Built-in sustainability of olive trees

Olive trees, like most plants, remove carbon dioxide from the atmosphere during photosynthesis, store carbon, and then release it in the soil. This is called *carbon sequestration* or *carbon sinking*. This process helps to mitigate or reverse the process of global warming and climate change as humans burn fossil fuels. Research has shown that a well-managed grove is capable of sinking 10 kilograms of carbon for each liter of olive oil produced.

Olive groves can serve as valuable and diverse ecosystems, providing secure habitats and encouraging the proliferation of numerous species of plants, animals, birds, and insects in a balanced environment. Olive trees and the vegetation in well-managed groves support pollinators, including bees and butterflies, which are crucial for the pollination of many other crops and wild plants.

Soil health can improve with organic methods of farming, with natural cycles of growth and decomposition of plant material beneath the canopies of the trees. The land is enriched and made more fertile and productive. The trees themselves can prevent soil erosion, their presence on sloping hills stabilizing the soil.

Olive trees are very drought resistant, which is important as pressures on water supplies increase in many regions of the world. There is much less dependence on using water compared with other crops.

FROM THE AUTHORS

Simon has particularly fond memories of a visit to the award-winning Maida olive grove in the Jordanian desert. As the 4-x-4 vehicles drove across rough tracks in the sand and dust and climbed the final hill, the sight of the lush olive groves below that circled a natural oasis, traditional tents, and an elegantly constructed modern mill was truly a sight to behold. Amy also has witnessed this type orchard in Egypt's Wadi Natroun oasis, which produces olive trees enriched with regenerated salt water in an area that was once famous for hosting ancient Roman aristocrats.

Using olive oil in recipes can also encourage a shift towards a more vegetarian or plant-based diet because it makes vegetables more palatable and enhances their flavor and texture. Substituting meat for vegetables reduces the carbon footprint of a meal.

Sustainable farming

There are some groves that are committed to sustainable farming. Mindful of past agricultural practices, which have often significantly altered the land, this concept involves working to restore environments to their most natural state. This means enhancing biodiversity, investing in soil health, and working with nature to a new level.

Sustainable farming goes beyond maintaining a healthy ecosystem to improving it and making it resilient and sustainable for future generations. These farming techniques include adoption of composting, an integrated pest- and disease-management system, maximization of the water usage efficiency, and the active encouragement and reintroduction of native pollinators as well as other species that may have been lost.

FROM THE AUTHORS

One of the strangest sights you may see in an olive grove is the introduction of a certain species of wasp in order to reduce the use of chemical pesticides. Parasitic wasps have been shown to successfully reduce the effects of the olive fruit fly, which can cause significant damage to olive trees. First, the tiny wasps lay their eggs in the fruit fly larvae. When the wasps hatch, they will feed and eventually destroy the host, reducing the numbers of fruit flies. As with all biological pest control, it's important to monitor the effect to achieve a balance.

Modern mills

Many mills are focusing on their carbon footprint and putting in place strategies to become more environmentally sustainable. There are a number of ways this can be achieved:

>> **Installing solar panels.** Olive mills are often located in sun-drenched regions, especially in the summer months. The sun's energy can be captured, stored, and used in the mill or added to the local electricity grid.

>> **Recycling of wood and olive leaves.** Pruning olive trees can produce substantial amounts of wood, which can be used in various forms for biomass fuel, mulch for soil improvement, erosion control, habitat improvement, or even bedding for animals. Larger pieces can be recycled for handicrafts or even furniture or building material construction.

Olive leaves can be used as mulch or stock feed, or they can be roasted to produce olive leaf teas or further treated to produce olive leaf extracts. These extracts, which are similar to a concentrated olive leaf tea, are quite rich in polyphenols, although largely different than those antioxidants present in extra-virgin olive oil.

>> **Using pomace.** The solid material that is left after extraction of the oil can be further refined into pomace oil, skin and soap products, animal feed, fertilizer, mulch, or biomass fuel.

>> **Composting biomaterials.** Small twigs and leaves separated from the olives on arrival at the mill may be composted and used as fertilizer material.

>> **Improving machinery efficiency.** The milling equipment and other machinery used in the production of olive oil is constantly evolving to become more efficient, with electric powered harvesters replacing older diesel models on some farms.

>> **Packaging that is ecofriendly.** Research continues to explore improvements in packaging. There are some advantages of recyclable glass over plastic, but the cost to manufacture and the carbon footprint of transporting heavier materials is part of the equation. "Bag in a box" technology is being used to decrease the weight and reduce the cost of packaging. This may also have some advantages in increased shelf life of the oil due to added protection from light and oxygen. Recycled materials may be used for packaging, and it's also important to make sure that the used container can be easily recycled by the consumer.

>> **Optimizing logistics.** Efficient methods and routes of transportation can reduce carbon emissions associated with logistics of getting the olive oil to the consumer.

>> **Treating wastewater.** The water produced from milling is very rich in organic material. If it's simply released into the environment, it can disturb the balance of established ecosystems. Alternatively, the water can be treated similar to sewerage to create gases that can be used as fuel. Some producers send the water away for any useful biological compounds to be extracted. Most modern mills utilize two-phase technology, which significantly reduces the use of water and the consequent water *effluent* (waste released into the environment).

Chapter **4**

Explaining Quality and Comparisons with Other Oils

The olive oil production process is one of the most heavily regulated of any food, yet there are still headlines in the media that describe the dramatic exposure of fraud or *adulteration* (impure because of an added substance) of olive oil. Industry experts, who have written articles about their investigation of olive oils on supermarket shelves, have revealed that all is not as some brands claim to be. However, when you find an excellent quality extra-virgin olive oil (EVOO), it is perhaps the most precious ingredient in your kitchen and on your table. There is no comparison with other oils.

In this chapter, we discuss everything there is to know about fraud, how to judge quality, and the reasons why extra-virgin olive oil is superior to other oils.

Recognizing Quality Olive Oil

Olive oil has been central to the economies of many civilizations for thousands of years, traded between cultures and across continents.

No other food contributes to the diet of the Mediterranean region in the same way as olive oil — a standard part of breakfast, lunch, and dinner. As the main source of fat, it represents a significant proportion of calories and is the primary cooking medium of the Mediterranean diet, adding taste and texture to foods from beginning to end of meal preparation and presentation. It has also been prized for its nutritional qualities, and research over the last 50 years has confirmed its unique and extraordinary benefits to health.

It takes time, commitment, and investment to plant, nurture, and harvest olives and mill them for their oil.

Getting to know the difference between a genuinely wonderful extra-virgin olive oil and the signs of a low-quality, defective or even fraudulently produced oil is an important first step in understanding how to choose the best for taste and health.

Olive oil fraud

Any valuable commodity market is likely to attract fraudsters and unscrupulous traders. The most common fraud has been to replace or mix extra-virgin olive oil with cheaper vegetable oils. This adulteration is sometimes known as *cutting* an oil. Extra-virgin olive oil has to be pure for it to meet the strict defining criteria introduced and regulated by the IOC and Codex (refer back to Chapter 2 for more information). Illegally tampering with extra-virgin olive oil and attempting to pass it off as a genuine product has a number of very serious consequences. Any such practice may

>> Cause serious harm to health.

>> Deceive and deny the consumer the valued health and flavor of a high-quality product.

>> Damage the reputation of anyone unwittingly involved.

>> Violate labeling and trading laws.

>> Reduce confidence in the olive oil market as a whole.

WARNING

Extra-virgin olive oil may be adulterated by adding refined olive oil or olive pomace oil, or it may be diluted with less expensive oils. The cheaper oils used to cut olive oil can include a variety of vegetable oils such as sunflower, soybean, corn, nut oils or even non-food grade oils that are not meant for consumption.

Traceability and value have always been important to people involved in the trading of olive oil. Ancient Rome was built on seven hills, but modern-day Romans often refer playfully to an "eighth" hill known as Monte Testaccio, which was an ancient Roman garbage heap that is so large it has the appearance of a hill. It's full of the remnants of *amphorae* (clay jars used to transport wine and olive oil to the city). What's striking is the frequent appearance of a producer's stamp or mark on shards of the pottery, indicating that the ancient Romans were very interested in knowing the provenance and authenticity of olive oil.

TIP

It is easy to trace the origins and practices of a single estate olive oil. Oftentimes, you can go to that company's website, or even visit the estate in person, to view their certifications, claims, and quality practices.

In 1981, the adulteration of olive oil in Spain had very tragic and lethal consequences. Olive oil was cut with industrially produced rapeseed oil that was unfit for human consumption; it contained a toxic chemical called aniline. A series of black-market transactions that also involved deception resulted in the oil being sold in local markets and retailers as "olive oil" mainly in the Madrid area. The result was an estimated 20,000 people affected with various symptoms, many of which were severe. Between 300 and 600 people are believed to have lost their lives as a result of the tainted oil. In 1987, the Spanish Supreme Court found several executives from the companies involved guilty of manslaughter and fraud. The court proceedings and investigations highlighted significant failures in regulatory oversight and the dangers of food adulteration.

Other cases of deliberate fraud have been reported over the years, including successful prosecutions by the Italian police in

"Operation Golden Oil" and "Operation Terra Nostra" (meaning "Our Land") where significant quantities of poor-quality olive oil from other countries have been falsely claimed to be premium Italian extra-virgin olive oil. Unfortunately, geographical fraud can still be difficult to identify.

In Italy, there is a unique unit of law enforcement officers known as the "Olive Oil Fraud Squad," which is under the watchful eye of the Guardia di Finanza (roughly translates as the "Finance Police"). This specialized unit specifically combats olive oil fraud and its officers are trained to understand the chemical and taste profile of unadulterated extra-virgin olive oil.

The police authorities hope that they can demonstrate a serious approach to combatting fraud, which not only enforces the laws and deters criminals but also ensures that consumers can have faith in the safety and authenticity of what they are buying.

Defective olive oil

Deliberate fraud with the mixing of olive oils with cheaper vegetable or seed oils is not only criminal but also potentially very dangerous. However, quality can be recognized rather easily by taste, chemistry, and sophisticated technology that analyzes plant DNA.

What is more difficult to identify is when olive oil does not pass the standards for "extra virgin." Chapter 2 explores the different classifications of olive oil, and we discuss the chemical and sensory criteria for oils to be defined as extra virgin in the following section. However, sometimes defective oils are passed off as high-quality extra-virgin olive oil on purpose, but on other occasions a change in the extra-virgin olive oil may simply represent deterioration that can be beyond the control of the producer.

It's possible for a producer or retailer to sell an oil that is defective and does not meet extra-virgin olive oil standards despite being labeled as such —knowingly or unwittingly. It gets even more complicated than this. Extra-virgin olive oil is a natural product that can deteriorate over time, especially if it is handled or stored improperly.

A compliant extra-virgin olive oil may have left its producer in good condition but was exposed to light, heat, and oxygen in transit, at a retail outlet, or in the consumer's home. The result may be in oxidative deterioration, and the oil becomes rancid and loses much of its healthfulness.

A 2010 report from the University of California, Davis cited research, which appeared to demonstrate that a majority of imported extra-virgin olive oils in California retail did not pass the tests required to be defined as extra-virgin oils. There was some controversy about the methodology and results of the research, but it resulted in a review of standards by producers to improve the quality of oils in the supermarkets.

TIP

An early harvest extra-virgin olive oil that is high in antioxidant polyphenol compounds will most likely retain its status when it's packaged to protect the oil from heat, light, and oxygen. Conversely, a poorer quality oil, which may have only just met the extra-virgin olive oil grade, can fall below the standards soon after it leaves the producer.

Testing Criteria for EVOO

Despite newspaper stories of fraud, "busts" by Italian police and the problems of being able to predict whether an extra-virgin olive oil has deteriorated, the olive oil industry is in fact one of the most robustly defined and regulated foods among the food production industry.

The International Olive Council (IOC) and Codex are charged by their membership with defining olive oil standards, but their implementation is the responsibility of governments and local authorities. (See Chapter 2 for more on olive oil standards.)

Any producer selling olive oil labeled as *extra virgin* must be able to provide evidence that it has passed the stringent chemical and sensory or *organoleptic* tests (appearance, flavor, mouthfeel, or aroma) necessary to achieve its classification.

Tasting panels and laboratory tests

The extra-virgin olive oil is tested by a trained tasting panel in a systematic process to implement the standards defined by the IOC and Codex. Each panel is comprised of rigorously trained individuals, and there are checks and balances in place to make sure that their conclusions are regularly calibrated with other testing panels. The tasting test is done with samples that are presented at a specific temperature with no identifiers, so the panel isn't aware of the source. Special blue or red glasses are used to prevent the color of the oil from influencing the tasters' perceptions. (Even professionals can be susceptible to unconscious bias.)

REMEMBER

For some people, a green oil may look more attractive than one that is more yellow, but there is no evidence that the color makes any difference to the sensory qualities. In order to appease the misconceptions of some consumers regarding color of olive oil, some less scrupulous producers add chlorophyll to their oil to give it a fake green appearance. For this reason, it's especially important to not be influenced by color.

Each panel member scores the olive oil for its attributes (negative and positive). These scores are then compiled to produce a final assessment, which defines the oil grade and may award it the prestigious status of extra virgin.

TECHNICAL
STUFF

The chemical criteria for extra-virgin olive oil status is an acidity of less than 0.8 percent, which is described in more detail in Chapter 2. Other tests that can determine whether the oil has not been oxidized or adulterated include:

>> **Peroxide Value (PV).** PV measures the degree in which the oil has undergone an early stage of oxidation. Extra-virgin olive oil should have a PV of less than 20 milliequivalents of oxygen per kilogram of oil.

>> **K232 and K270 levels.** These levels measure ultraviolet (UV) light absorption by the oil, which can detect the presence of secondary oxidation products that are not measured by PV.

>> **Delta K.** As a very generic indicator of the oil's purity, the values of Delta K should be close to zero indicating no adulteration.

>> **Fatty acid and sterol composition.** Although these vary with different extra-virgin olive oils, specific ratios and percentages of fatty acids and sterols can indicate the oil's authenticity and whether it has been mixed with oils from other sources. The presence of certain chemicals called *stigmastadienes* can detect adulteration with refined oils, like vegetable oils or lower grade refined olive oil.

There are numerous accredited laboratories and tasting panels in producing and consuming countries where extra-virgin olive oil can be sent for assessments and monitoring testing levels.

Sensory categories

For olive oil to fulfill the sensory criteria to be classified as extra-virgin olive oil, it must have acceptable elements of fruitiness, bitterness, and pungency and no organoleptic defects. While there isn't a specific flavor or aroma, the overall balance between fruitiness, bitterness, and pungency, as well as the harmony among the various flavors and aromas, are critical attributes of a high-quality extra-virgin olive oil.

The fruitiness of an olive oil is defined by several different flavors that can be present in extra-virgin olive oil and may include notes of different fresh produce, such as unprocessed olives, cut grass, artichokes, tomato leaves, almonds, or bananas.

Sensory defects are very important because an oil will fail to pass extra-virgin standards and a panel will reject it, if such defects are present. The number of defects that can be detected may have particular causes, which represent failures in the production or preservation process.

>> **Earthy.** This describes the flavor of olive oil produced from olives that have been collected with/from the ground or mud and not washed before processing.

>> **Frozen.** This defect is characterized by a rather flat mouthfeel and flavors, such as stewed fruit or wet hay,

occurring when the oil is produced from olives that have been exposed to freezing temperatures before milling.

>> **Fustiness.** This defect is the result of anaerobic fermentation, where oxygen isn't present, often because olives are piled up and left to sit too long before being processed. It gives the oil a fermented smell and taste reminiscent of brined olives, tapenade, and even horse poo, if the fermentation is really severe.

>> **Greasy.** If the oil feels greasy or heavy, it may be due to poor processing techniques or storage that are closely linked to the development of rancidity as defined above.

>> **Hay-wood.** Olives that were dried out before pressing or that have been milled with an excess of twigs and leaves can be a defect, leading to a flavor reminiscent of dry grass, olive pit, or wood.

>> **Heated or burnt.** This defect occurs when the olives or the olive paste gets too hot during the extraction process, giving the oil a taste that is reminiscent of boiled or cooked vegetables and burnt caramel.

>> **Metallic.** A metallic taste can occur if the oil has been in contact with reactive metal surfaces during processing and/or storage.

>> **Muddy sediment.** Oil that has been in contact with the sediment in the storage tanks for too long, leading to a swampy, cheesy, soapy, and acidic taste.

>> **Mustiness.** Mustiness occurs when olives develop mold and yeast before being pressed due to being stored in a damp/humid environment for several days or weeks. The oil will have a damp/humid, moldy, acidic, or musty aroma and flavor.

>> **Rancidity.** This is perhaps the most common defect, characterized by a flavor of old, stale nuts. It occurs when the oil oxidizes, a process that can be sped up by exposure to light, heat, and air.

>> **Winey-vinegary.** This defect is a result of the aerobic fermentation, where oxygen is present in the olives or olive paste, leading to a sour, acetic acid, vinegar, or bad wine taste.

Comparing EVOO to Other Oils

Oils or fats for cooking or dressing foods have been created from many different types of plants. They are collectively called *vegetable oils*, and they are often made from the nuts or seeds of plants. These oils are distinct from animal fats — like butter or lard — which contain a high proportion of saturated fats and are solids at room temperature. Examples of vegetable oils include sunflower oil, safflower oil, canola oil (also includes a variety known as rapeseed oil), palm oil, corn oil, sesame oil, coconut, avocado, peanut oil, and grapeseed oil. This list is by no means exhaustive. Some have a long history in cuisines of different countries or are relatively new products, while others have been the subject of significant marketing efforts. Vegetable oils have been promoted as part of public health campaigns in many countries to replace the predominantly saturated fat in animal products with the mostly unsaturated fats — polyunsaturated and monounsaturated fats of vegetable oils. The implications for health are explored in more detail in Chapter 5.

What makes EVOO different

Extra-virgin olive oil is different from most other vegetable oils. In addition to its health and flavor virtues, extra-virgin olive oil is created at low temperatures by separating the oil, effectively the juice, of the olive fruit from the solid parts solely by mechanical means.

Most other oils need extraction by chemical means and/or utilizing high temperatures during the separation process or for further processing in a refinery.

Some manufacturers of vegetable or seed oils understand the marketing potential of using language associated with the olive oil. Some rapeseed oils, avocado and coconut oils for example, are described as "extra virgin," which has no equivalent meaning or regulation comparted with the stringent definition and production criteria applied to extra-virgin olive oil. "First cold pressed" is also sometimes added, although it isn't a legal definition. It simply describes the high-pressure processes under temperatures of 50 degrees centigrade (122 degrees Fahrenheit) to extract the oil from the seed.

Each different oil has an average profile of fat composition. Some, like coconut and palm oil, have high levels of saturated fat, and others have higher levels of polyunsaturated or mono-unsaturated fats.

REMEMBER

The environmental impact of an oil is extremely important. Much of the world's palm oil is produced at the expense of important natural habitats, which are cleared for planting and oil production. Extra-virgin olive oil is an extremely sustainable product, which is discussed in depth in Chapter 3.

Finally, there is nothing that compares with the exquisite taste of a good-quality extra-virgin olive oil. Each grove produces an oil with unique characteristics that reflect the olive trees, their age, the *terroir* (soil, environment, and climate), variety, and time of year as well as the way in which the olives have been harvested and milled. Some of these flavors derive from the significant compounds called polyphenols, which are discussed in detail in Chapter 6.

Bioactive compounds in EVOO

Vegetable oils are primarily made up of fats, but there are other molecules present, depending on the particular plant origins of the oil and also the method of processing that can alter and often destroy naturally occurring compounds, many of which have healthy properties.

Extra-virgin olive oil starts with an incomparable quantity, quality, and variety of *bioactive compounds*, which are chemicals found in plants that have health benefits such as antioxidant and anti-inflammatory properties. There may be some bioactive compounds in other vegetable oils including, but not limited to, vitamin E and sulfur compounds called *glucosinolates* found in brassica plants (related to rapeseed). Most refined oils, however, have very low levels of these compounds following chemical and thermal processing during which they're destroyed. Extra-virgin olive oil is produced naturally so does not have potentially harmful chemicals like trans fats, stigmastadienes and other breakdown products of oxidation which can form in the refining process.

Contrary to the myths that extra-virgin olive oil is unsafe when heated, it has a high-temperature tolerance and its naturally high levels of resistant monounsaturated fatty acids are further protected from breakdown by its antioxidants. Research also shows that extra-virgin olive oil is unique in its ability to increase *nutrient exchange*, where healthy compounds of ingredients are shared and enhanced during cooking. This is explored in greater detail in Chapter 15.

2
How Olive Oil Improves Health

Chapter 5

Choosing Healthy Fats

ats have had a lot bad press. Low-fat diets have been promoted so much in the media over the last half-century that the mention of "good" or healthy fats still seems like a misnomer. Many governments and public-health professionals were recommending low-fat diets because of concerns about high-fat foods contributing to raised blood cholesterol, resulting in *atherosclerosis* (the buildup of fat deposits or plaque within arteries or blood vessels in the form of cholesterol).

It turns out that the "dietary fats" discussion is more complex than that. While some types of fats in the diet can damage blood vessels, other types of fat are protective and actually improve blood cholesterol levels. Clinical research has shown that problems arise when plaque becomes inflamed, which causes blood clots that can fill and block blood vessels. The good news is that there are foods that can help reverse that inflammation.

Fortunately, olive oil contains healthy fats that promote a beneficial ratio of the different types of circulating cholesterol, which will be discussed later in this chapter. Additionally, bioactive compounds in extra-virgin olive oil, including poly-phenols, prevent the inflammation of plaque. This dual effect is the reason why the Olive Wellness Institute cites studies demonstrating that enjoying 2 tablespoons of extra-virgin olive oil each day may be associated with reducing the risk of developing heart disease by an average of 30 percent.

In this chapter, we examine the important role of fats in our diets, and find out how to choose healthy fats while avoiding those that are less healthy.

Identifying Different Types of Fat

Eating healthy fats is essential for life. Fats are one of the three *macronutrients* in our diets — the nutrients that comprise most of our diets and that provide us with energy (calories).

Macronutrients are

>> **Fats.** Important for many functions in the body, which include storing energy, forming cell structures and membranes, providing insulation, and involving the production of many types of hormones.

>> **Carbohydrates.** Carbs provide a more immediate form of energy or can be converted into fats for energy storage, and their fiber is vital for gut health.

>> **Proteins.** Building and maintenance of cell structures require proteins, which are also used in the creation of hormones and molecules involved in transportation and immune defense.

Micronutrients (nutrients needed in much smaller quantities, which include vitamins and minerals), especially those in an olive oil–rich Mediterranean diet are discussed in more detail in Chapter 7.

TECHNICAL
STUFF

Most fats in foods are in the form of *triglycerides*, three fatty acids held together by a smaller molecule called *glycerol*. These fatty acids are made up of carbon, hydrogen, and oxygen atoms. They can be saturated, polyunsaturated, or monounsaturated. A *saturated fatty acid* has no double bonds between the carbon atoms of the fatty-acid chain. Each carbon atom is "saturated" with hydrogen atoms. *Polyunsaturated fatty acids* (PUFAs) have two or more double bonds, which can become single if one of those bonds attached to an added hydrogen atom, and *monounsaturated fatty acids* (MUFAs) have one double bond. PUFAs and MUFAs are sometimes described together as *unsaturated fats*.

Animal fats, butter, and coconut oil contain mostly saturated fats and are typically solid at room temperature. Foods that contain mostly polyunsaturated fats include fish oil, sunflower oil, and corn oil. Olive oil, avocados, and many tree nuts contain high proportions of monounsaturated fats.

The effects of saturated, polyunsaturated, and monounsaturated fats have been studied over the years and have resulted in recommendations for dietary fat. The advice to reduce fat consumption because of concerns that fats contribute more to weight gain than other macronutrients and that they cause a harmful rise in blood cholesterol levels and heart disease, has been updated to reflect the evidence which shows that different types of fats have very different, and sometimes entirely opposite results.

WARNING

Another type of fat called *trans fats* rarely occur in nature, only in some meat and dairy products. They are created in an industrial process called *hydrogenation* that adds hydrogen to liquid vegetable oils to make them solid. Partially hydrogenated oils are a major source of artificial trans fats in processed foods and in recent years have been found to be a significant risk factor for heart disease.

Partially hydrogenated fats have been used by the food industry in baked goods, snacks, refrigerator dough, nondairy creamers, margarine, and fried foods where cheap refined hydrogenated soybean oil is used. They also can form when cooking oils are heated for prolonged times and/or on repeated occasions. Many countries including the United States, Canada and some European countries have taken steps to make laws to ban or limit their use by the food industry.

Correlating fats to cholesterol and health

The association of fat in the diet to high blood cholesterol levels and heart disease is called the *lipid hypothesis; lipid* is another word for fats. For example, your doctor may have taken a lipid profile to measure your cholesterol levels in order to assess your risk of heart disease.

Cholesterol is manufactured in the liver to perform specific important functions. It's vital for the cell membranes, which protect the interiors of cells from harmful effects, and hormone production. Clinical research has shown that there are different types of cholesterol in the blood as well as different types of dietary fat, and that this association really does matter.

Circulating cholesterol: LDL and HDL

Earlier in this chapter, we refer to the term *circulating cholesterol.* The most important types of circulating cholesterol are *low density lipoprotein* (LDL), which is associated with an increased risk of heart disease, and *high density lipoproteins* (HDL), which transports cholesterol away from blood vessels and back to the liver, thereby protecting us from the formation of plaque in blood vessels and reducing the risk of heart disease. Knowing the ratio between "bad" LDL cholesterol and "good" HDL cholesterol is a better reflection of heart-disease risk than a simple total cholesterol level, which is made up of both good and bad cholesterols.

While dietary fats themselves are not directly converted to cholesterol, the fatty acids and triglycerides from fats can influence the liver's production of cholesterol, leading to more circulating "good" or "bad" cholesterol.

Saturated fats and trans fats are harmful because they raise "bad" LDL cholesterol and, in the case of trans fats, also lower "good" HDL cholesterol, which increases the risk of heart disease.

Monounsaturated and polyunsaturated fats are beneficial for cholesterol management and heart health, helping to lower LDL levels and maintain or increase HDL levels. Incorporating these healthier fats into the diet while reducing intake of saturated and trans fats is widely recommended for cardiovascular health.

Increasing polyunsaturated fats in the diet must be done with care because there are two types called omega-6 and omega-3 polyunsaturated fats and an excess of omega-6 in relation to omega-3 can result an increased tendency for harmful chronic inflammation. The pro-inflammatory effect of the abundance of omega-6 polyunsaturated fats in foods, such as many types of vegetable oils and in processed foods, means that it's important to focus on the particularly healthy omega-3s found in oily fish and some plants like flaxseeds, chia seeds, walnuts, kale, spinach, and *purslane* (a succulent herb).

Cholesterol in its natural form can occur in foods, and it is particularly rich in shrimps, prawns, and eggs, for example. It has been shown that the cholesterol directly from our diet does not contribute to our blood cholesterol levels to the extent that was first assumed. It's perfectly fine to eat these foods in moderation without being concerned about the effect on your cholesterol levels.

Examining the lipid hypothesis

The lipid hypothesis remains a subject of debate, and at times, fierce controversy. Some researchers argue that the role of saturated fat and raised LDL cholesterol in the development of heart disease has been overstated. The effects of eating a moderate amount of full-fat dairy products appear to include protection from diabetes without increasing the risk of heart disease — despite the saturated fat content.

Not all saturated fats have the same adverse effects on LDL cholesterol. Some saturated fatty acids are absorbed and rapidly used for energy. So, they don't increase LDL cholesterol levels.

Critics of the lipid hypothesis argue that the focus on cholesterol has overshadowed other important aspects of heart health, such as the role of genetics, dietary sugar and refined carbohydrates, inflammation, and a process called *oxidation of LDL cholesterol*. It's important to understand what happens when LDL cholesterol is oxidized and how this process occurs.

When LDL cholesterol particles travel through the bloodstream, they can become oxidized by molecules known as free radicals. *Free radicals* are often by-products of normal metabolism but can also result from exposure to environmental toxins, pathogens, radiation, or our own body's inflammatory processes. Many free radicals contain oxygen atoms and are specifically referred to as reactive oxygen species (ROS), which are highly reactive due to their unpaired electrons. They can initiate the oxidation of LDL particles. This oxidized LDL is more likely to contribute to the development of atherosclerosis, which is associated with cardiovascular diseases.

The immune system recognizes ROS as potentially harmful, which may lead to inflammation, plaque instability, rupture, and the formation of blood clots. Where there is an excess of ROS and other free radicals from our diet, the environment, or a sedentary lifestyle, there is chronic inflammation and a state called *oxidative stress* (an imbalance of free radicals and antioxidants in the body), which risks chronic illness and disease.

Finally, the bioactive compounds like the polyphenols in extra-virgin olive oil, which have antioxidant and anti-inflammatory properties, adds to the evidence that the lipid hypothesis must also consider the effects of our diet. The power of polyphenols is discussed in more detail in Chapter 6.

Understanding how fats relate to calories and weight

You may put off eating foods that contain fat because you have heard the oversimplistic advice to reduce the amount of fat in your diet; or perhaps you thought the term *dietary fat* implies that eating it will make you fat.

Most health professionals now recognize that the different types of fats in foods not only have different effects on cholesterol but also on the likelihood of you putting on extra weight.

Fat calories

Among the three macronutrients, it's fats that contain the most calories. The calorie content of a food is the amount of energy a food can provide. Excess calories in our diet may result in that energy being stored as body fat. However, it's a bit more complicated than that. Our bodies don't simply add up the calories consumed, subtract the energy used, and put the difference onto our waistlines.

Calories from different sources can affect the body's hormonal balance and energy usage differently, influencing hunger, satiety, and overall metabolic health. For example, it's been shown that the fat from olive oil helps to reduce the speed of sugar absorption from carbohydrates and makes the hormone insulin more sensitive to the rise in blood sugar following a meal. Calories from the sugars in refined carbohydrates can be more likely to result in weight gain than calories from dietary fat.

Good evidence from an analysis published in 2018 shows that the monounsaturated fats in olive oil help to stimulate body fat breakdown known as *lipolysis* and inhibit body fat production or *lipogenesis*. A diet rich in monounsaturated fats may modify the body composition of obese individuals by increasing their lean body mass and decreasing the percentage of body fat.

REMEMBER

The typical fat content of a healthy Mediterranean diet is 35 to 40 percent of total calories, which is a relatively high-fat diet. However, the Mediterranean diet is dominated by healthy fats that contrasts with many Western diets, which may also have high-fat content but with larger proportions of saturated fats, trans fats, and refined carbohydrates from processed foods. The Mediterranean diet's specific composition of fats, as well as the other powerful compounds in extra-virgin olive oil, is one of the key factors in its associated health benefits of supporting heart health and weight management.

Weight

It's also important to understand what we mean by being overweight. Your doctor may measure your weight and height and use a calculation to work out your *body mass index* (BMI.) Your BMI will define whether you fall into the category of being underweight, normal weight, overweight, or obese. With a Western diet and a sedentary lifestyle, being overweight or obese increases the likelihood of developing health problems such as diabetes, heart disease, and certain types of cancers.

There are some limitations to the use of the BMI calculation to assess risk for health problems. It is unable to make distinctions between excess body fat and the presence of more lean muscle for example. Very fit American NFL or Australian rugby players each may have a high BMI, but their weight will have a greater proportion of muscle.

Bone density and lean muscle are also important contributors to weight, which protect older people, contributing to core strength and reducing the likelihood of fracturing bones after a fall.

Another limitation of simply using BMI as a guide to risk of becoming ill is the evidence that a good diet and lifestyle can mitigate the increased risk of health complications of being overweight.

Research from Uppsala University in Sweden, which was published in 2020, studied 79,000 individuals over 21 years. Each person's BMI was measured along with their adherence to a Mediterranean diet. The researchers found that individuals classified as overweight with high Mediterranean diet adherence had the lowest risk of all-cause mortality or death from any cause. Obese individuals who followed a Mediterranean diet did not have a higher mortality risk but did have an increased risk of heart disease. By contrast, individuals with a healthy weight but low Mediterranean diet adherence had higher mortality rates compared to people in the same weight range who regularly adhered to a Mediterranean-style diet.

TIP

If you are overweight, a Mediterranean-style diet with olive oil, even if it is relatively high in fat, can support a sustainable move to a lower weight. It's most important to have a healthy diet to reduce the risks of diabetes, heart disease, cancers and chronic inflammation which may be associated with being overweight on a Western diet.

Determining the Benefits of Eating Healthy Fats

Fats are definitely important in the diet, and the right types of fat-containing foods are essential for good health. By replacing highly processed foods that are full of unhealthy fats with natural foods that have a high monounsaturated content, you can reduce your cholesterol and improve your health. The healthy fats will also provide the building blocks of cell membranes and important hormones while aiding the absorption of fat-soluble vitamins.

Olive oil: A fat for life

Extra-virgin olive oil has gained the reputation of being one of the healthiest foods on the planet. Olive oil generally contains between 55 and 83 percent monounsaturated fat, with the rest being made up of smaller amounts of polyunsaturated and saturated fats. The monounsaturated fat in olive oil is called *oleic acid*. The word *oleic* is derived from the Latin term *oleum*, which means oil.

TECHNICAL STUFF

Oleic acid is widely regarded as healthy for the heart. It is the most common monounsaturated fat in the human diet. Oleic acid is chemically designated as an omega-9 fatty acid because the double bond in its structure is located at the ninth carbon atom from the omega end of the molecule.

Oleic acid in olive oil has been shown to have the following effects:

>> Lowering "bad" LDL cholesterol and possibly raising "good" HDL cholesterol.

>> Reducing the risk of obesity by inducing a feeling of fullness, aiding in weight management, increasing insulin sensitivity, and slowing the absorption of glucose during and after a meal.

>> Inhibiting the growth of certain types of cancer by suppressing the expression of genes associated with the metastasis of cancerous cells.

>> Preserving brain function and reducing the decline of cognition in early dementia.

>> Lowering levels of inflammation through stabilization of cell membranes, production of anti-inflammatory molecules, and suppression of pathways of chronic inflammation. Diets high in oleic acid are associated with lower levels of markers for inflammation.

>> Improving the functioning of blood vessels. Oleic acid has been shown to increase the production of nitric oxide (NO), a signaling molecule that helps dilate blood vessels, thus improving blood flow and reducing blood pressure.

Extra-virgin olive oil also contains bioactive compounds including polyphenols, which make it even more powerful. Polyphenols play an important part in reducing the oxidation and inflammation of LDL cholesterol, which contributes to the risk of heart disease and strokes. The important effects of polyphenols are explored more fully in Chapter 6.

REMEMBER

Increasing polyunsaturated fats can also contribute to health, but it's best to focus on omega-3s rather than omega-6s to make sure a healthy balance. Western diets have a ratio of approximately 16:1 omega-6 to omega-3 whereas a more healthy, anti-inflammatory Mediterranean-style diet has a ratio of 4:1. So it's best to limit vegetable oils and highly processed foods in your diet and make sure you eat plenty of the following foods, which are rich in omega -3 fatty acids.

>> **Fatty fish (such as salmon, mackerel, sardines, and trout).** An excellent source of high-quality protein and vitamin D.

>> **Flaxseeds.** Rich in fiber, protein, and magnesium.

>> **Chia seeds.** Great source of fiber, protein, calcium, and magnesium.

>> **Walnuts.** Contains high levels of fiber and vitamin E.

>> **Hemp seeds.** Good source of protein, magnesium, and iron.

>> **Green leafy vegetables (such as kale, spinach, and watercress).** Contain vitamins A, C, K, as well as significant amounts of minerals like calcium and manganese.

Other foods that contain nutrient-rich fats

Foods are more than just their macronutrients. Here is a list of healthy foods containing monounsaturated fats with additional nutrients:

>> **Olives and olive oil.** Contains vitamin E and numerous bioactive compounds including polyphenols and *squalene* (anti-inflammatory, provides skin hydration) in extra-virgin olive oil.

>> **Avocados.** Rich in fiber, vitamins E, K, C, and B-vitamins, and potassium.

>> **Nuts (particularly almonds, cashews, and hazelnuts).** Good sources of fiber, protein, vitamin E, and magnesium.

>> **Peanuts and pure peanut butter.** High in protein, fiber, and vitamin E.

>> **Seeds (such as sesame seeds).** Provides fiber, protein, calcium, and iron.

Chapter **6**

Incorporating Antioxidant and Anti-Inflammatory Polyphenols

Ahealthy diet has a good balance of foods consisting of quality *macronutrients* (fats, carbohydrates, and proteins) and crucial *micronutrients* (vitamins and minerals). Because there are a number of unrecognizable and largely unnecessary ingredients in highly processed foods, many health professionals recommend that their patients eat more whole, natural foods — mainly from plants. The troublesome ingredients in highly processed food include artificial sweeteners, colorings, nitrite preservatives, stabilizers, and emulsifiers.

In this chapter, we examine plant polyphenols and their healing properties. Although polyphenols are not macronutrients or micronutrients, they have extraordinary potential to preserve good health and protect us from becoming sick.

Understanding Polyphenols

The vast majority of polyphenols come from plants directly. They are often found in colorful vegetables and most abundant in the outer protective layers of plants. Herbs and spices, though we eat them in small amounts, have particularly high levels of polyphenols that add pleasant bitter and pungent flavors to our foods. Extra-virgin olive oil (EVOO) also contains polyphenols.

Raw honey is a rare example of a good source of polyphenols, not directly from plants. Bees concentrate the protective polyphenols in the honeycomb to preserve and protect their valuable honey stores.

Polyphenols also have very beneficial effects on our health. They belong to a group of chemicals called bioactive compounds. *Bioactive compounds,* as the name suggests, have biological activity that is important for the maintenance of health. They have powerful potential to protect us from harmful inflammation and many chronic diseases, which so commonly lead to disability and preventable deaths. We may rely on nutrients to survive, but we need bioactive compounds to flourish.

Besides polyphenols, bioactive compounds also include glucosinolates and carotenoids. *Glucosinolates* are sulfur-containing compounds found in cruciferous vegetables like broccoli, cauliflower, and kale and are known for their potential cancer-protective properties as well as a distinctive pungent aroma. *Carotenoids* are pigmented substances found predominantly in plants, imparting red, yellow, and orange colors to fruits and vegetables and are important for vision, immune function, and skin health.

But it's polyphenols that are the most abundant of bioactive compounds in plants with more than 8,000 identified so far. There is clinical evidence of their extraordinary ability to contribute to health in numerous ways, potentially helping to protect us from heart disease, stroke, diabetes, cancers, obesity, and other debilitating illnesses.

Polyphenols are classified into different groups, such as flavonoids, phenolic acids, stilbenes, and lignans. Extra-virgin olive oil contains polyphenols from all of these groups.

REMEMBER

You may hear polyphenols referred to as *phenols* or *biophenols*. In this book, we use the term polyphenol. They are sometimes incorrectly called *phytonutrients*. This is a misnomer because literally translated it simply means "plant nutrient." Polyphenols and other bioactive compounds are not nutrients because the definition of a nutrient is something necessary for growth and maintenance of life.

TECHNICAL STUFF

The science of polyphenols is still young. There are many things yet to be fully explained. Scientists are not sure exactly how they work in the body, what contributions are made by the new compounds formed after they have been processed by our gut microbes (the fungi, bacteria, and viruses in our digestive systems), and to what extent the power of polyphenols is affected by our individual genetic blueprints.

Plants have a survival instinct

Plants are often taken for granted and considered simple organisms. Yet for a plant to survive, it must adapt and have resilience to be able to grow and propagate. Most plants, rooted to the land, have developed sophisticated defenses because they can't just move to a more comfortable environment. An olive tree, for example, must survive and produce fruit despite extreme variations in temperatures and weather and the threat of disease— perhaps while clinging to a dry, rocky cliff leading down to the sea. If an olive tree is able to defend itself from these challenging conditions, it's likely to have a lifespan of many hundreds, or even thousands of years.

Self-protection

While polyphenols have an important role in providing health benefits to humans, they are primarily used in plants for their defense.

Here are some of the ways in which polyphenols help safeguard plants:

>> **Antioxidant protection.** Polyphenols have strong antioxidant properties that help plants combat oxidative stress caused by environmental factors, such as ultraviolet (UV) radiation or pollution. They neutralize free radicals and prevent them from damaging cells, which will be explored in greater detail later in this chapter.

>> **UV radiation absorption.** Some polyphenols can absorb UV light, protecting plant tissues from UV-induced damage. This is particularly important for plants exposed to high levels of sunlight.

>> **Defense against pathogens.** Polyphenols contribute to the plant's immune defense by providing resistance against various pathogens, including fungi, bacteria, and viruses. They can inhibit the growth of these organisms, acting as antimicrobial agents.

>> **Pest deterrence.** The bitter taste and potential toxicity of certain polyphenols serve as natural deterrents to herbivores and insects, reducing the likelihood of being eaten.

>> **Structural integrity.** Some classes of polyphenols are integral to the structural support of plants, forming the cell walls — particularly in wood and bark to increase its physical strength.

>> **Water absorption.** Some plants, including the olive tree, produce polyphenols that help in the absorption of water from the soil, increasing the levels of these polyphenols in periods of stress when water is scarce and needed for the production of its fruit.

>> **Allelopathy.** Polyphenols can also play a role in *allelopathy*, where plants release chemicals into the environment to inhibit the growth of competing plant species nearby. This process can give them a competitive advantage for resources like light, water, and nutrients. On other occasions, plants can help each other when they face a common threat by communicating through polyphenols to warn other nearby plants of imminent dangers. The result may be an increased production of a neighbor's protective polyphenols to form a community of plant defenses.

Plants can exist in an ever-changing environment. When there is greater challenge, they respond by increasing levels of polyphenols. The way plants are grown will also have a significant impact on their polyphenol levels.

Seed distribution

Many plants rely on a symbiotic relationship with animals or birds that eat ripe fruits when the seeds are matured and ready for distribution. Because the seeds are resistant to absorption, they are deposited back on the ground, neatly packaged in natural fertilizer. Different polyphenols often appear in colors that change as the seeds mature to signal the fruit is ready to eat. At this stage, any bitter-tasting polyphenols will decrease in concentration as the nutritious sugars and fats increase to attract animals or birds. Plants can even, to some degree, choose the animals that eat them by altering the taste to attract the animals.

Bitterness in the olive fruit is designed to put off animals from eating the olives before the seed is mature. The reward for waiting until the seed matures is that the olive tastes more palatable and has a higher nutritious oil content. Sometimes plants like olives and chilies have evolved to be in *symbiosis* (a close relationship between two organisms) with certain types of birds that are impervious to the pungency in polyphenols. This may be an adaption to environments that are especially tough, so that the offspring of the parent tree are seeded a farther distance away to decrease the competition for nutrients.

Polyphenols and inflammation

Oxygen is a powerfully reactive atom in the world around us. It's in the air we breathe and is involved in many of the chemical processes in our bodies, which include producing energy from *glucose* (sugar from carbohydrates). A key part of these reactions is a process of exchange of electrons between atoms, with oxygen taking away electrons from other atoms. This process is known as *oxidation*.

The power of oxidation is evident in the world around us. It can be observed in the way air and water can oxidize metals, causing rust and even destroying objects. It is also visible within minutes when the protective outer layer of an apple is peeled away, or it's cut open. The flesh soon changes color and browns (or oxidizes) with exposure to air.

Particularly reactive forms of oxygen are called free radicals or *reactive oxygen species* (ROS). Unlike the more stable oxygen molecule consisting of a balance of two oxygen atoms, ROS have one or more unpaired electrons that can "steal" electrons from other molecules, setting off a chain reaction of damage to chemical structures.

In small and controlled quantities, ROS are used by cells for specific purposes. They can act as chemical messengers, or they can be created by cells of our immune system to destroy invading bacteria in a regulated, localized, and confined *oxidative burst*. Once they have had the desired effect in the chemical defense against a harmful bacterial incursion, ROS levels return to normal. The processes involve acute inflammation designed to damage the bacteria in the vicinity to make a way for restorative healing to occur.

ROS are always in our bodies — from environmental sources, such as pollution and UV radiation. ROS are also by-products of inflammation as well as the complex chemistry of our metabolism. Acute inflammation also produces ROS as part of the body's defense against infection or injury. In healthy circumstances, this process reverses and healing occurs. However, an excess of ROS in the body causes *oxidative stress* that can lead to cell damage and chronic inflammation, which results in a number of chronic illnesses. Figure 6-1 shows the imbalance between ROS and antioxidants (that work to inhibit free radicals) in the body, resulting in oxidative stress.

Foods in our diet also have the capacity to increase ROS. High sugar levels can lead to an excessive production of ROS during glucose metabolism. The metabolism of saturated and trans fats also leads to the production of free radicals and ROS. Heme iron in red meat and the preservatives in processed meats may also contribute to ROS formation. Excessive alcohol consumption can induce ROS production and impair the body's defense system to handle the overload. Pesticides and chemicals in foods can also lead to ROS production.

The body has its own systems for controlling and neutralizing excess of ROS with rebalancing systems called *redox homeostasis*. If this response is insufficient to cope with the presence of ROS in an unhealthy lifestyle, a state of *oxidative stress* is said to exist, where there is a risk of damage to internal structures of our bodies. Oxidative stress, with circulating ROS hungry for electrons, can impact delicate fat molecules in cell wall membranes, LDL cholesterol molecules, and DNA. The result can be a risk of damage, inflammation and cancerous changes to cells.

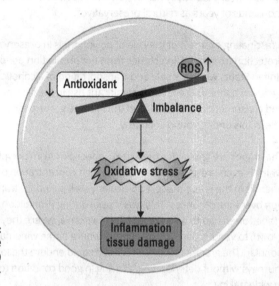

FIGURE 6-1:
Oxidative
stress in
a cell.

Here's where polyphenols come into play. Polyphenols are well-known for their antioxidant activity, which can neutralize ROS and prevent them from damaging cells in the body.

When we eat plants with polyphenols, they have an antioxidant and anti-inflammatory effect. They can modify the pathways of inflammation by switching on and off good or bad genes. We need them to work with our own internal systems to combat damaging oxidative stress. This is what makes them such powerful allies in the protection against disease. What is good for plants, is good for us.

A diet rich in a wide variety of polyphenols has been shown to reduce oxidative stress, chronic inflammation, and many chronic diseases. Such diets are associated with a healthy and diverse gut microbiome, improved mental health and well-being, and reduced markers of aging. The best example of a polyphenol-rich diet is the Mediterranean diet, discussed in more detail in Chapter 7.

GRAPE POLYPHENOLS AND THE PROHIBITION

The antioxidant protection of structures from oxidation and degradation by polyphenols means they are great for food preservation. Spices that are especially rich in polyphenols have been used for thousands of years as natural preservatives.

A fascinating example of the role of polyphenols in preservation and protection from oxidation comes from the prohibition period in the United States when the sale and transportation of alcoholic beverages was banned. There was a significant rise in the illicit production and consumption of alcohol, and the Alicante grape played a unique role in this underground economy.

The grapes are known for their deep, dark color from polyphenols, which is even present in the flesh. The high concentration of polyphenols in the grape made it particularly well-suited for transportation over long distances. This was crucial during Prohibition, as grapes often had to be shipped from California, where they were grown, to various parts of the country where home winemaking was popular. The grape's resilience meant it could endure the long rail journeys without deteriorating, arriving in good condition to be used in winemaking.

Knowing the Extraordinary Polyphenols in EVOO

Extra-virgin olive oil is a healthy fat because it is rich in oleic acid. (The beneficial effects of oleic acid are discussed in Chapter 5.) But most researchers who study extra-virgin olive oil believe that it's the polyphenols that make it so extraordinarily powerful, especially its antioxidant and anti-inflammatory effects.

Naturally high in polyphenols

The olive tree survives in some of the most challenging environments on earth. It can flourish where other plants would die from lack of water or nutrients. It can grow in varying temperatures and different microclimates within Mediterranean conditions. The resilience of the olive tree is the subject of awe and legend.

Unlike most fruit bearing plants, the olive tree produces fruit rich in oil rather than sugars. It has evolved specific traits that adapt to its environmental conditions and survival needs. Producing oil rather than sugar in its fruits is a reflection of the challenges of water scarcity and heat. Oils are denser in energy compared to sugars. Oils also help in reducing water loss from the seeds within the fruit and are more tolerant of extremes of temperatures, protecting the seeds from freezing or extreme heat.

The olive tree further protects its fruit by producing unique and exceptional polyphenol compounds in high concentrations. A high polyphenol extra-virgin olive oil will have levels of total polyphenols compared to pomegranate, cranberry, and grape juices, which have also been studied for their health benefits. But there are very specific fat-soluble polyphenols in extra-virgin olive oil, meaning they are probably more efficiently absorbed in the body without being broken down like the mainly water-soluble polyphenols in other fruits. That's why it's important to consume extra-virgin olive oil rather than taking a polyphenol supplement.

Conditions that effect the levels of olive polyphenols

As noted earlier in this chapter, plants produce polyphenols for their own protection against the stresses in their environment. They are often bitter, pungent, and spicy to deter animals from eating too much of the plant. Since the olive fruit develops in a changing environment, the following factors can influence its levels of polyphenols at any time.

>> **Olive variety:** Different olive varieties naturally contain varying levels of polyphenols. Examples of varieties that have particularly high polyphenol content include Coratina, Picual, and Koroneiki.

>> **Climate and environment:** The local climate and soil conditions (or *terroir*) can significantly affect polyphenol

levels. Generally, olives grown in harsher conditions with less water, higher altitude, and greater day-night temperature variations tend to produce more polyphenols.

>> **Irrigation management:** Controlled water stress, especially during the final stages of fruit maturation (also known as the oil accumulation period), has been shown to increase polyphenol content. Limited irrigation strategies can stress the olive tree in a way that boosts the concentration of these compounds.

>> **Harvest timing:** Polyphenol levels are higher when olives are harvested early in the season. These olives yield less oil compared to fully ripe olives, but the oil is richer in polyphenols.

>> **Harvesting techniques:** The method and speed of harvesting also affect polyphenol content. Mechanical harvesting can reduce the time between picking and processing, which is crucial because polyphenols degrade as olives begin to ferment. This is explored in more detail in Chapter 3.

It is fortunate for us that the careful process of milling retains the majority of the olive fruit's polyphenols in the extra-virgin olive oil produced. At the same time, milling transforms many of the polyphenols and decreases the bitterness and pungency to palatable levels for us to enjoy, especially when mixed with other foods. The taste of extra-virgin olive oil is explored in more detail in Chapters 9 and 10. The specific polyphenols in extra-virgin olive oil and their contribution to health are discussed in more detail in Chapter 8.

IN THIS CHAPTER

» Defining the foods in the
Mediterranean diet

» Understanding the importance of
extra-virgin olive oil in the diet

» Finding the medicinal and cultural
uses of extra-virgin olive oil

Chapter 7

Recognizing Olive Oil's Role in the Mediterranean Diet

The Mediterranean diet is heralded as the world's most healthy dietary pattern. When experts compare it with other diets, for example for the annual *U.S. News & World Report* "Best diets overall" list, it consistently ranks as the best. The foods of the Mediterranean diet are enjoyed as part of a wholesome and fulfilled lifestyle.

We like to say, you can take the extra-virgin olive oil out of the Mediterranean diet, but you can't take the Mediterranean diet out of extra-virgin olive oil. In other words, extra-virgin olive oil is a key component of the diet, but it can also be incorporated into other dietary patterns to complement and enhance ingredients that are native to other regions of the world and other traditional or heritage diets.

In this chapter, we provide more information about how extra-virgin olive oil is the most important ingredient in the Mediterranean diet and its contribution to the diet's extraordinary benefits. If you want more information on this wonderful way of life, check out Amy's book *Mediterranean Lifestyle For Dummies*.

Focusing on Olive Oil as the Primary Ingredient

The Mediterranean diet has never been static. It has evolved over many millennia, embracing new ingredients as trade routes expanded and cultures shared different practices of food preparation and enjoyment. The precious oil from its fruit of the olive tree has always been central to the diet as the main source of fat. And it can be considered the "heart and soul" of the diet. As olive groves were planted in new continents, the unique health benefits of the fruit were discovered and incorporated into other cuisines.

Reflecting on the extraordinary benefits

When someone says they are "on a diet," they usually mean that they're trying to lose weight and restricting what they eat. Because people who are overweight and eat a Western diet are more likely to develop illnesses like high blood pressure, heart disease, cancers, stroke, and diabetes, a specialized diet may be a good thing to do. Different diets come and go — some are endorsed by celebrities or are very expensive, while others are downright dangerous. However, a diet can only be successful if it's sustainable and effective.

The people who are living long and healthy lives with a Mediterranean pattern of eating would not consider themselves to be on, or following, a diet. Their congenial way of life is intuitive, passed down through the generations, and is aligned with cultural norms that relate to their own sense of well-being and the health of the world around them. It's quite simply their way of being.

This lifestyle goes beyond the characteristics of the diet, which is defined by UNESCO (the United Nations Educational, Scientific and Cultural Organization) as "a set of skills, knowledge, rituals, symbols, and traditions concerning crops, harvesting, fishing, animal husbandry, conservation, processing, cooking, and particularly the sharing and consumption of food."

It extends to prioritizing the community, with respect of age, religion, a positive relationship with activity on the land, and an attitude to life that sustains good health. Olive trees and olive oil are an integral and inseparable part of the Mediterranean landscape (see Figure 7-1).

FIGURE 7-1: Tenute Cristiano farm in Calabria, Italy.

The diet guidelines

The diet is characterized by the predominance of plant foods: extra-virgin olive oil, diverse colorful vegetables, fruits, whole grains, legumes including beans, nuts, herbs, and spices. A moderate intake of full-fat fermented dairy products is also a feature, including cheese and yogurt, mainly from the milk of sheep and goats. Fish is consumed perhaps once or twice a week, especially in communities living by the sea, with poultry and game animals eaten more often than red meat. Red meat is eaten less frequently and in smaller quantities. A modest amount of wine, especially red wine, is enjoyed with a meal in some parts of the

Mediterranean with herbal teas after meals. Sweets made with ingredients, such as local raw honey, are reserved for special occasions. Highly processed foods have no place in the traditional Mediterranean diet. The way food is grown and produced should be taken into consideration to maximize the quality and reduce the inclusion of industrial chemicals from processing or contamination by pesticides.

This pattern of eating provides *low-glycemic index* (a scale for how foods affect blood sugar), high-fiber carbohydrates with healthy monounsaturated fats, and a good omega-6 to omega-3 ratio of polyunsaturated fats (approximately 4 to 1). Proteins are often from plant sources packed with fiber. The diet is also rich in minerals, vitamins, and anti-inflammatory and antioxidant bioactive compounds and encourages a diverse and healthy *gut microbiome* (microbes that occupy our gastrointestinal tract).

The health benefits

The Mediterranean diet was first described by the American physician and professor Ancel Keys and his colleagues, referring to the traditional eating patterns that stretched back thousands of years, which he observed in communities in Southern Italy and Greece in the 1950s and 1960s. The diet appeared to have a powerful effect in preventing chronic diseases like heart disease, stroke, and diabetes that were beginning to increase statistically in the United States and Northern Europe at the time.

Since then, thousands of studies have consistently and robustly established that the Mediterranean diet is associated with reduced risks of heart disease, stroke, diabetes, obesity, high blood pressure, many types of cancer, arthritis and other inflammatory conditions, Alzheimer's disease, Parkinson's disease and vascular dementia, depression, and premature death.

Certainly, there are benefits over a long period but also in the short term with factors in the diet protecting from inflammation and supporting a healthy immune system to improve outcomes in people who acquire acute illnesses including infections like

COVID-19. A 2023 study published in the journal *Advances in Nutrition* showed that dietary patterns like the Mediterranean diet reduced the severity of consequences of COVID-19 by more than 70 percent.

A Mediterranean-style diet can improve blood vessel function and reverse preexisting *atherosclerosis* (the buildup of fat deposits or plaque within blood vessels in the form of cholesterol). It's also associated with a lower risk of erectile dysfunction and better overall sexual health. The benefits start almost immediately, with improvements of some measurements often discernible in weeks, and benefits can be seen even when changes are made in later life. The Mediterranean diet works outside the Mediterranean. It has been studied in populations of diverse ethnicity in many parts of the world, across continents and cultures, and shown to carry its extraordinary effectiveness far beyond the shores of the Mediterranean.

There have been many papers published on the subject, but perhaps the most quoted is the PREDIMED study (Prevención con Dieta Mediterránea). The study was a randomized controlled trial of 7,447 individuals aged 55 to 80 years who were at high cardiovascular risk but had no established disease. Groups adhered to a Mediterranean diet supplemented with extra-virgin olive oil or nuts, or a standard low-fat diet. The risk of heart attack, stroke, or death from either vascular event was reduced by more than 30 percent with the Mediterranean diet. There was a 40 percent reduction in risk of developing type 2 diabetes and 68 percent reduction on breast cancer. There were significantly lower levels of cognitive impairment and dementia as well as a number of other chronic diseases.

Several regions in the Mediterranean have become emblematic of the benefits of the Mediterranean lifestyle. The Greek Island of Crete and the region of Calabria in Southern Italy were included in Ancel Key's Seven Countries Study, and Sardinia and Ikaria have been noted for the exceptional number of centenarians, remarkable even by Mediterranean standards. The Greek islanders of Ikaria enjoy an 8 to 10 year-longer lifespan when compared with the United States; Ikarians' chances of celebrating their 90th birthday are doubled in comparison, and one in three residents live beyond that 90th birthday. Their quality of life is much better, with low levels of chronic diseases, preserved mental health and active participation in community life. More than 80 percent over 65 years report regular and active sex lives.

It can't be a coincidence that many of the benefits of the Mediterranean diet can be shown to be characteristic of extra-virgin olive oil as a single ingredient, and that studies of the diet rely on measuring and sometimes supplementing with extra-virgin olive oil as a key factor. In Chapter 8, the nutritional science of olive oil is more deeply explored and shown to align precisely with the Mediterranean diet as a whole.

The first paragraphs of this section described how many people view the idea of a diet, which is often limited to a desire to lose weight. The Mediterranean diet has been shown to help people achieve a healthy weight, but at the same time it achieves what a healthy pattern of eating should do. It protects from illnesses, keeps people in excellent mental and physical health to be able to enjoy a life of many high-quality years. If the pharmaceutical industry was able to replicate this kind of effect with a medicine, everyone would certainly be taking it!

ENVIRONMENTAL SUSTAINABILITY AND PERSONAL FULFILLMENT

Whenever the subject of discussion is diet and lifestyle, it's important to consider the effect on the environment.

Studies have shown that the carbon footprint of a Mediterranean diet can be up to 60 percent lower than that of a Western diet due to the reduced consumption of red and processed meats. It has been estimated that the water footprint of a Mediterranean diet is approximately 60 percent less than that of a meat-based diet. It also naturally promotes biodiversity, soil enrichment rather than erosion, and an ethos of preparing whole foods with minimal wastage.

The integration of seasonal food production into local economies reduces the carbon footprint of transportation and sustains communities. The planting and nurturing of olive trees in groves has been studied, showing that it can support important ecosystems and reduce water usage in comparison with other types of farming. Every hectare of active olive production neutralizes the annual carbon footprint of a person. An olive grove gives back to our Earth.

The Mediterranean diet lifestyle is also sustainable for individuals. In research surveys, people report better health, describe improved criteria of well-being, and have been shown to be much more likely to continue the diet and adopt the lifestyle in the long term.

In Simon's medical practice, patients who adopted the Mediterranean diet reported feeling happy, fulfilled, and had better health outcomes — often avoiding the need for medications. This anecdotal experience aligns with the scientific research that underlines the extraordinary benefits of this enjoyable and delicious way of living.

Measuring the effects of the diet

Researchers have always recognized that the Mediterranean diet is built on the foundations of combining extra-virgin olive oil with vegetables in every meal — whether raw or cooked. When scientists measure the effects of the Mediterranean diet and show its impressive powers to prevent and reverse illnesses, they base this on a *Mediterranean Diet Adherence Score*. This scoring system is a way of measuring how closely a person is following the pattern and comparing the health of those who achieve a high score with those with a lower score who eat fewer of the typical food in the Mediterranean diet.

No single food contributes to the diet as much as extra-virgin olive oil, and this is reflected in the weighting of the scoring systems, with the regular consumption of extra-virgin olive oil having an equivalent value of eating vegetable servings through the day. An example of a typical scoring system is shown in Table 7-1.

TABLE 7-1   **Mediterranean Diet Adherence Scoring System**

Foods	Servings*	Score
Olive oil (for bread, frying, salads)	1 servings/main meal**	3
Fruit	1–2 servings/main meal**	3
Vegetables	≥2 servings/main meal**	3
Cereals (bread, breakfast cereals, pasta, rice)	1–2 servings/main meal**	3
Nuts	1–2 servings/day	2
Dairy products (cheese, ice cream, milk, yogurt)	2 servings/day	2
Potatoes	≤3 servings/week	1
Legumes	≥2 servings/week	1
Eggs	2–4 servings/week	1
Fish	≥2 servings/week	1
White meat (poultry)	2 servings/week	1
Red meat (beef, lamb, pork)	<2 servings/week	1
Sweets (candies, pastries, soft drinks, sugar, sweetened fruit juices)	≤2 servings/week	1
Fermented beverages (beer, wine)	1–2 glasses/day	1
	Total score	**24**

* Servings are standardized amounts for each food group
** Main meals: breakfast, lunch, and dinner

When it comes to trials designed to measure outcomes of the Mediterranean diet over a period of years, studies have been set up with people eating the typical foods of the diet and being provided with extra-virgin olive oil to make sure they meet the criteria. Extra-virgin olive oil, with its culinary applications in cooking and flavoring in the diet, is the reason why it's possible to sustain eating the appropriate amount of healthy and nutritious plant ingredients over time. In one of the landmark studies of the Mediterranean diet, researchers did not simply rely on the participants reported intake but checked up on their high

Mediterranean diet compliance by measuring extra-virgin olive oil polyphenols in their urine. The importance of extra-virgin olive oil's polyphenols is discussed in detail in Chapter 6.

Considering Olive Oil as Medicine

While researchers continue to study the effects of a healthful diet on overall health, many doctors and patients are turning to culinary medicine to prevent and transform illness.

The modern definition of culinary medicine refers to the combination of the science of nutrition and the art of cooking. In the United States, universities are beginning to offer culinary medicine as a course of study. However, knowing the medicinal properties of certain plants isn't new. Historically, culinary medicine was the only way in which people treated and prevented illness before chemically derived medicines were invented. And it's important to remember that many modern medicines were derived from culinary ingredients.

For example, Thymol, an ingredient in many cough medicines, is a chemical version of the herb thyme, which has been used for millennia to treat respiratory issues. Camphor and eucalyptus oil have been used for thousands of years to treat congestion. Contemporary research has shown that a substantial proportion of these treatments had therapeutic value.

Ancient olive-oil treatments

One medical text from ancient Egypt was called the Ebers Papyrus, and it prescribed numerous foods to transform illness. Dating back to 1550 BCE, it contains recipes and remedies for various ailments, many of which involve the use of oils and ointments made from plants and other natural materials, including olive oil. There are recipes for ointments made with olive oil to treat skin conditions, such as eczema and psoriasis, as well as to soothe insect bites and stings. It is also mentioned as a treatment for joint pain and eye infections. The Ancient Greeks and Romans also believed that olive oil had distinct medicinal properties, especially the most bitter and pungent early harvest oils.

Hippocrates used to prescribe olive oil to treat gastric ulcers, muscular pain, and cholera. In Persian culture, Traditional Persian Medicine (TPM) is a specific type of medicine with a holistic approach to medicine and the treatment of various diseases. TPM originates from humoral medicine in which an imbalance of four bodily fluids was used to prevent illness. Olives and olive oil are prescribed in TPM for the treatment of several diseases.

The ancient Indian ayurvedic concept of using food to improve overall wellness also views good-quality olive oil as an internal detoxicant with nutrient and tonic qualities that are believed to help the liver and gallbladder. Currently, ayurveda is enjoying widespread popularity among integrative medicine practitioners in the United States and Europe.

Mediterranean cultural practices

First, it's important to describe just how rich and deeply rooted the various cultures of the region are. Oxford Languages defines *culture* as "the customs, arts, social institutions, and achievements of a particular nation, people, or other social group." Many of the customs and arts of the communities in the Mediterranean region have been practiced and celebrated for millennia. During the entire time, olive oil has played a key role in folkloric, religious, sporting, and festive ceremonies.

Olive oil is so embedded in Mediterranean literature, poetry, spirituality, lore, traditions, rituals, and memories in people of the region that it's difficult to separate them. Olive oil was and, in many cases, still is seen as not only an important staple but a remedy, a prized elixir, and a font of flavor and health. In many communities, it was and still is viewed as miraculous and as a way of heightening spirituality and supernatural powers.

FROM THE AUTHORS

Amy was once the guest of a Palestinian family living in Jeddah, Saudi Arabia. They gave her a gift of the superb olive oil that their family would ship to them each year. When they gave it to her, they reminded her to say the name of God over it, and to blow in it before consuming it in order to enhance its benefits and offer spiritual protection. The "evil eye" is also a core concept in Mediterranean culture, which means that someone can cause you harm by looking at you and wishing evil thoughts upon you. It is believed that a headache is a common symptom of being afflicted with this type of curse. Growing up, whenever Amy had a headache, there was an older lady who would be called to "boil the oil" on her account. In a traditional Southern Italian ceremony, the woman would say prayers and stir the oil in a certain direction in order to dissolve the negative energy. In Amy's household, olive oil was used to treat ear infections, skin ailments, congestion, pain, and just about everything you can think of.

In some parts of the Mediterranean, it is customary to apply olive oil to a baby's gums when teething. In Italy, after babies' nails are clipped for the first time, olive oil is rubbed on their nails and money is placed in their hand as a sign to ensure health, abundance, and prosperity. While the significance of these customs may seem strange to some, they do a good job of highlighting just how deeply integrated olive oil is outside of the kitchen and in other daily living traditions in the Mediterranean.

Chapter 8

Maximizing the Health Benefits of Olive Oil

The nutritional benefits that come from olive oil, especially of the finest, freshest quality, have been the subject of folklore and medical writing for many thousands of years. Modern scientific research, however, requires rigorous methodology and scrutiny. All the evidence we quote in this book has been published in peer-reviewed journals, abiding by the highest standard. The results of such studies in recent years have shown extraordinary benefits of consuming olive oil, especially extra-virgin olive oil.

In this chapter, we help you gain a greater understanding why extra-virgin olive oil (EVOO) is the most valuable ingredient in the Mediterranean diet, with its unique and extraordinary health benefits. Alternatively, the health benefits can become accessible if extra-virgin olive oil is incorporated into any traditional dietary pattern that has similar amounts of fats, carbs, proteins, vitamins, and minerals.

We also discuss the way in which the polyphenols in extra-virgin olive oil contribute to health, how to learn to recognize and enjoy the taste, and how to maximize the positive impact on your health and well-being.

Examining the Benefits of EVOO

In Chapter 7, we discuss how extra-virgin olive oil is a fundamental part of the Mediterranean diet. This section reviews the effects that are solely attributable to this ubiquitous and emblematic ingredient of the diet.

TECHNICAL STUFF

The information in this chapter is generally referring to "risk reduction" or *relative risk*, which is a decrease in the chances of something happening in one scenario in comparison or *relative* to another. A decrease in relative risk is usually quoted in percentages. It's also important to consider how great the risk is in the first place. For example, one situation may be associated with a reduced risk of developing a particular disease of 50 percent. This halving of a risk may sound impressive, but if it's halving from a baseline 2 in 10,000, the chance of getting a particular rare illness is still only 1 in 10,000. It's important to remember that for most people it has little relevance. On the other hand, the lifetime chances of developing conditions, such as heart disease, stroke, diabetes, high blood pressure, and many types of cancer are quite high, especially in the "Western world."

REMEMBER

When researchers study the effects food have on our health, they need to consider lots of other variables that may give misleading results. Although there may seem to be a link between particular eating patterns and an outcome, it doesn't necessarily mean that researchers are observing a cause and effect. There may be other coincidental factors at work. Drug trials can be set up with a *placebo* (a dummy pill), so participants won't know whether they're taking the active ingredient or not. However, this method isn't possible to do with nutritional science. This is why it's very important that studies are well designed and reviewed to make sure the findings and interpretations are accurate.

The protective power of olive oil

In the case of olive oil, there is plenty of convincing evidence to show its extraordinarily beneficial effects on health. Some small studies look at very focused effects of specific compounds in olive oil, while other studies are part of large, ongoing scientific initiatives that are researching broader aspects of dietary patterns and health outcomes.

From time to time, it's helpful for experts in a field to publish a review of the best quality research that is available summarizing and interpreting that data. One such review by researchers Mary Flynn, Audrey Tierney, and Catherine Itsiopoulos was published in the journal *Nutrients* in 2023. The article titled, "Is Extra Virgin Olive Oil the Critical Ingredient Driving the Health Benefits of a Mediterranean Diet?" also compared the effects of higher and lower polyphenol extra-virgin olive oils.

The evidence for the benefits of extra-virgin olive oil are compelling and cover many aspects of health. Thousands of articles are published about its effects on immunity, blood clotting, *oxidative stress* (an imbalance of free radicals and antioxidants in the body), and inflammation. But the most important conclusion is how regular consumption of olive oil can keep us healthy by reducing the risk of actual diseases. Chapter 6 has more details about oxidative stress and free radicals.

You may be aware that extra-virgin olive oil is good for you, but be prepared for some extraordinary revelations in the science. The following sections are just a few highlights.

Heart disease

Reductions in heart disease with olive oil, especially extra-virgin olive oil, are due to its fats, which improve cholesterol profiles and reduce blood pressure, alongside the polyphenols that protect from oxidative stress and inflammation and improve blood vessel function and flow. (Polyphenols will be discussed later in this chapter.)

The Nurses' Health Study — ongoing research into women's risk factors for chronic diseases — showed that participants in the highest category of olive-oil consumption (more than 7 grams/around 1½ teaspoons per day) experienced a 19 percent lower risk of cardiovascular disease mortality compared to those who never or rarely consumed olive oil. The PREDIMED study found that by increasing extra-virgin olive oil consumption to 10 grams (around 2 teaspoons) per day, cardiovascular disease and mortality risk decreased by 10 percent and 7 percent respectively. The European Prospective Investigation into Cancer and Nutrition (EPIC) Study, with participants from ten European countries, found that regular consumption of 2 tablespoons of olive oil was associated with a near halved risk of heart disease.

Stroke

Numerous studies of the Mediterranean diet with olive oil have shown reductions in the risk of stroke, with a 30 percent decrease seen in the PREDIMED study (Prevención con Dieta Mediterránea; see Chapter 7 for study details). The study involving older adults found that those who used olive oil intensively, particularly for both cooking and dressings, had a 41 percent lower risk of stroke compared to those who never used olive oil. This study used dietary questionnaires and followed participants for about 5 years, adjusting for dietary and lifestyle factors.

Type 2 diabetes

Consuming olive oil reduces the risk of developing type 2 diabetes in a number of ways. It lowers and slows the rise in sugars from carbohydrates in a meal and improves the sensitivity of the hormone that regulates blood glucose. For more information on olive oil and diabetes, you can read Amy and Simon's book *Diabetes For Dummies* and *Diabetes Meal Planning and Nutrition For Dummies*.

Among participants who followed a Mediterranean diet supplemented with extra-virgin olive oil in the PREDIMED study, there was about a 40 percent reduction in the risk of developing diabetes compared to those on a low-fat diet. An Italian study published in 2007 in the journal *Diabetes Care* observed that individuals who consumed at least 8 grams (around 2 teaspoons) per day of olive oil had a 12 percent lower risk of developing type 2 diabetes compared to those who consumed less than 1 gram (around ¼ teaspoon) per day. An analysis combining several studies found that higher olive-oil consumption was associated with a lower risk of type 2 diabetes. Specifically, the study indicated that each tablespoon (approximately 13.5 grams) of olive oil consumed per day within the study quantities was linked to a 10 percent decreased risk of diabetes.

Obesity and weight management

The theories about how olive oil contributes to a good weight are explored in more detail in Chapter 5. Several studies have shown more gradual but better sustained weight loss on a Mediterranean diet when compared with a low-fat or low-carbohydrate diet. A 2018 review of several studies where diets were enriched with olive oil also showed a significant benefit in terms of weight reduction.

Cognition and neurodegenerative diseases

Olive oil, particularly extra-virgin olive oil rich in polyphenols, protects the brain from conditions including Alzheimer's disease and Parkinsons disease through its preservation of healthy blood vessels in combination with anti-inflammatory and anti-oxidant effects. The Italian Longitudinal Study on Aging (ILSA), a long-term study following the health status of Italians aged 65 to 84 years, found a significant association between olive-oil consumption and cognitive benefits. Participants with the highest olive-oil consumption had a 38 percent reduced risk of developing Alzheimer's disease over an 8-year period compared to those with the lowest consumption.

The PREDIMED study showed a 35 percent lower risk of cognitive impairment in participants consuming a Mediterranean diet with extra-virgin olive oil compared to those following a low-fat diet.

The Moli-sani project, a large-scale epidemiological cohort study, is aimed at investigating the genetic and environmental risk factors for chronic degenerative diseases, including cancer, cardiovascular, cerebrovascular, and neurodegenerative diseases. Conducted in the Molise region of Italy, the study recruited 24,325 participants aged 35 and older between March 2005 and April 2010. The study has observed that consuming at least 7 grams (a bit over 1½ teaspoons) of olive oil daily was linked with a 28 percent lower risk of dementia-related death, compared with those who never or rarely ate olive oil.

There is even some evidence that high polyphenol extra-virgin olive oil is more protective than low polyphenol extra-virgin olive oil. A study from the University of Thessaloniki published in the *Journal of Alzheimer's Disease* in 2020 showed better outcomes of participants with early cognitive decline using high polyphenol oils.

Cancer

The antioxidant and anti-inflammatory properties of extra-virgin olive oil may have a role in preventing the formation and spread of some types of cancer cells. It may also affect the ways in which genes behave, suppressing the effects of genes related to an increased risk of cancer and increasing the influence of protective genes.

A review of numerous studies showed that high olive-oil intake is associated with a significantly lower risk of breast cancer, comparing the highest level of olive-oil consumption to the lowest level being associated with a 36 percent reduction in breast cancer risk. The PREDIMED study with the Mediterranean diet supplemented with extra-virgin olive oil observed a 68 percent reduction. An analysis from European studies found that higher olive-oil intake can reduce colorectal cancer risk by approximately 9 percent for each 10-gram (around 2 teaspoons) increase in daily intake within the study quantities. Research has been done across a broad range of cancers and shown beneficial associations with olive oil. A comprehensive systematic review looking at 45 individual studies revealed that the highest versus lowest olive-oil consumption was associated with a 31 percent lower cancer risk overall. This reduction spanned various cancer types, illustrating olive oil's broad protective effect.

Mental health

Olive oil can improve symptoms of depression and anxiety, although the ways in which it does this are not entirely clear. The SMILES (Supporting the Modification of lifestyle in Lowered Emotional States) trial, conducted in 2017, was a pioneering study that found a Mediterranean diet rich in olive oil significantly reduced symptoms of depression. About 32 percent of participants in the diet intervention group achieved remission of major depression compared to 8 percent in the control group, which focused on social support without dietary change.

Bone health

Research suggests that a diet enriched with olive oil can improve bone mineralization and prevent bone loss that leads to osteoporosis. This effect is attributed to the anti-inflammatory and antioxidant properties of the polyphenols in olive oil. A study of seniors in Spain observed that those who consumed olive oil frequently had higher levels of *serum osteocalcin*, which is a marker of bone formation.

Pregnancy and fertility

Olive-oil consumption has been linked with increased chances of reversing infertility as well as improving symptoms of menopause. Olive oil appears to have protective effects on many pregnancy outcomes. Higher olive-oil consumption is associated with lowering the occurrence of *gestational diabetes* (diabetes that can emerge in pregnancy) as well as protecting from preeclampsia and cardiovascular risk. In a study on the influence on the baby's health, olive-oil consumption was associated with a lower risk for small- or large-for-gestational-age infants and a reduced incidence of wheezing in the first year of a baby's life.

Premature death

It is no surprise that the contribution from olive oil in reducing the risk of many serious illnesses results in it preventing premature deaths. The PREDIMED study demonstrated a reduction in mortality of 30 percent during the period of participant follow-up. Outcomes from the large Valencia Nutrition Study published in the journal *Frontiers in Nutrition* in 2022 showed that compared to less than once per month olive-oil consumption, the consumption of up to 1 tablespoon per day was associated with a 9 percent lower risk of all-cause mortality (death from any cause) and the inclusion of 2 or more tablespoons per day, with a 31 percent lower risk of all-cause mortality.

Other conditions, especially inflammation-related disease, such as arthritis, asthma, and inflammatory bowel disease have been shown to improve with a Mediterranean diet where olive oil is included. However, it is difficult to show an effect of olive oil on its own.

Discovering the compounds in EVOO

Apart from the fat content, there are a number of other important compounds found in extra-virgin olive oil. These include

>> **Pigments.** Including chlorophyll and carotenoids, which contribute to the color. Carotenoids have some antioxidant activity and are classified as bioactive compounds. which are discussed in Chapter 4.

>> **Vitamin E.** Also known as tocopherol, which has antioxidant and anti-inflammatory effects and is beneficial for heart, eye, skin, immune, and nervous system health.

>> **Volatile compounds.** Including hexanals and terpenes, which are responsible for the aromas and flavors in extra-virgin olive oil.

>> **Sterols.** Naturally present in extra-virgin olive oil, which are compounds sometimes added to functional foods (foods with added ingredients claimed to benefit health) to reduce LDL cholesterol levels and may contribute to the LDL lowering effects of extra-virgin olive oil.

>> **Squalene.** A compound that has antioxidant properties and tends to concentrate in skin tissue. It may help to protect for skin cancers.

>> **Polyphenols.** Antioxidant and anti-inflammatory compounds, which are discussed in greater detail in Chapter 6.

There are between 30 and 40 distinct polyphenols in extra-virgin olive oil, depending on how they are measured and classified. The diversity of polyphenols is important for the health benefits of extra-virgin olive oil, and there is even an entire group of polyphenols that is unique to the olive.

The bioactive polyphenols in extra-virgin olive oil can be classified into different groups (see Figure 8-1), but they all have antioxidant effects.

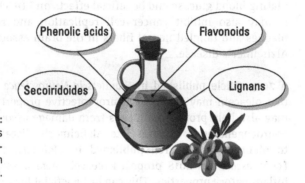

FIGURE 8-1:
Polyphenols in extra-virgin olive oil.

TECHNICAL
STUFF

Most sources cite five major groups of polyphenols (see Chapter 6). However, there are other polyphenols that don't fit neatly into any subgroup because they are structurally quite distinct, including tannins (found in tea and wine), curcuminoids (found in curcumin), and secoiridoides (found in extra-virgin olive oil).

Here are the main ones:

>> **Flavonoids.** Examples are luteolin and apigenin. Flavonoids are polyphenols that are present in many fruits and vegetables.

>> **Lignans.** Examples are pinoresinol and acetoxypinoresinol. Lignans are protective polyphenols that often contribute to the structure and strength of plants. The majority originate from the seed and outer skin of the olive.

>> **Simple phenols.** Examples include tyrosol and hydroxytyrosol. Simple phenols are often derived from more complex molecules.

>> **Secoiridoides.** Examples include oleuropein, oleacein and oleocanthal (see the sidebar). These polyphenols are unique to extra-virgin olive oil and have some very specific and special qualities.

Oleuropein and oleacein are two polyphenols unique to extra-virgin olive oil that have significant potential health benefits.

A review of the research on oleuropein published in the journal *Antioxidants* in 2019 summarized its antioxidant and anti-inflammatory effects as well as its likely contribution to protection from heart disease by reducing blood pressure, regulating blood glucose and beneficial effects on LDL cholesterol. It may also inhibit cancer cell replication and reduce the plaques and tangled neural fibers in the brain associated with Alzheimer's disease.

A 2017 article published in *Frontiers in Neuroscience* suggested that oleacein may also have neuroprotective properties. And it may also help protect brain cells from damage associated with neurodegenerative diseases like Alzheimer's disease. Similar to oleuropein, research published in *Molecular Nutrition & Food Research* in 2018 proposed oleacein also possesses anti-inflammatory properties. This can be beneficial for various conditions where chronic inflammation plays a role.

Oleocanthal is another very potent anti-inflammatory secoiridoid polyphenol. Its mechanism of action is similar to that of non-steroidal anti-inflammatory drugs (NSAIDs) like ibuprofen. It also may reduce the risk of Alzheimer's and other neurodegenerative diseases by preventing amyloid plaque formation and neuroinflammation. Oleocanthal is being investigated for a possible role in cancer prevention and treatment because of its ability in laboratory experiments to inhibit cancer growth. The National Cancer Institute in the United States has identified oleocanthal as a potential nutraceutical (a naturally occurring chemical that can be developed into a medicine) in the fight against cancer, specifically breast cancer.

POLYPHENOL DISCOVERY

Simon had the privilege to meet the scientists who first identified the new polyphenol *oleocanthal* and described its anti-inflammatory effects. Gary K. Beauchamp, PhD and Paul Breslin, PhD tested the sensory properties of liquid anti-inflammatory ibuprofen, which has the tendency to produce mild irritation or burning of the throat and sometimes a cough. Following a trip to Sicily, Dr. Beauchamp noticed that a local extra-virgin olive oil produced a similar effect, inducing a pronounced but not unpleasant burning of the throat. After extensive further investigation, he discovered the polyphenol that had this effect and describe its anti-inflammatory effects comparable to ibuprofen, calling it oleocanthal — *oleum* meaning oil and *kanthos* being the ancient Greek for sting or irritation.

In some Italian circles, particularly among olive oil producers and connoisseurs, extra-virgin olive oil is colloquially described as a "one-cough," "two-cough," or "three-cough" oil. This terminology relates to the distinctive pungency or "bite" that high-quality extra-virgin olive oil often possesses, which is primarily due to the presence of the polyphenol oleocanthal. Like so much in olive oil lore, this has been described by Italians who know their olive oil for generations before oleocanthal was discovered and its effects known.

Tasting the polyphenols of EVOO

Plant polyphenols often taste bitter and pungent, peppery, or spicy to protect the plant from being eaten. Humans, having evolved alongside the plant world, understand that these flavors often belong to plants that are nutritious, healthy, and sometimes medicinal. The antioxidant and anti-inflammatory compounds that possess these taste characteristics can keep us healthy. And these foods and their flavors are regarded as interesting and enjoyable.

There is some evidence that highly palatable ingredients such as the sugars, saturated fats, and salt in highly processed foods stimulate the brain's reward system, conceived in times of food-energy scarcity and potentially reducing the appeal of other flavors. Highly processed foods are often created with more standardized and often milder flavors to appeal to a broad audience. This may condition people to prefer less intense flavors over time and have less tolerance for spicy foods.

It is time to recapture our taste for spiciness and pepperiness. Chapter 10 explores our current understanding of how individual polyphenols influence the taste of extra-virgin olive oil, making healthy and delicious extra-virgin olive oil an excellent place to start to celebrate the abundance of delicious and vibrant flavors in our foods.

REMEMBER

Every bottle of extra-virgin olive oil doesn't have the same quantity of polyphenols. The levels of polyphenols in extra-virgin olive oil are variable. Different olive varieties have different proportions of each polyphenol and levels of total polyphenols. Also, each year's harvest produces different levels of polyphenols, depending on growing and climatic conditions of the olive tree. Polyphenols are likely to be abundant in fresh high-quality extra-virgin olive oil that is harvested early in the season, processed quickly and carefully, and stored correctly. Cumulative exposure to oxygen, heat, and light over time will diminish polyphenol levels and reduce many of the potential health benefits that are dependent on the biological activities of polyphenols.

Knowing Your Daily Intake

Most studies of the health benefits of extra-virgin olive oil are based on between 2 and 3 tablespoons a day. Some research shows that positive effects increase with increasing quantities of extra-virgin olive oil or up to the maximum amounts used in the study. It's commonplace in traditional Mediterranean diets to consume 5 tablespoons a day for cooking and flavoring meals on the dining table.

Oxidative stress and *pro-inflammatory* (causing inflammation) conditions can occur throughout the day. Evidence suggests that it's wise to consume extra-virgin olive oil regularly and with every meal. Starting the day with a "shot" of extra-virgin olive oil on an empty stomach may currently be in vogue and practiced from time to time in some Mediterranean cultures, but there is little evidence to support this as a particularly desirable way to consume extra-virgin olive oil. Extra-virgin olive oil is a food and not a supplement.

TIP

It's also very trendy to have extra-virgin olive oil in ice cream or mixed into cocktails or coffee, which can be fun to try from time to time. But remember that extra-virgin olive oil's protective characteristics are not limitless. It's best to enjoy extra-virgin olive oil at the heart of a healthy Mediterranean-style dietary pattern in order to maximize the benefits of both.

Increasing the Efficacy

Extra-virgin olive oil is a beautiful food at the center of Mediterranean culture and cuisine and is an essential component of the Mediterranean diet. As we mention in Chapter 7, scientists can measure some of its individual effects with experiments in laboratories and with trials in humans. Further research shows how extra-virgin olive oil works in combination with other foods.

Combining EVOO with other nutritional foods

Compounds in extra-virgin olive oil have benefits on their own. However, when extra-virgin olive oil is combined with other foods, those effects are often multiplied. The powerful antioxidant properties of extra-virgin olive oil when used as a marinade or cooking oil can protect other foods from heat-related changes, which may result in the formation of free radicals and other chemicals that have been implicated as possible carcinogens.

For centuries, olive oil has been used to preserve foods that otherwise may become rancid. Nutrients and bioactive compounds like polyphenols are exchanged between foods during cooking, especially with vegetables and extra-virgin olive oil. The end result is that both the olive oil and the food have higher levels of available micronutrients and bioactive compounds. When red wine and extra-virgin olive oil are enjoyed together at a meal, research has demonstrated that the polyphenols from both the wine and the extra-virgin olive oil are more available for absorption — greater than the sum of the individual ingredients.

Experiments have shown fascinating insights into the relationship between diet and biomarkers of inflammation. A 2024 UK-based study published in *The Journal of Nutrition* found convincing evidence that higher dietary polyphenol intake is associated with lower blood inflammatory markers, confirming other research. Findings from an experiment published in the journals *Nutrients* in 2019 showed quite extraordinary and rapid changes in inflammatory markers. A group of people without any apparent inflammatory condition were fed a low-quality diet high with highly processed foods, refined sugars, and saturated fat for 48 hours and had baseline measurements of their biomarkers of inflammation. Following a single meal of sofrito rich in bioactive compounds from the ingredients of extra-virgin olive oil, tomatoes, onions, and garlic, researchers were able to demonstrate a significant and sustained reduction in the participants' biomarkers of inflammation. (For Amy's sofrito recipe, see Chapter 17.)

This experiment is an extraordinary testament to the relevance of the type of food consumed at each meal. Overall health does not simply depend on the cumulative effect of our lifestyle over many years but can be affected by your food choices today.

TECHNICAL
STUFF

As a physician, Simon is used to measuring *biomarkers of inflammation* in the blood of patients who have chronic inflammatory conditions, such as arthritis. These chemicals indicate the level of background inflammation that may be raised in a patient with a chronic inflammatory illness. The biomarkers can also be within the normal range but perhaps higher than average in a person with an overabundance of oxidative stress and pro-inflammatory factors in their lifestyle. Examples of these biomarkers include C-Reactive Protein (CRP) and Interleukin 6 (IL-6).

FROM THE
AUTHORS

It's important to note that the average person in the Mediterranean region (unless they are a renowned olive-oil producer) wouldn't have scientific knowledge of the amazing health benefits of extra-virgin olive oil. What they do have, however, are time-honored traditions that are passed down from generation to generation. Using a combination of olive oil and other anti-inflammatory ingredients to ease pain, appreciating the role of olive oil in folkloric and religious ceremonies, and skillfully coaxing the maximum amount of flavor out of olive oil are common knowledge, which are now backed up by science.

Having a healthy gut

Our gut microbiome — the trillions of microbes that occupy our gastrointestinal tract —plays a vital role in processing our foods and regulating hormones, including the ones that manage our metabolism and others that regulate our mental health and well-being. A diverse gut microbiome that supports good health is dependent on a diet that feeds them plenty of fiber and plant compounds including polyphenols. Extra-virgin olive oil combined with vegetables contributes to a healthy gut environment in which "friendly" microbes can flourish.

3

Incorporating Olive Oil into Your Daily Life

IN THIS PART . . .

Practice how to taste olive oil properly.

Identify the flavor features, taste, and health properties. Choose different varieties based on their taste.

Determine how to pair extra-virgin olive oil with food and wine.

Chapter **9**

Tasting Olive Oil Properly

Olive oil that fulfils the strict criteria required to be described as extra-virgin olive oil will have features of fruitiness, bitterness, and pungency and have no defective aromas or taste characteristics, indicating contamination, rancidity or fermentation. But there's much more to the taste of extra-virgin olive oil (EVOO) than these characteristics. In particular, taste profiles can indicate the presence of health-giving polyphenols.

In this chapter, we explore the myriad of taste sensations you can experience with a good extra-virgin olive oil. We hope that you'll embrace a journey to discover the diverse and exquisite taste experiences with extra-virgin olive oil.

Considering the Flavor Profiles

Tasting extra-virgin olive oil is a skill that you can cultivate at home, but there are also various courses and qualifications available for those who want to take their knowledge further. Experts who are employed to taste extra-virgin olive oils for organizations that regulate the sensory standards, judge competitions, or are involved in the assessing standards in production or importing of extra-virgin olive oil will have undergone more rigorous training.

This section will help you become familiar with the language of taste and introduce you to the exciting range of flavors waiting to be discovered.

Enjoying the flavor

The most important thing about tasting EVOOs is to recognize the flavors you most enjoy. It's always good to experiment with new oils, because you'll find something different in the profile of a good-quality oil, and our tastes need not be static or set in stone. For many people, the first time they taste a good-quality extra-virgin olive oil, the bitterness and spiciness may not be what they expect or are used to. But most will come to enjoy and value those characteristics.

For people who like milder extra-virgin olive oils, Chapter 10 explores the olive varieties that are used to create "softer" oil.

TIP

It's the polyphenols in extra-virgin olive oil that tend to give it the bitterness and pungency, but that doesn't mean you need to always have a strong oil. Differences in polyphenol levels may not always be entirely discernible by the taste of an oil because other flavors can change how an oil is perceived. It is probably best to find several good-quality extra-virgin olive oils that you like and vary them with different foods. There's no doubt that if you enjoy your extra-virgin olive oil throughout the day, you will get a healthy amount of those precious polyphenols.

REMEMBER

There is a difference between a low-quality blended oil with bland, uninteresting flavors and a high-quality mild, "gentle," "soft," or "delicate" extra-virgin olive oil, which combines complex and harmonious positive features with gentle bitterness and pungency. Mild extra-virgin olive oils can win awards for sophistication and elegance.

Understanding flavor features

The first thing to remember about tasting a good-quality extra-virgin olive oil is that the experience is very personal and intimate. It's also influenced by many factors, including our previous experience of flavors, cultural background, ability to recognize and compare our sensations with other foods we are familiar with, and the many psychological aspects of our perception. If you can't quite discern the descriptions in the tasting notes on the bottle, there's no need to feel that you are wrong. Sommeliers have years of training, and sometimes even the experts politely disagree.

You may have some information about the oil and its provenance, or you may be tasting it "blind." There is nothing wrong with knowing where the oil comes from — being able to imagine its origins may add to the enjoyment of tasting it. Professional tasters need to be as objective as possible. They will often have little or no information about the oil that is presented in standardized glass tasting cups that are often in dark blue or red to disguise the color of the oil, which may introduce prejudices or preconceptions.

TECHNICAL STUFF

When an extra-virgin olive oil has a description of how it tastes, this usually includes aromas and tactile perceptions. Flavors refer specifically to the sensations perceived by the taste buds on the tongue (sweet, sour, salty, bitter, umami). Aromas are the sensations through the nose, and pungency is a tactile sensation often in the throat.

In order to pass the sensory criteria for extra-virgin olive oil, an oil must have no defects, which are considered later in this chapter. It must have fruitiness and some bitterness and pungency. Within the definition of fruitiness are many different positive flavor experiences; the flavors may be present in an extra-virgin olive oil, depending on the variety or varieties and the growing conditions, which can vary from year to year. Examples include "green fruitiness," such as grassy or herbaceous notes, "ripe fruitiness" reminiscent of ripe apples or tropical fruits, "citrus" features that bring to mind berries or lemons, and other "vegetal" notes like almonds or artichoke.

You can use Figure 9-1 to note the different aromas and taste in the olive oil.

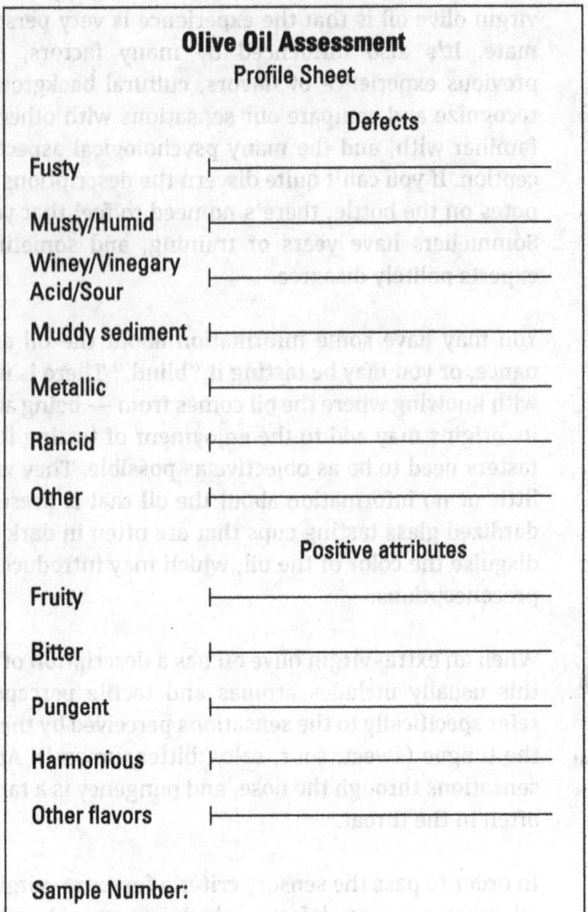

Olive Oil Assessment
Profile Sheet

Defects

Fusty

Musty/Humid

Winey/Vinegary
Acid/Sour

Muddy sediment

Metallic

Rancid

Other

Positive attributes

Fruity

Bitter

Pungent

Harmonious

Other flavors

Sample Number:

FIGURE 9-1:
Olive oil assessment form.

Features in extra-virgin olive oil can be particularly recognizable from the same region. For example, EVOOs from Sicily are often noted to have a particular taste reminiscent of tomato leaf or tomato on the vine due to the presence of the Nocellara del Belice variety of olive used for many oils.

It's best to try an extra-virgin olive oil by itself initially and there are ways to maximize that experience. Tasting extra-virgin olive oil is an art that mirrors wine tasting in its attention to sensory details (see Figure 9-2).

Here's a guide on how to properly taste extra-virgin olive oil to appreciate its complex aromas and flavors:

1. **Choose the right environment.** Make sure the environment is free from strong odors or distractions. Neutral conditions help in accurately identifying the subtle nuances of the oil. Avoid eating or drinking foods or drinks immediately before you taste the extra-virgin olive oil.

2. **Use the appropriate glassware.** Ideally use a small, dark glass to taste the oil. The darkness of the glass prevents color from influencing your perception of quality. A tulip-shaped glass is ideal as it helps to concentrate the aromas. If you can't access this type of glass, don't worry; this method is mainly for the professionals.

3. **Pour the oil.** Pour a small amount of olive oil into the glass, just enough to swirl around and cover the bottom.

4. **Warm the oil.** Cup the glass in your hands and cover the top with your other hand. The warmth of your hands will help release the oil's aromas. Let it warm for a minute or so.

5. **Swirl the oil.** Gently swirl the oil in the glass to further release its aromas. This action helps the volatile compounds that contribute to the oil's scent to evaporate.

6. **Smell the oil.** Bring the glass up to your nose and inhale gently. Take note of the first aromas that hit your senses. Look for descriptors like fruity, grassy, nutty, or fresh. Also, be aware of any off-odors that may indicate spoilage, such as mustiness or a rancid smell.

7. Sip the oil. Take a small amount of oil into your mouth but do not swallow immediately. Instead, slurp it — drawing air into your mouth to help spread the oil across your palate. This action enhances flavor detection as it aerates the oil and releases more flavor compounds. Feel free to make a noise when you bring air into your mouth. The Italians call this *strippaggio* so it must be cool!

8. Taste and feel. As you hold the oil in your mouth, focus on the flavors and the tactile sensations. Notice if it feels smooth, stinging, or thick. Pay attention to whether it tastes bitter or peppery, which is sometimes a delayed sensation or mild warmth in the throat. This may be most pronounced as you swallow.

9. Swallow. Finally, swallow the oil to notice any lingering flavors and the sensation as you complete the tasting.

10. Cleanse your palate. Cleanse your palate between different oils with a small piece of apple or plain water. Sparkling water is particularly good to refresh your taste buds.

REMEMBER

When you start tasting, use small amounts of oil. You may be surprised by the pungency after tasting extra-virgin olive oils without any food for the first time. The tasting experience may bring tears to your eyes!

Extra-virgin olive oil can have delightful flavor attributes like grassy and herbaceous notes, reminiscent of freshly cut grass or green leaves. You may also encounter fruity flavors, ranging from the sweet, mild taste of ripe apples to the zesty, citrus-like brightness of lemons. Nutty flavors can emerge, bringing to mind almonds or walnuts, while subtle bitterness adds complexity, akin to artichokes or leafy greens.

Figure 9-3 shows how an extra-virgin olive oil can be "mapped" using a chart to visualize the different flavor contributions.

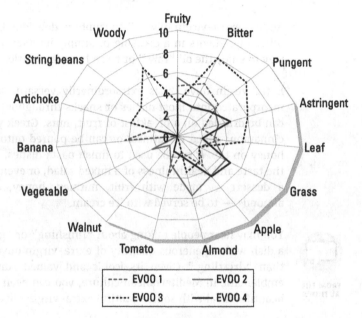

FIGURE 9-3: A spider chart illustrating different flavors of EVOO.

A good extra-virgin olive oil will be "balanced," referring to the even distribution of positive flavor attributes like bitterness, fruitiness, and pungency, creating a well-rounded taste. It should also be "harmonious," when these flavors complement each other seamlessly, resulting in a unified, pleasing taste experience that enhances the overall enjoyment of the oil.

TIP

If you are tasting more than one extra-virgin olive oil and you expect to be tasting delicate and more robust oils, it's a good idea to taste the mildest oil first. That way your palate won't be overwhelmed by the stronger oil.

Matching taste with health benefits

The contribution of extra-virgin olive oil to health is through its credentials as a nutrient-rich fat with a unique profile of protective polyphenols, to preserve and protect the olive fruit in its changing and challenging environment. The oleic acid monounsaturated fat gives a mild buttery flavor; volatile compounds provide many of the complex aromas and sensations; and the polyphenols tend to impart some bitterness and pungency. This is discussed in detail in Chapter 6.

Adding extra-virgin olive oil to combine delicious flavors with other ingredients in a dressing or simply by itself is a healthy way to enjoy the oil "raw," or fresh from the bottle.

Extra-virgin olive oil is extraordinarily versatile and can be incorporated into most dishes or snacks throughout the day. It can be drizzled on a breakfast of fruit, nuts, Greek yogurt, and cinnamon; added to oatmeal or can be poured onto toast with honey on top. It can be used to finish pasta dishes, to enhance the taste and healthfulness of a mixed salad, or even baked into a dessert — made with fruit, nutmeg, honey, and flaked almonds — to be served with ice cream.

FROM THE AUTHORS

You may hear people talking about "finishing" or "garnishing" a dish with a generous quantity of extra-virgin olive oil rather than "drizzling." Given its iconic and valued status that is emblematic in Mediterranean culture, you can even "anoint" a beautiful meal with some beautiful extra-virgin olive oil.

Using extra-virgin olive oil as a cooking medium combines flavors with other ingredients to produce delicious and healthy meals. For example, when extra-virgin olive oil and vegetables are cooked together, several beneficial processes occur. The oil coats the vegetables, which helps distribute the heat evenly, preventing the vegetables from burning and ensuring they cook uniformly. This is particularly important in methods like sautéing, where even exposure to heat can make a significant difference in vegetables' texture and taste.

As the cooking continues, the oil aids in breaking down and softening the vegetables' fibers, making them more tender and easier to chew and digest. The oil facilitates this process, allowing heat to penetrate more deeply into the vegetables, enhancing their texture and bringing out their natural flavors. There is also exchange of nutrients and bioactive compounds between the ingredients. Finally, the oil contributes flavor to the vegetables, infusing them with its own unique aroma and taste. This combination of enhanced texture, even cooking, and flavor enrichment leads to a dish where the vegetables are palatable, appealing and extraordinarily healthy.

Try simply roasting a mixture of chopped colorful mixed vegetables, red onions, garlic, and some herbs or spices in a generous amount of good extra-virgin olive oil to complement fish or marinated meat also roasted in the oil.

After you get used to the ubiquitous presence of extra-virgin olive oil in your kitchen and on the table, you can try Amy's delicious sauces and recipes in Part 6 of this book.

FROM THE
AUTHORS

Many restaurants follow the trend of mixing extra-virgin olive oil with balsamic vinegar to serve with bread, believing the pre-appetizer is the height of "good taste." However, mixing the two condiments in this way masks the taste of a high-quality extra-virgin olive oil and a high-quality balsamic vinegar. It may even be a ploy to use poor-quality versions of both, which is difficult to recognize when mixed together.

Working with the Best EVOO

The chances are that you may have a bottle of extra-virgin olive oil in your kitchen. Now you can taste it and see if you like it, or if there are others you may want to try. It's possible that a bottle labeled as extra-virgin olive oil has defects because it has been exposed to air, light, and/or heat. It may even be rancid. It's important to know how to recognize that these defects have occurred because it certainly will diminish the taste and also health qualities.

Becoming a defect detective

We are naturally optimistic and expect the extra-virgin olive oil we buy to be excellent quality, but sadly there are times when this doesn't happen. Any defects will mean the oil is no longer "extra virgin" in quality, because the criteria for extra-virgin olive oil are based on taste tests as well as laboratory chemical analysis.

Chapter 2 provides a complete guide to the standards necessary and defines in detail the most common defects, which include rancidity, fustiness, mustiness, a muddy sediment flavor; and evidence of oxidation or contamination through poor handling, overripe olives, or improper storage conditions. An aroma that reminds you of the smell of nail varnish remover may be the most obvious recognizable defect or a taste similar to stale nuts or vinegar will also provide you with the awareness that the oil has deteriorated.

REMEMBER

Hydrolysis of an extra-virgin olive oil degrades it, breaking down the fatty acids bound together to become free fatty acids and increasing the measurable acidity of the oil. Oxidation will consume the protective polyphenols, therefore reducing in concentration as the oil deteriorates. So a defective oil will not be as healthy as an oil that is protected from oxidation, although it will still retain the monounsaturated fats.

Taking a deeper dive into EVOOs chemistry

Focusing on the science of extra-virgin olive oil connects its flavor and aroma characteristics with its health benefits, and you can use this information to determine when an extra-virgin olive oil has qualities of excellence. Considering how taste and smell relate to the chemical properties of extra-virgin olive oil, it's no surprise that people have grown up for generations using it for food and medicinal purposes. (Refer back to Chapter 7 for more detailed information on olive oil's role in the Mediterranean diet.)

Modern sensory science, which aims to explain perceptions of smell and taste, is a relatively new area of research and is important for us to be able to gain insight into the links between chemistry, taste, and quality.

Here are a few examples of compounds we know contribute to the experience of extra-virgin olive oil:

» *Terpenes* such as limonene provide a citrus-like aroma, indirectly adding freshness to the flavor. Alpha-Pinene gives a pine-like, resinous aroma also adding freshness.

» *Alcohols* like hexanols provide fresh, green, grassy aromas.

» *Volatile phenols,* such as eugenol, give a clove-like aroma that adds to our perception of spiciness, with a sweetness in the vanilla-like aroma of vanillin.

» *Squalene* is associated with a nutty aroma, contributing to a mild nutty flavor.

Non-polyphenol compounds in extra-virgin olive oil have been identified with following tastes:

» *Aldehydes,* like hexanals, contribute to fresh, grassy and green flavors

» *Ketones,* such as 1-Penten-3-one, provides a fruity and almond-like taste, with 6-Methyl-5-hepten-2-one giving a citrus-like flavor.

» *Esters,* which include ethyl acetate and methyl acetate, impart sweet, fruity flavors.

» *Fatty Acids,* including oleic acid and linoleic acid, also give flavor including nutty and sweet or bitter tones.

Polyphenols in extra-virgin olive oil have been studied individually for their flavor contribution and other sensations. Table 9-1 lists the flavor contributions in the group of polyphenols known as *secoiridoides*, which also have antioxidant and anti-inflammatory effects.

TABLE 9-1 Flavors of a Group of Polyphenols: Secoiridoides

Polyphenols	Flavor Contributions
Oleuropein	Bitter
Oleuropein Aglycone (from the breakdown of oleuropein)	Bitter
Deacetoxyoleuropein Aglycone (from the breakdown of oleuropein)	Bitter
Oleocanthal	Pungent, peppery (similar to ibuprofen's stinging sensation)
Ligstroside	Bitter
Ligstroside Aglycone (from the breakdown of ligstroside)	Bitter
Oleacein	Bitter, pungent

These compounds shown in Table 9-1 are sometimes broken down to the simpler phenols called *tyrosol* and *hydroxytyrosol*, which provide a milder bitterness. Other compounds related to polyphenols may also contribute to bitterness or spiciness including vanillic acid, p-coumaric acid, and ferulic acid.

As we deepen our understanding of extra-virgin olive oil's complex chemistry, the better we are able to choose and enjoy extra-virgin olive oil based on its taste, smell, and corresponding health benefits.

IN THIS CHAPTER

» Understanding different olive
varieties

» Recognizing that variety plays a role
in taste and polyphenol levels

» Exploring how to combine foods
with extra-virgin olive oils

Chapter **10**

Deciphering the Taste of Different Varieties

t's estimated that there are more than a thousand olive varieties or *cultivars* in the world. The criteria and process required for confirmation of the existence of a new variety is rigorous and sometimes takes many years. The tree and its fruit must be distinct from others in its physical characteristics and chemistry, with genetic traits being stable over several generations.

All olives are initially green in color before maturing and darkening to purple and black as they ripen. Each variety has its own traits including the conditions in which it flourishes, its hardiness, its water needs and ultimately in its taste profile.

Some cultivars are used exclusively for table olives, others solely for oil production, and a number of varieties are so versatile that they can be used for both. More than half of the recognized varieties are considered to be suitable for oil production. The International Olive Council (IOC) currently estimates that 85 percent of world olive oil production is from 139 varieties, illustrating the remarkable choice and contrast in oils available on the international markets. Some countries have even greater diversity of cultivars especially where local traditional farming practices are protected and valued, with Spain estimated to use 250 varieties, Greece 170, and Italy cited as having up to 500 cultivars used for the production of olive oil.

REMEMBER

An olive oil made from a particular variety of olive tends to have characteristic flavors associated with that cultivar, but there are many other variables that affect the flavor such as the cultivating method, harvesting time, and processing techniques.

In this chapter, we discuss a little more about these varieties, their usual countries of origin, typical innate polyphenol content, and most likely flavor attributes. This will help you choose the best extra-virgin olive oils (EVOOs) and determine how their flavors are likely to interact with other foods.

Checking Out Varieties of Olive Oil

As olive trees of the species Olea Europaea have evolved with human cultivation over many thousands of years, selective breeding to find the most resilient and productive trees has resulted in distinctive varieties emerging in particular parts of the world.

TIP

If you visit an olive grove, you can find out how to recognize different olive varieties from their physical appearance. For example, in Spain, the Picudo variety, known for its fine, fruity oil with hints of apple and almond flavors, bears an olive with a tapered end. Picudo means "pointed" in Spanish. The Hojiblanca cultivar, which generally produces a more intense oil, may be grown alongside the Picudo. It's distinctive because the greater intensity of silver coloring on the underside to its leaves — an adaption to preserve water— is so bright they almost look white in appearance. *Hoja* is the Spanish word for leaf and *blanca* means white.

Different olive varieties not only possess specific physical attributes, but also produce different flavors in their oil. Additionally, their oils have variations in their chemistry, including the levels of polyphenols.

Discovering cultivars in different countries

Extra-virgin olive oils that come from particular geographical regions or individual estates will have sufficient traceability to be able to describe the trees from which the olives were harvested. Producers of good extra-virgin olive oils appreciate that some consumers wish to know the variety or varieties of olives used to make the oil in order to anticipate its likely qualities.

The choice of cultivar used depends on a number of factors. Tradition often dictates planting strategies in countries with a long history of olive oil production. More recently, climate change may affect the choice of varieties used, with the introduction of non-native cultivars or an increase in the proportion of existing trees that are more resistant to drought or disease in future.

With the demand for common and recognizable varieties increasing and the tendency of new groves to plant trees of those cultivars, it's important that older, heritage varieties are preserved. They may have as yet undiscovered health or resilience benefits, and certainly have an important place in local culture as well as unique flavor profiles. Diversity in olive oil cultivars is something to be celebrated and enjoyed and must be protected.

FROM THE AUTHORS

Biodiversity is paramount in Italy, which is known for having the largest number of cultivars of olives and varieties of grapes. The Italian government and the European Union offer special incentive programs for farmers, in various regions of the country, to continue growing indigenous cultivars in an effort to improve the environment. Healthy ecosystems that provide clean air, water, and food depend on a wide range of animals, plants, and microorganism. Some of the most unique cultivars that Amy has seen are completely white olives. In Calabria, Italy, there are several varieties including the Leucocarpa, Leucolea, and the Olivo della Madonna (the Madonna's Olive).

REMEMBER

Some varieties have different names in different countries but may be very similar or even the same cultivar. Conversely, there may be diverse varieties that are simply named the equivalent of "local olive" in a language. Throughout history, in fact, olives were referred to in that way. Only in more modern times, when olives and olive oils are sold across regional and national borders, did it become important for farmers to identify the olives and classify them by their cultivars.

The traditional world of olive oil

The following is an alphabetized list of countries from the "old world" of olive oil, which includes the most common, distinct, original native olive varieties and some of their features. This is by no means exhaustive and does not necessarily reflect the percentage of production. Some countries in the Mediterranean, for example, are planting Greek or Spanish varieties cultivars in preference to their own native ones. In addition, Italian, Greek, and Spanish cultivars are being planted and harvested in places as far away as North and South America, Australia, Africa, and Asia. There are over 60 countries that are members of the IOC, and more in the process of applying to be members.

>> **Algeria.** With a rich tradition of olive oil production that dates back to before Roman times, Algeria dramatically increased production to supply oil to Rome and its empire. It is used extensively in local cuisine and, in common with neighboring countries such as Libya, olive oil is regarded as symbolizing health and hospitality.

- **Chemlali:** The most widely grown variety in Algeria, in common with Tunisia; produces a light and fruity oil with a delicate flavor

- **Sigoise:** Known for its balanced and slightly bitter oil, popular as a table olive

- **Azeradj:** Produces a robust and aromatic oil with a strong flavor profile

- **Blanquette:** Characterized by its mild and fruity oil, often used for blending with other varieties

- **Rougette de Mitidja:** Produces a medium-intensity oil with a balanced and slightly peppery flavor

Croatia. Particularly the Istrian Peninsula, Croatia has a long tradition of olive oil production dating back to ancient times. The Adriatic coast provides an ideal climate for olive growing, with its mild winters and hot, dry summers. Olive oil is a key ingredient in Croatian cuisine, used in everything from salads and marinades to traditional dishes like *pašticada* (beef stew). The production of olive oil is also a significant cultural heritage in Croatia, with many family-run groves and small-scale producers maintaining traditional methods.

- **Oblica:** The most common variety in Croatia and known for its mild and fruity oil

- **Buza:** Indigenous to the Istria region of Croatia, produces a robust and aromatic oil with a complex flavor profile

- **Istarska Bjelica:** Known for its high polyphenol content and strong, peppery oil; also common in Istria

- **Soltanka or Levantinka:** Has two different names; produces green, aromatic, herbaceous, and spicy oils

Egypt. The long history of olive oil production in Egypt dates back to the time of the Pharaohs. Egyptian olive oil is typically mild and slightly fruity, with a smooth finish. The Mediterranean climate of the northern coast, with its hot summers and mild winters, provides ideal conditions for olive cultivation. Olive oil is an essential ingredient in Egyptian cuisine, used in dishes like koshari and various salads. Beyond its culinary uses, olive oil has historical significance in Egypt, having been used in ancient rituals and as a symbol of purity and vitality.

- **Aggizi:** Distinctive for its large fruit size, produces a mild and fruity oil, also popular as a table olive

- **Toffahi:** Produces a high-quality oil with a delicate and slightly sweet flavor, used as a table olive

- **Maraki:** Recognized for its robust and aromatic oil with a balanced flavor profile

- **Wardy:** Known for its smooth and mild oil, widely cultivated in Egypt

- **Sewani:** Produces a mild and slightly fruity oil, commonly used as a table olive

>> **France.** Olive oil production and consumption has been traditionally associated with the warmer climate along the Mediterranean coastline of France. In regions such as Provence, it's celebrated in the distinctive cuisine of the area.

- **Picholine:** Famous for its robust and peppery oil, popular as a table olive

- **Aglandau:** Produces a fruity and slightly bitter oil, common in Provence

- **Salonenque:** Creates a mild and aromatic oil, often blended with other varieties

- **Bouteillan:** Produces a balanced and fruity oil with hints of almond and artichoke

- **Tanche:** A rarer variety mainly found in the Nyons region, produces a mild and delicate oil

>> **Greece.** Considering its origins trace back to the Minoan civilization on Crete, Greece has been producing olive oil for many millennia. Greek olive oil is known for its robust and fruity flavor, often with a peppery finish. Its most common cultivars are a reflection of the country's hot climate and rocky soil. In Greek culture, olive oil has deep symbolic meanings — representing peace, wisdom, and victory — and is used in various religious ceremonies and traditional practices, making it more than just a culinary staple.

- **Koroneiki:** Dominant in Greek olive oil production and known for its high polyphenol content and robust flavor

- **Kalamata:** Famous as a table olive, used to produce a fruity and rich oil (Kalamata is also the name of a region of Greece.)

- **Athinolia:** Creates a balanced oil with slight bitterness, common in the Peloponnese area

- **Manaki:** Produces a mild and aromatic oil, which is popular in central Greece

- **Lianolia:** A specialty of Corfu; often produces a mild, sweet oil with hints of bitterness

>> **Iran.** Although Iran doesn't have a border with the Mediterranean Sea, its climate of moderate temperatures and ample rainfall in the northern regions and on the

Caspian Sea coast, like Gilan and Zanjan, is conducive to olive growing. The cultural significance of olive oil in Iran is growing, with increasing appreciation for its health benefits and culinary versatility.

- **Zard:** A traditional Iranian variety, known for its robust and slightly bitter oil with a fruity aroma
- **Mari:** Produces a mild and sweet oil with a delicate flavor, popular in Iranian olive oil production
- **Rowghani:** Recognized for its smooth and balanced oil
- **Shengeh:** Known for its strong and aromatic oil

>> **Israel.** The cultural significance of olive oil in Israel is profound, with the olive tree symbolizing peace and abundance in Jewish tradition. Israel is also associated with the rich Biblical heritage and ancient symbols of the relationship between humans and the olive tree. It's a staple in all aspects of local cuisine.

- **Barnea:** The most widely grown olive in Israel, known for its mild and balanced oil
- **Souri:** An ancient variety common in the wider geo-graphical region, produces a robust and peppery oil
- **Muhasan:** Produces high-quality oil that is very delicate though aromatic and quite sweet

>> **Italy.** Synonymous with premium, small estate olive oil, Italy's oil production methods are steeped in tradition and artistry. Regions like Tuscany, Calabria, Sicily, and Puglia — the area with the biggest production — are renowned for their distinct styles of olive oil, each influenced by the local cultivars and *terroir* (the soil, environment, and climate). The history of olive oil in Italy dates back thousands of years and is entwined with the influence of classical Greek culture in its southern regions, once called Magna Grecia. Olive oil is an integral part of Italian cuisine and culture, celebrated in dishes from simple bruschetta to elaborate pastas.

- **Frantoio:** Found in many combined variety olive oils from Tuscany, produces a fruity and slightly bitter oil
- **Leccino:** Produces a delicate and mild oil, often blended with others

- **Moraiolo:** Known for its robust and slightly spicy sensations, especially common in central Italy

- **Coratina:** Produces a strong, peppery oil, typically found in regions like Puglia and Calabria in southern Italy

- **Taggiasca:** Tends to result in a mild, fruity oil; mainly found in Liguria

- **Nocellara:** Sought after for its delicate fruity flavor with hints of green apple, almond, and artichoke

- **Biancolilla:** A common variety in Sicily; has a medium-fruity profile with well-balanced notes of almond, green banana, and sometimes citrus

- **Carolea:** Grown in regions of Southern Italy, a medium-fruity with balanced bitterness and peppery notes, sometimes accompanied by hints of apple or almond

>> **Lebanon.** Perhaps Lebanon can claim to be the country from which the Mediterranean-wide culture of olive oil production began. It was probably from Phoenician ports that the colonies around the Mediterranean were supplied with the knowledge of olive cultivation and uses before the birth of the Roman empire. The country's diverse microclimates, from coastal regions to mountainous areas, contribute to the unique qualities of its olive oil. Olive oil is integral to Lebanese cuisine, used in traditional dishes like tabbouleh, baba ghanoush, and various mezes. It also holds cultural significance, often symbolizing health, peace, and hospitality in Lebanese society.

- **Souri:** The primary variety in Lebanon, produces a robust and peppery oil with a fruity flavor

- **Abyad:** Known for its mild and sweet oil

- **Baladi:** Produces a rich and aromatic oil, often used for its balanced and smooth flavor

- **Ayrouni:** Recognized for its high-quality oil, with a distinctive fruity and slightly peppery taste

>> **Morocco.** As another big North African contributor to worldwide supply, Morocco's history also stretches back to Phoenician settlers who brought the olive tree from the eastern Mediterranean. Olive oil is a fundamental

component of Moroccan cuisine, used in dishes like tagine and couscous, and as a dip with bread.

- **Picholine Marocaine:** The dominant variety, known for its robust and fruity oil
- **Menara:** Known for its balanced and aromatic oil
- **Haouzia:** Produces a fruity and slightly bitter oil, common in new plantations

>> **Palestine and Jordan.** Due to their geographical proximity, Palestine and Jordan share many local varieties, and this is whereyou can see some of the most impressive archeological evidence of the earliest production of olive oil. The varieties in this region are a cornerstone of Palestinian and Jordanian cuisine, used in dishes like maqluba and mansaf, and as a dip with bread. Olive trees also hold significant cultural and economic importance, often representing resilience and identity.

- **Souri:** One of the oldest oil varieties; known for its robust, fruity, and slightly peppery oil
- **Nabali:** Produces a mild and sweet oil, with a unique buttery flavor
- **Rumi:** An ancient variety that produces a robust and slightly bitter oil; less common but valued for its historical significance and flavor profile

>> **Portugal.** Olive trees were planted in Portugal before the Romans arrived. Portugal is an Atlantic country rather than a Mediterranean one, but olive trees flourish in the country's diverse landscape, ranging from the Douro Valley to the Alentejo region. The varying climates and soils influence the flavor of the olive oil.

- **Galega:** The most traditional Portuguese variety, known for its delicate and sweet oil
- **Cobrançosa:** Produces a balanced and slightly peppery oil, often blended with other varieties
- **Cordovil de Serpa:** Recognized for its robust and slightly bitter oil
- **Verdeal:** Tends to create a fruity and aromatic oil, common in northern Portugal

>> **Spain.** As The world's largest producer of olive oil, Spain has a deep-rooted history that dates back to before Roman times. The country's diverse climates, from the arid plains of Andalusia to the lush regions of Catalonia, contribute to the unique characteristics of Spanish olive oil. Andalusia alone accounts for a significant portion of the world's olive oil production. Festivals and traditions celebrate the olive harvest, such as the Fiesta del Olivo in Jaén.

- **Picual:** Known for its robust pungent and bitter notes, and high polyphenols; the most widely cultivated olive in the world

- **Arbequina:** A small, sweet olive that produces a mild and fruity oil, popular for its delicate flavor

- **Hojiblanca:** Characterized by its balanced flavor with hints of bitterness and spiciness

- **Cornicabra:** Recognized for its strong flavor and stability, commonly cultivated in central Spain

- **Manzanillo:** Famous in Spain for its balanced flavor, used as a table olive and for oil

>> **Syria.** The olive tree was first cultivated by humankind for its fruit and olive oil in a region that includes Syria. Olive oil is an essential part of Syrian cuisine that is used in a variety of dishes, such as hummus, baba ghanoush, and fattoush. Beyond its culinary uses, olive oil holds cultural significance in Syria, symbolizing peace and prosperity, and is often used in traditional rituals and ceremonies.

- **Qaisi:** Produces a mild and sweet oil, and is popular in many regions of olive oil production

- **Sorani:** Known for its balanced and slightly bitter oil, often found in the northern regions of Syria

- **Zaity.** Another local variety that produces a strong and aromatic oil

>> **Tunisia.** Another country that contributes very significantly to world olive oil production is Tunisia. Ever since the Phoenicians established settlements such as Carthage and introduced the olive tree, the climate and soil of Tunisia has been an environment conducive to oil production. Tunisian

oil and grain production was essential for the prosperity of the Roman Empire. Tunisia now produces world class oils, winning international awards.

- **Chemlali:** The most widely grown olive in Tunisia, produces a light and fruity oil

- **Chetoui:** Known for its intense and slightly bitter flavor profile

- **Zalmati:** Produces a robust and peppery oil, less common but distinctive

>> **Turkey.** Long-standing traditions in Turkey are associated with olive oil and its production. The ancient lands of Anatolia provide archeological evidence of olive oil production dating back to 6000 BCE. Olive oil has been prized as a key ingredient in cooking and marinating as well as its use in salads and accompanying mezes. It has been valued as a medicine and is used in ceremonies and celebrated in local festivals.

- **Memecik:** Known for its balanced and fruity oil, commonly found in western Turkey

- **Ayvalik:** Produces a delicate and aromatic oil, used for table olives

- **Gemlik:** Primarily a table olive but also used on occasions for a smooth and mild oil

- **Nizip Yaglik:** Generally creates a robust and slightly spicy oil

New olive cultivators

For countries that are relatively new to olive cultivation — like the United States, South Africa, Australia, New Zealand, Japan, China and those in South America such as Chile, Peru, and Argentina — varieties that are easy to import and establish are chosen. The olive trees have to flourish in each country's terroir. Tree selection is sometimes a matter of trial and error, with a final mix of varieties evolving as the grove matures.

The cultivars that have been favored in the global rise of olive groves include Arbequina, Coratina, Leccino, Picual, and Koroneiki. Even countries like Egypt, which have a multi-millennial history of producing olive oil, now produce some of these varieties.

Argentina and the United States may have evolved their "own" unique varieties over time: Arauco, a fruity intense oil from Argentina; and the Mission olive, which was introduced by the Spanish to California hundreds of years ago and also has genetic roots in Morocco and Spain.

Blending flavors

Oils may be produced using one type of olive. These are called *monocultivar* or *monovarietal* oils. Alternatively, more than one variety may be used in different proportions to achieve the properties the producer is looking for.

Some farmers will cultivate more than one variety, as long as the conditions are favorable, because the average yield for each cultivar tends to vary. This will also depend on the time of harvesting and weather conditions, but it may be a way for the grove to ensure that a certain volume of oil can be met to guarantee supplies. In recent years, unprecedented climate changes have meant that even the varieties known for the high levels of oil formation have produced less, leading to shortages worldwide and dramatic price fluctuations in extra-virgin olive oil.

Considering total polyphenol levels

It's said that "variety is the spice of life." This is quite literally true when it comes to olive oil.

The effects of polyphenols in extra-virgin olive oil on health are discussed in greater detail in Chapter 6. Many of these compounds contribute to the valuable bitter, spicy, and pungent flavors in the oil. Milder, more delicate oils may have lower levels of total polyphenols (or TPs) than more intense, robust oils.

Average levels of polyphenols in oils of different varieties have been calculated. Most extra-virgin olive oils have levels of TPs somewhere in the region of between 100 and 1,000 milligrams per kilogram (mg/kg). Higher levels can be achieved with particular varieties, which are grown and harvested in specific ways, but the oils produced may be too bitter and pungent for consumption. There is no research to support any claims that they are better for health than oils with, for example, 200 to 600mg/kg.

Typical levels of TPs in some common olive oil varieties, which are usually measured a few weeks after harvest, include

>> **Arbequina.** A delicate Spanish variety: 100 to 200mg/kg

>> **Leccino.** A mild Italian variety: 100 to 250mg/kg

>> **Frantoio.** A moderately intense Italian variety: 200 to 400mg/kg

>> **Hojiblanca.** A moderately intense Spanish variety: 200 to 400mg/kg

>> **Picual.** A robust Spanish variety: 300 to 500mg/kg

>> **Koroneiki.** A robust Greek variety: 300 to 600mg/kg

WARNING

These ranges are useful guidelines but must be treated with care, because TP levels depend on many other factors as well as the variety. It's also important to note that each harvest year produces different polyphenol levels. Fresh, excellent, and carefully produced extra-virgin olive oils will have TP levels in the higher ranges, and may commonly exceed these average numbers.

Extra-virgin olive oils that are produced by larger brands for a mass market are more likely to have lower TPs of 80 to 150mg/kg. This lower polyphenol content is often due to the blending process, which aims to achieve a consistently mild taste and low price point rather than focusing on a high polyphenol content. These oils may also come from less carefully selected olives and may include oils that have been stored for longer periods before blending, further reducing their polyphenol levels.

Refined olive oils have TP levels of 0 to 20mg/kg. The refining process destroys the polyphenols, although sometimes there are small amounts in the final product from adding a virgin oil back in to give a little flavor to an otherwise tasteless fat.

REMEMBER

Polyphenols in foods can interact with other ingredients and undergo complex changes when they meet our gut microbes. The evidence is clear that they're beneficial for health when consumed regularly through the day, combined with a Mediterranean or similar diet and lifestyle.

TIP

If you enjoy the minimum recommendation of 2 tablespoons each day recommended for the health benefits attributed to extra-virgin olive oil, you can easily achieve this with good-quality extra-virgin olive oils especially if they have TP levels of 250mg/kg or greater and if you mix delicate and more intense oils, depending on your preference and food choices.

Beginning to Combine EVOOs with Foods

Choosing an extra-virgin olive oil that best complements certain foods is easy when you get the hang of it. Ultimately, it comes down to preference and what you have available. There are no hard-and-fast rules, but there are general principles to be considered, which are outlined in Table 10-1. (More details about pairing different oils with foods are discussed in Chapter 11.)

FROM THE AUTHORS

Adding a drizzle of extra-virgin olive oil to "finish" a dish, whether it's prepared raw or cooked, is a beautiful way to add a healthy burst of fresh flavor. We recommend you do this at every meal. And while we love the flavors of all extra-virgin olive oils at all times, we recommend it's best to choose an extra-virgin olive oil that enhances, elevates, and balances the dish without overwhelming any flavors of other ingredients.

TABLE 10-1   How to Use Different Intensity Oils

EVOOs	Characteristics	Uses	Food Pairings
Delicate oils: a gentler flavor profile, especially suited for drizzling and very short or low temperature cooking.	Light, buttery, smooth, and subtle with low bitterness and pungency	Ideal for delicate dishes where you don't want the oil to overpower the other flavors	Seafood, as a butter substitute, mashed potatoes, popcorn, baked goods, and light pasta dishes
Moderate intensity oils: medium strength can be used for cooking or flavoring and are very adaptable.	Balanced with a bit more fruitiness, slight peppery notes, and moderate bitterness	Versatile and can be used in a variety of dishes	Grilled vegetables, poultry, soups, stews, salads, and tomato and herb-based or meat-based pasta sauces
Robust oils: The flavors of intense oils can still shine after more prolonged or higher temperature cooking, and complement stronger tasting dishes as finishing oils.	Strong, bold, peppery, and bitter with pronounced fruity flavors	Best for dishes that can stand up to a strong oil, adding depth and complexity	Red meats, hearty salads, cooked greens, legumes, robust soups, and dips like hummus, baba ghanouj, tapenade, aioli, and so on.

Chapter **11**

Pairing Extra-Virgin Olive Oil with Food and Wine

T raditionally, olive oil–producing regions relied on their own oils for all of their needs, and places that didn't produce olive oil locally couldn't use it at all. Fortunately, things have changed. Good-quality olive oil is available all over the world, and many consumers and home cooks are interested in experimenting with new flavors.

While the popularity of extra-virgin olive oil continues to grow, many people still use the same extra-virgin olive oil (EVOO) for everything that they eat. There's no harm in using the same good-quality oil all the time, but it can be fun and interesting to enjoy a variety of oils.

Mixing cultivars and flavors in the kitchen helps to promote a greater daily consumption of extra-virgin olive oil that will, in turn, benefit your health. In addition, just like with wine, when you begin to pair extra-virgin olive oil and food properly, your food will develop deeper levels of flavor and complexity.

In this chapter, we show you different varieties of olive oils that pair best with specific foods and wine.

Understanding How to Complement Flavors

In Italy, the largest professional chefs' organization known as la Federazione Italiana Cuochi, or the Federation of Italian Cooks (https://fic.it) pairs different olive oils with different dishes in the same way that it pairs different wines with them. This healthful and tasty trend has already caught on in upscale restaurants, and we expect that it will eventually trickle down to mainstream restaurants and home kitchens around the world. You don't need to be a professional chef or olive oil sommelier to pair foods and wine. Just follow the tips in this chapter, and you'll be off to a great start.

TIP

Becoming familiar with the aromas and tastes of all the single ingredients that you use — extra-virgin olive oil, individual herbs, spices, fruits, vegetables, and so on — is the best way to educate yourself to be a master at pairing. If you're just starting out, take the opportunity to smell and taste fresh herbs and everything that you're cooking with when you can. Having these aroma and flavor profiles committed to memory will help you to pair them with the oils and wines that best compliment them easily.

Pairing EVOO with Food

There are two ways of pairing food with olive oil: One is to select the olive oil first (perhaps using what you have on hand) and then decide on the food you'll have with it, or decide on the foods first and then select the olive-oil pairing. The suggestions in this section can help you with pairings using either method.

In Table 11-1, olive oils are divided into three flavor categories: Low/Delicate, Medium, and Robust/Intense. For each flavor "strength," we provide a list some of the most popular global olive cultivars and the foods that work best to complement them.

TABLE 11-1 Flavor Categories of EVOOs

EVOOs	Low/Delicate	Medium	Robust/Intense
Best Use	**Foods that have or need a light, buttery olive flavor:** Baking, dessert, chocolate, green salads, mayonnaise, aioli, eggs, fish, pesto, mashed potatoes. Try swapping out for butter in your favorite recipes.	**Foods that benefit from fruity and peppery flavors:** Tomato sauce, salad dressings; grilled, sautéed, or roasted chicken, beef, veal, goat, and lamb; salads, vegetables; firm fish dishes; creamy soups	**Foods that are strongly flavored or need to be enhanced with strong flavor:** Complex tomato and other sauces, legume-based dishes such as beans and greens, stewed lentils, minestrone-style soups, hummus, baba ghanouj and other creamy dips, aged-cheese based dishes, roasted potatoes, grilled vegetables, bitter greens, stews and classic Mediterranean recipes
Attributes and Tasting Notes	Pair with: Taggiasca, Leccino, Casaliva, Olivastro Seggianese, Gentile di Chieti, Picholine, and blends labelled as "delicate"	Pair with Moraiolo, Frantoio, Itrano, Mission, Ascolano, Coratina, Koroneiki, Beldi, Arbequina	Pair with Picual, Carolea, Intosso, Biancolilla, Nocellara del Belice, Lianoli, Chetoui, Manzanillo, Hojiblanca, Cerasuola

Alternatively, you can select the meals first, and then pair it with an extra-virgin olive oil. Table 11-2 shows a few food examples — making a salad, meat, fish, and so on — and the flavor profile of extra-virgin olive oil that works best with that dish.

TABLE 11-2 **Food Combinations with EVOOs**

Foods	Low/Delicate	Medium	Robust/Intense
Salads	Light greens, fresh herbs, and citrus dressings	Greens, tomatoes, cucumber, and vinaigrettes with a bit more acidity	Stronger greens like arugula or kale, and bold dressings with mustard or garlic
Seafood	Light fish like sole or cod, shrimp, and scallops	Salmon, tuna, and grilled seafood	Strong-flavored fish, such as mackerel or sardines
Vegetables	Steamed or lightly sautéed vegetables	Vegetables, including grilled vegetables like zucchini and bell peppers	Hearty vegetables like eggplant, artichokes, and mushrooms
Meats	Light poultry dishes and veal	Chicken, pork, and lamb	Beef, game meats, and barbecued meats
Pasta and Grains	Simple pasta dishes, rice, and couscous	Pasta with tomato-based sauces and risotto	Pesto and pasta with hearty sauces like Bolognese or ragù
Breads and Dips	Lightly toasted bread or simple dipping breads with a sprinkle of salt	Bruschetta and tapenades	Strong dips like spicy harissa hummus

REMEMBER

There's no "wrong" way to pair good-quality extra-virgin olive oil with different foods, especially if you like the way oil tastes. Our sense of taste is affected and influenced by many factors, and what appeals to one person may not be as appreciated by another. We are much more interested in helping people to consume more extra-virgin olive oil and reap the benefits of it than worry about which cultivar they're pairing with their foods.

Taste perceptions depend upon genetics, cultural backgrounds, where we grew up, and even where we live now. In addition, our moods, mentality, and memories can influence the way we taste food. A culinary education, or simply understanding the nuances of flavors, can also change the way we taste things. One of the most pleasurable aspects of cooking and baking for yourself and those you love is that you can combine all these unique aspects into the food preparation and create something that uniquely expresses your own state of being.

**FROM THE
AUTHORS**

Chef Amy tends to pair her menus and recipes using memories, *terroir* (the soil, environment, and climate), and nostalgia as her main inspiration. She enjoys creating dishes that combine flavors that hail from the same parts of the world together to conjure up warm memories of experiencing them there. This gives a trademark "sense of place" to her cuisine. She has also noticed many clients and students who purchase their olive oils based on both quality and nostalgia. Having an olive oil that comes from a place they love, where they have ancestral origins, or want to visit on vacation is meaningful for many people, and a great way to start your food and olive oil pairings.

Matching EVOOs with Wine

There are good wines, very good or great, but with time you can forget them simply because there are many. Then there are unforgettable wines, decidedly only a few, that populate a restricted personal list which we have put them on because they struck us; maybe because of an unexpected organoleptic nuance. Then there are emotional wines, very difficult to find, but easy to recognize. They are the wines which go beyond harmony and sensory complexity because they touch that profound personal emotional sphere which is often reluctant

*to reveal itself. The emotional wines are those wines that
disarm every technical approach, they mix all convictions
and preconceptions to a point that they almost stop the
chaos that surrounds us in a suspended atmosphere!*

— DR. SANTE LAVIOLA, ITALIAN RESEARCH SCIENTIST,
SOMMELIER, AND OFFICIAL TASTER
FOR THE SLOW WINE GUIDE

**FROM THE
AUTHORS**

It's hard for Amy to think about wine pairing without mentioning her dear friend and colleague Dr. Sante Laviola who created
the wine pairings for *Italian Recipes For Dummies.* The previous
quote does a good job of summing up the complex process of
pairing wine with food. It also explains how the emotional pairings have a logic all of their own, and that the goal of a good
pairing is to inspire a delicious moment in time where we can do
nothing else but savor the sensational combination of food and
wine itself.

If you enjoy drinking wine and are comfortable pairing various
olive oils with foods, the next step is to complement your olive
oil and food pairings with wine.

While it's true that there are different styles of wine-pairing
principles, there are some general guidelines that, when
followed properly, can help to enhance the flavors of the food.
Chef Amy's goal, when creating recipes, is to coax the most
flavors out of the ingredients she uses by including the best
extra-virgin olive oil possible, and then build on another layer of
flavor and balance with the right wine.

When extra-virgin olive oil and food are paired properly with
wine, they offer a beautiful balance. Your goal when pairing
them is to use ingredients that are perfect on their own, but
when paired together, they taste better than they did individually. If a paired meal does not meet these criteria flavor-wise, it
isn't properly paired.

Pairings are often combined into two categories — contrasting
and congruent. A *contrasting* pairing creates balance by contrasting tastes and flavors. A *congruent* pairing creates balance by
heightening shared flavors in recipes. Both methods work well
with all types of food.

In addition to flavor, there are health benefits to consuming extra-virgin olive oil with wine as well. Both red wine and extra-virgin olive oil contain polyphenols. The polyphenols in plants, which may have beneficial effects on health, play a role significant in color and taste of both wine and olive oil. Resveratrol is a polyphenol in the skin and juice of grapes. But for red wine specifically, the most important polyphenol may be the *tannins* belonging to the group called *proanthocyanidins*, which contribute to the color of the wine. These wine polyphenols also impart pleasant bitterness and astringency, which are especially rich in some grape cultivars like Tannat, Cannonau, and Nebbiolo. Polyphenol levels similarly increase if the wine is cultivated in a more challenging environment, for example in arid or high-altitude vineyards. A study published in the journal *Nutrients* in 2019 suggests that consuming wine with an extra-virgin olive oil–rich meal makes the polyphenols from wine more readily absorbed.

Here are some general guidelines to keep in mind if you're new at pairing wine:

>> **When in doubt, use terroir to your advantage.** The easiest and most accurate way of pairing a wine with a dish made with extra-virgin olive oil is to combine them with recipes that come from the same areas that they do.

   For example, if you are making a Sicilian pasta dish, such as Pasta alla Norma, you can rest assured that Biancolilla or Nocellara olive oil varieties will pair well with a Nero d'Avola wine because they're from the same region. This is the way the majority of recipes in Part 6 of this book are paired.

>> **Match the intensity of the wine to the intensity of the food and the extra-virgin olive oil.** For example, a delicate poached fish dish such as the Fresh Fish Poached in Olive Oil with Sun-dried Tomato Pesto and Broccolini (see recipe in Chapter 21) is paired with an Alberquiño extra-virgin olive oil because of its delicate flavor and herbaceous and fruity notes. Poaching a delicate fish in a highly robust oil would overwhelm the recipe.

   In addition, this recipe is paired with an Albariño wine from Spain. This pairing was made for several reasons. First, it's a Spanish varietal as is the extra-virgin olive oil. Second, this wine is a light-bodied white that grows in Spain and Portugal. It's loved for its high acidity and refreshing citrus flavors that complement fish perfectly. The second pairing option given is a dry rosé because it's light enough to not overwhelm the fish while offering a bit more intensity than white to complement the sun-dried red pesto sauce used in the recipe.

>> **Acidity has different meanings in different contexts.** It's important to remember that low acidity connotes good-quality extra-virgin olive oil. This does not refer to an acidic taste, but the acidity that is measured in extra-virgin olive oil, which are free fatty acids (FFA). This measure has nothing to do with an acidic flavor.

When people think about foods with acidic tastes, however, they think of citrus, tomatoes, vinegar, and fermented products. When pairing wines, on the other hand, acidity can be a good thing because acidity lends crispness on the palate.

A higher acidity content in wine will create a mouthwatering effect when drinking it. It refreshes the palate in the way that a bite of a crisp green apple would. Winemakers and sommeliers know that sweetness and acidity balance each other. A dry wine needs good levels of acid to provide liveliness and balance, while sweet wines need acidity, so they don't seem excessively sweet.

Sauvignon Blanc, Riesling, Grüner Veltliner, Pinot Noir, Sangiovese, and Nebbiolo are good examples of both white and red wines with higher acidity levels. When pairing acidic foods to extra-virgin olive oil, it's important to choose cultivars that pair best with each recipe. Acidic wines are usually paired with

- Foods with an acidic taste (meaning citrus, unless it's done by an Italian sommelier; see the bullet below), tomatoes, ceviche, fermented foods, and so on. These pair well with Moraiolo, Frantoio, Itrano, Mission, Ascolano, Coratina, Carolea, Koroneiki and Beldi, Arbequina olive cultivars.

- Rich, creamy foods because the acidity in the wine is believed to "cut through" and balance the citrus in the food. Taggiasca, Leccino, Casaliva, Olivastro Seggianese,

Gentile di Chieti, Picholine, Arbequina, and Chemlali each have a buttery flavor, which pairs well with these foods and balances with the acidity in the wine.

- Fish and fried foods: The acid in the wine complements these foods just as fresh lemon does. These items can also benefit from robust flavored olives such as Picual, Coratina, Intosso, Biancolilla, Nocellara del Belice, Lianolia, Chetoui, Manzanillo, Hojiblanca, and Cerasuola.
- Some examples of robust varieties that can stand up to the intensity of meats, sugar, and fatty proteins include Moraiolo, Frantoio, Itrano, Mission, Ascolano, Coratina, Intosso, and Picual.

>> **Tannins and acidity are known to reinforce each other.** A big, tannic red wine that is also high in acidity will seem even more tannic and/or acidic. For this reason, red wine is always paired with red meat. Picual, Carolea, Intosso, Biancolilla, Nocellara del Belice, Lianolia, Chetoui, Manzanillo, Hojiblanca, Cerasuola are some of the cultivars that pair best with strong flavors.

>> **Different cultures view citrus pairings differently.** According to the Italian Sommeliers Association (AIS), citrus is never paired with wine. In a traditional Italian salad course, wine would not be served because of the vinegar or citrus juice content. French and American wine pairing philosophies, on the other hand, include pairing citrus flavors with wine.

>> **When serving desserts, it's important to pair them with a sweet dessert wine.** Passito, Dolce, Marsala, Moscato d'Asti, Muscat, and Ice Wine are generally paired with different desserts. Generally delicate types of olive oil varieties such as Taggiasca, Leccino, Casaliva, Olivastro Seggianese, Gentile di Chieti, Picholine, and blends labeled as "delicate" are the best choices when making desserts, which don't compete but rather complement their sweetness as well as the sweetness of wine. In Chapter 22, Chef Amy also uses Hojiblanca and Koroneiki cultivars in different dessert recipes that benefit from additional intensity due to their simple ingredients.

>> **Sparkling wines can be paired with all types of foods.** If you've prepared a perfectly paired combo of food and extra-virgin olive oil but aren't quite sure of which wine to pair with it, remember that you can't go wrong with a little bubbly. Sparkling wines — including Champagne, Cava, and Prosecco — contain high levels of acidity and small amounts of sugar, which are two extremes that complement flavor elements in almost any food. They help to clean the palate and balance acidic foods, such as fried foods, and can stand up to spicy food, while remaining tame enough to enjoy with dessert. Sparkling wines are often served at the beginning because they pair well with a variety of appetizers and can be followed by heavier wines, or are served at the end to finish a meal. In this case, the bubbles help to refresh the palate for the sweet course. Chocolates and bubbly, anyone?

Pairing is extremely intimidating for a lot of people, even professional chefs, yet they may be embarrassed to admit it. That's because to pair food/extra-virgin olive oil with wine/extra-virgin olive oil effortlessly, you have to either have grown up in a culture that uses those pairings; or have taken culinary, wine, and extra-virgin olive oil education courses. Of course, you could have also spent a lot of time researching on your own.

The suggestions in this chapter are just the beginning. If you're new to extra-virgin olive oil, wine, or cooking, embarking on an educational odyssey can be rewarding and exciting. Start by experimenting with the recipes in Part 6 of this book and follow the suggested pairings to get a taste for the ones that you like best. Remember to keep a journal to write down notes of pairings that work particularly well for you and include favorite combinations from restaurants or trips. Brush up on terroir and its influences on wine varieties and olive cultivars that flourish in the places you love. Before you know it, you'll be well versed in one of the hottest new culinary trends that has its roots in the ancient Mediterranean! *Alla salute!*

4

Choosing Extra-Virgin Olive Oil

Discover what you need to know to buy the best olive oil for your money.

Find out how to recognize proper packaging and maximize freshness with the correct storage procedures.

Figure out where to purchase olive oil and take into account the price and quality.

Chapter **12**

Buying Extra-Virgin Olive Oil

It's important to understand the meaning of the myriad of terms and phrases commonly used on the packaging of extra-virgin olive oil (EVOO) and also on the websites and social media of producers and importers. Some of the words are mandatory and are regulated by local laws, while other descriptions are added by the producer to help customers understand the profile of their extra-virgin olive oil.

In this chapter, we show you how to become a discerning consumer of extra-virgin olive oil by decoding not only the label terminology but also the claims about olive oil's health properties, which are often made for marketing purposes. Although many of the health claims are legally allowed in most countries, this chapter will help you sort through the unjustified claims that are only hype and designed to entice you to buy one particular brand of extra-virgin olive oil over another.

Deciphering the Labels

Every bottle of olive oil should have a clear description on its label to indicate whether it's extra-virgin olive oil or refined olive oil. The words *extra-virgin olive oil* can only be used on the label if it has passed the rigorous chemical and sensory tests described in Chapters 2 and 4. Refined olive oil must be labelled as "olive oil," though it may be presented as "pure olive oil," "light olive oil," or "extra light olive oil."

Nutrition labels

In most countries, there are laws that requires a basic-nutrition panel to be written on foods labels, which are identified as *Nutrition Facts* for brands produced in the United States. This usually covers the energy in calories, the total macronutrients — fats, carbohydrates, and proteins — as well as saturated fats, sugar, and salt. There may be other requirements depending on local laws.

Olive oil is permitted to be described as 100-percent fat on nutritional labels, but it also has "negligible amounts" of carbohydrate, sugar, protein, and salt, although some regions allow the amounts to be listed as zero. Other important micronutrients and bioactive compounds in olive oil, like vitamin E and polyphenols, are also present in small amounts but generally not required to be included on nutritional labels.

The labeling requirements are different depending on the country where the olive oil is sold. In Europe, the nutritional information is expressed in grams per 100 milliliters of oil, and the fat is further divided into saturated, monounsaturated, and polyunsaturated fat. The United States has different guidelines, which are outlined in the following section.

Nutritional facts

In the United States, where the laws are regulated by the Food and Drug Administration (FDA), it's mandatory to quantify total fat and saturated fat, while monounsaturated and polyunsaturated levels are optional. The FDA also requires protein, carbohydrates, trans fats, cholesterol, dietary fiber, sugar, and sodium to be listed, though these will be zero or negligible for olive oil.

The nutrients are listed in grams and *percentage daily value* or *%DV*. The %DV is a guide to the nutrients' optimum recommended daily intake. This is distinct from the Recommended Dietary Allowance (RDA), which is based on age/sex. It reflects the amount of a nutrient an average individual should aim to consume in a day, based on public health recommendations. For some nutrients, like dietary fiber, vitamins, and minerals, the goal is to meet or, in some cases, exceed the %DV. For others, like saturated fat, cholesterol, and sodium, consumers are generally advised not to exceed the %DV.

In the United States, the nutrition label is expressed per serving rather than per 100 milliliters. For olive oil, a serving is defined as 1 tablespoon.

REMEMBER

Nutritional labels are limited in scope. In the case of %DV, they are designed for an "average person." The nutritional content on the label is based on the belief that calories are an accurate reflection on likelihood of gaining weight and saturated fats from all sources are harmful. Some of the false assumptions about calories and fats are explored in Chapter 5.

Additional categories in other countries

Some countries — like the United Kingdom, Australia, and Europe — encourage or enforce other systems of nutritional profiling designed to support consumers to make healthy choices. These may be in the form of traffic light colors, with red, amber, and green indicating a spectrum from least healthy to healthy. Unfortunately, because of the oversimplistic assumption that increased calories and total fat are unhealthy, in some instances this can result in extra-virgin olive oil receiving less than a complete endorsement of its health credentials. Until such categorization is more nuanced and includes beneficial nutrients and bioactive compounds such as polyphenols, we recommend that you "take them with a pinch of salt."

The energy content of food is usually expressed in calories (cal) in the United States and kilocalories (kcal) in most other countries, which are technically the same measurement. Additionally, energy content can also be listed in joules (J) or kilojoules (kJ), which is more common in countries using the metric system — 1 kcal equals 4.184 kJ. The energy content in olive oil, like in other foods, is derived from its macronutrient composition — primarily fats. Since fats provide about 9 kcal per gram, the calculation for olive oil (which is nearly 100 percent fat) is straightforward. For example, if a tablespoon of olive oil (about 14 grams) contains 14 grams of fat, it would provide approximately 126 kcal (14 grams x 9 kcal/gram). In terms of weight and volume, a milliliter of volume is approximately equivalent to a 0.9 gram in weight.

Legal necessities

In order to fulfill the criteria for extra-virgin olive oil, there must be guarantees of purity. While this isn't widely practiced, the International Olive Council (IOC) advises that extra-virgin olive oil is further defined on the label with the words "superior olive oil obtained from olives and solely by mechanical means." This phrase clarifies that the oil is exclusively from olives and is in the superior category classed as "extra virgin." Refined olive oil is usually processed with chemicals and heat rather than solely by mechanical methods.

This also has relevance for infused, flavored, or gourmet oils that have ingredients like garlic, chiles, lemon, or herbs. There are numerous variations on those themes. Sometimes a flavor is added to the oil after milling, but more often the process is done *agrumato*, (processing a small percentage of the added ingredient with the olives at the mill). For example, whole lemons may be added to the olives at the beginning of the process. These products, while appealing to many, may not be described as being made with extra-virgin olive oil because the end product will not fulfill the criteria of extra-virgin olive oil. The chemistry and taste characteristic will be altered. In Europe, the oil may have the quality and health benefits of extra-virgin olive oil, but since it has been altered beyond the recognition of the standards set by the IOC and Codex for extra-virgin olive oil, it must bear the words "olive oil" without reference to "extra virgin."

Unnecessary or misleading phrases on labels

Many olive oils have potentially misleading phrases on their labels. Here are a few examples:

>> **Cold pressed:** This term, often seen on bottles of extra-virgin olive oil, originally referred to olives being pressed without heat to produce oil, preserving the olive oil's flavor and nutritional quality. However, most modern olive oil is produced using centrifugation rather than pressing, and temperature levels are generally kept to between 20 and 25 degrees centigrade to guarantee the oil will be *extra virgin*. The term persists for historical reasons and marketing appeal, but it doesn't necessarily indicate superior quality in today's context.

>> **First pressed:** Before the use of modern technology, the milling process involved the crushing of olives using circular stones. It was often possible to take the crushed olives from the first run and press them for a second time to extract more oil, with a lower-quality oil being the likely result. The first press was therefore an indicator of a fresher, better quality oil. Extra-virgin olive oil will, there-fore, always be from the "first press." Second centrifugation of the remaining paste from first extraction may be done with the resulting oil usually classified as "virgin" or "lampante," and further refined, depending on the initial quality of the fruit and how quickly the paste is reprocessed.

>> **Pure olive oil, light olive oil, or extra light olive oil:** These terms may imply that the olive oil is somehow healthier or of better quality. In reality, "pure olive oil" is a blend of refined olive oil and virgin olive oil, and "light or extra light olive oil" refers to its lighter flavor, not fewer calories or fat content, relying on the misperceptions when it comes to olive oil that lower calories and fat are healthier. These oils are of lower quality compared to extra-virgin olive oil.

>> **Made from refined olives:** This phrase suggests a quality aspect that doesn't exist; it's trying to mask the fact that the oil is produced from olives that needed refining due to

inferior quality. Refined olive oil lacks the flavor, aroma, and health benefits of extra-virgin olive oil.

>> **Product of Italy:** This label, where Italy is used as an example, may imply that the olives were grown, harvested, and pressed in Italy. This may be perceived by consumers as meaning the oil may compare with the best Italian extra-virgin olive oil — the reputation of which is high. However, it often only indicates *where* the blending or bottling took place because the actual olives could've come from various countries, affecting the oil's quality and character. Of course, olives from any country can be made into fine extra-virgin olive oil.

>> **Grand Cru:** While "special reserve" or "family selection" are phrases that may be used for marketing olive oil, some olive producers label their bottles with the term "Grand Cru," which is literally translated as "great growth." Grand cru originated in the wine industry and applied to specific wines of quality; the description is a part of an official and regulated classification. This is not the case for olive oil.

Harvest and "best before" dates

Extra-virgin olive oil is best consumed fresh. Following the harvest, it's stored away from heat, light, and oxygen in order to reduce the speed of the oxidation reactions that will lead to defective and finally rancid oil. The antioxidant polyphenols that are so valuable for health will act to reduce and slow the inevitable oxidation and so by the time an extra-virgin olive oil has deteriorated, the polyphenols will have acted as antioxidants, chemically changed and diminished. Polyphenols neutralize free radicals which otherwise "scavenge" the chemistry of normal cells and damage them. Once that occurs, the polyphenols may lose any further abilities to neutralize free radicals. If all of their antioxidant capacity is consumed, polyphenol antioxidant levels will reduce.

Some oils, while still passing extra-virgin olive oil quality standards, may be stored from the previous year's harvest or made with a blend of 2 harvest years.

Try to find an extra-virgin olive oil with the most recent year's harvest date on the label. Some producers even label their very first oils as *olio nuovo* or new oil. With northern and southern hemisphere olive oils available in many countries, it's possible to buy an extra-virgin olive oil within 6 months of the most recent harvest by buying alternating hemisphere oils according to the seasons.

Extra-virgin olive oil will deteriorate over time, and so it's best to consume it as close to the most recent harvest as possible. *Best before date (BBD)* is measured and regulated differently depending on where you are in the world. Because all forms of olive oil are reasonably stable, this may be 12 to 24 months from the date of bottling. It's common that oils do not display a harvest date on their labels, which is usually a first warning sign of the fact that old oils and/or a blend of multiple season's oils are being used for that bottle.

REMEMBER

Although oxidation may be a slow process, by the time a BBD is reached, an extra-virgin olive oil may not actually be at its best. It's possible, depending on the original quality and the level of antioxidants and storage conditions, that the oil may be defective and will certainly have seen a reduction in antioxidants and positive flavor attributes.

The polyphenols in extra-virgin olive oil and their effect on the oxidation process are explained in greater detail in Chapter 6.

Acidity and other values

You may see other values displayed on extra-virgin olive oils. Some producers recognize that their consumers can have some understanding of the chemical standards applied to oils and may include the information on product labels and on their websites.

Chapter 4 has a list of testing results that a laboratory may provide when an olive oil is analyzed to confirm it is extra virgin. Lower levels of acidity or free fatty acids and peroxide levels indicate that the oil has not been produced from olives that suffered fermentation or are oxidized.

Total polyphenol levels may also be included on the label. This is usually expressed in milligrams per kilogram (mg/kg). It's commonly accepted that a high polyphenol oil is one where the levels are greater than 250mg/kg. This may be part of a health claim discussed later in this chapter.

As a result of closely collaborating with artisan olive-oil producers, we understand their perspective and industry challenges as well. It's especially difficult for a smaller estate to include the low acidity rates and high phenolic content on the labels of their extra-virgin olive oil because labels are costly to reproduce. Although labels are usually purchased in bulk to reduce the cost, acidity and polyphenol rates are different during yearly harvests or even between different batches of oil of the same season. For these reasons, label collars have become popular. That way, estates can use the same label from year to year while creating a sticker or collar (see Figure 12-1) to call attention to their low acidity or high phenolic rates.

FIGURE 12-1:
A bottle collar for an extra-virgin olive oil.

HIGH PHENOLIC
EXTRA VIRGIN OLIVE OIL

COLD EXTRACTION
LOW ACIDITY

PRODUCT OF ITALY

Getting to Know Your EVOO

Now that you know the meaningful (and meaningless) phrases you may see on olive oils, it's time to get to know some of the individual oils a little better. When you buy extra-virgin olive, you'll probably be looking at several items on the bottle in addition to the nutritional information.

Region of origin

The label should clearly identify where the extra-virgin olive oil has been produced. Any extra-virgin olive oil that is the product of many countries is likely to have been transported and blended. The chances of oxidation are higher because of transportation and because lower-quality oils are intentionally sourced for the cheaper end of the market. They tend to have less intense and interesting flavor profiles than higher-quality extra-virgin olive oils, and low levels of polyphenols.

Many brands in the marketplace don't own a single olive tree or have a direct relationship with a particular mill. They are simply trading companies that buy oil from different places and blend them.

Excellent extra-virgin olive oils will often display not only their country of origin but also a region of production. In Spain and Greece particularly, it's common for a mill to be owned and operated by a cooperative of farmers spread over many acres (or hectares). The mill may be based at a local town or city. An extra-virgin olive oil may also be from a single estate, which may have been owned by many generations of the same family.

Telling the origin story

Producers are generally very proud of their extra-virgin olive oil and want to communicate its qualities on their packaging label, websites, and social media. There is, of course, more information that can be provided on websites than in the limited space on product labels. Yet labels can help you determine where and how your extra-virgin olive oil is produced, as noted in the following list.

>> **Olive varieties.** It is always a good sign to see the varieties of olive on the label. The extra-virgin olive oil may be *monocultivar,* which means it's made exclusively from one variety of olive. Alternatively, it may be created by a combination of more than one type. In Spain, you can often see a gentle monocultivar oil made from the Arbequina variety, or a more robust one from Picual olives. In Tuscany, it's traditional to combine several varieties — Frantoio, Moraiolo, Coratina, and Leccino. The proportions of each will define the flavor of the oil.

>> **Harvesting and production methods.** Sometimes there are detailed descriptions of the local terrain and *terroir* (soil, environment, and climate), which contribute to the unique nature of an oil. Methods and timing of the harvesting and production are often included on labels.

>> **Olive oil classifications.** Labels can include specific designations such as organic and protected origin standards, which are described in detail in Chapter 2.

>> **Tasting notes.** The official tasting notes are sometimes summarized on the label, which helps consumers to understand whether the oil is a gentle or more robust oil and to recognize some of the flavors that have been identified by a trained taster. This is explored more in Part 3 of this book.

There are regulations about what producers can say about their extra-virgin olive oil on websites and social media as well as the obligatory and the permitted descriptors allowed on labels. Producers should not make false, misleading, or exaggerated claims. The Internet is less easily monitored by agencies that are responsible for advertising standards, and this results in exaggerated claims being quite commonplace. Sometimes there is genuine ignorance of the law and sometimes unsubstantiated statements are made by those who should know better. The subject of these false claims often relate to the effects of extra-virgin olive oil on health.

Health claims on labels and advertising

In most countries, there are strict laws about what food manufacturers are allowed to state about their products on the label and in any supporting advertising, including on websites and social media. Rules are particularly strict about claims that relate to health. It's important that consumers are not misled or persuaded to buy expensive foods because they are advertised with vague or inaccurate statements about health benefits that are not backed up by robust evidence.

In the United States, the FDA is responsible for assessing health-claim submissions by food producers. In Europe, this task falls to the European Food Safety Authority (EFSA). These organizations have scientific committees that scrutinize the proposed wording of a claim, assess the published research data to support it, review the quantity and context in which the food should be consumed, and then form an opinion on the merits of the claim. As expected, the process is a very rigorous. Many submissions don't meet the criteria to be included on the list of allowed claims, although there is debate about whether the standard of evidence required is too high.

The enforcement of the law on health claims — including the interpretation on the exact way in which they are communicated to consumers and using any flexibility to help with understanding of their meaning — is the task of national or regional agencies in Europe. Interpretation of the regulations is complex, and there are a number of other strict rules that must be followed. For example, it's not permitted to discuss the reduction of a disease on European health claims. The organizations responsible for trading and advertising standards can work with producers and also act in response to consumer complaints, but they're often understaffed, and it's a huge task to monitor the Internet and online content.

There is a wealth of evidence to support the health benefits of olive oil both on its own and as part of a Mediterranean-style diet. These effects are discussed in Part 2. So far, there are only limited claims that can be presented to consumers on bottles of olive oil. It's the responsibility of producers to make sure they are compliant with the regulations.

The FDA has concluded that consuming oils rich in the monounsaturated fat oleic acid, such as olive oil, may reduce the risk of coronary heart disease when replacing fats and oils higher in saturated fat. The amount to be consumed should equate to 2 tablespoons per day.

EFSA has a similar permissible claim with *oleic acid*, the predominant monounsaturated fat in olive oil. It has gone further with recognition that there is significant biological activity of polyphenols found in extra-virgin olive oil, but only if there's enough of them in the oil. EFSA concluded that "the consumption of olive oil polyphenols contributes to the protection of blood lipids from oxidative stress. This claim is applicable to extra-virgin olive oils that contain more than 250 mg/kg of olive oil polyphenols."

This claim distinguishes between extra-virgin olive oils that are high in polyphenols, which will have the desired health effect, and those that have lower levels.

TECHNICAL
STUFF

The EFSA polyphenol claim goes into further detail. The claim, under EU Regulation 432/2012, is applicable to olive oils that contain at least 5mg of hydroxytyrosol and its derivatives (for example, oleuropein complex and tyrosol) per 20g of olive oil. The claim indicates that the beneficial effect is obtained with a daily intake of 20g of olive oil. This equates to total polyphenol levels of approximately 250mg/kg.

Most consumers do not understand the EFSA polyphenol claim, the wording of which is complicated and technical. The purpose of the FDA and EFSA should be not only to prevent false, unsubstantiated or misleading claims but also to support consumers in benefitting from health gains where they are identified and substantiated. So, in order for the general public to be able to understand the acknowledged effects of polyphenols, trading standards organizations can work in cooperation with producers to ensure that the communication of the health claim is understandable and accessible for everyone.

IN THIS CHAPTER

» Knowing the ten quality indicators

» Exploring different types of packaging

» Identifying the best way to store extra-virgin olive oil at home

Chapter **13**

Recognizing Proper Packaging and Storage

I n this chapter, we discuss the different packaging and presentation of olive oils. These storage and labeling options are important to understand because they'll help you decide which oil is best for you and how to make sure it's preserved to taste fresh and deliciously healthy until the last drop.

While the details that producers are required to put on labels is explained in Chapter 12, this chapter summarizes those mandatory descriptions and explores other indications of quality and the different types of containers you may find. Packaging and storage play crucial roles in maintaining the olive oil's freshness, flavor, and nutritional properties by protecting it from light, air, and temperature fluctuations.

Recognizing a Good EVOO Label

The label on the finished product gives the producer the opportunity to describe the product, fulfill the legal obligations, and communicate information about their extra-virgin olive oil (EVOO). The label requirements vary depending on laws in the country or region where the oil is produced. This section provides a few labeling guidelines for selecting high-quality extra-virgin olive oil among a myriad of oils.

Looking out for quality indicators

Knowing what to look for on a label is a skill that enables you to choose the right extra-virgin olive oil for cooking, dressing, or for giving to friends and family as gifts. Here's a quick-reference guide to good-quality indicators that can be present on the labels of extra-virgin olive oils:

>> **Extra-virgin classification.** The olive oil fulfills the requirements of the International Olive Council's definitions of "extra virgin" is the first indicator of quality (see Chapter 2).

>> **Origin.** Every region can produce any quality of extra-virgin olive oil but a single region, estate, or designated area of origin tends to be a marker of a good-quality oil and better traceability.

>> **Acidity.** Having an acidity level of below 0.8 percent is necessary for all extra-virgin olive oils, but some producers indicate much lower levels to denote superior standards.

>> **Tasting notes.** Professional descriptions of positive attributes of aromas and flavors describing the oil and/or style are sometimes added to the label. (Refer to Chapter 9 for specific tasting descriptions.)

>> **Variety.** No variety of olive is a higher quality than another. Blends of extra-virgin olive oil can be equally excellent as single varieties, although single varieties have typically higher polyphenol levels than others. Indication of variety or varieties can help consumers to understand the likely taste profile and demonstrate a producer's interest in informing consumers.

>> **Harvest date.** A high-quality extra-virgin olive oil will remain fresh for months, but most recently harvested oil is likely to retain the highest taste and health qualities. Always look for oils within 12 months of their harvest dates.

>> **Polyphenol level.** Research shows that a minimum level of polyphenols in an extra-virgin olive oil is associated with specific health benefits beyond those attributed to it as a healthy fat. A level of above 250mg/kg (milligrams per kilogram) of total polyphenols may be present on the extra-virgin olive oil to indicate reaching those critical levels.

>> **Permitted health claim.** An extra-virgin olive oil with the minimum required unsaturated fat and polyphenol levels may, with the permission of the local regulatory authority, carry a health claim. To ensure that consumers understand the health claim, the wording should be in agreement with trading standards organizations and also make reference to the original permitted claim. (See Chapter 12 for more label information on health claims.)

>> **Organic.** Indication of organic production is an indicator of oils produced or involving production without the use of chemical fertilizers or artificial pesticides and fungicides.

>> **Competition prizes.** Just like wine, there are competitions for olive oils. Competition organizers, which are usually commercial ventures, charge an entrance fee and appoint a panel of tasters or judges who then award gold, silver, or bronze awards that producers are allowed to display on their labels. Industry "insiders" and the top sommeliers who have many years of experience will have a view on the merits of the competition, including the criteria for selection of the judges. These competitions are not regulated by any official overseeing organization, but olive oil competitions in New York, Los Angeles, and Tokyo in addition to the Mario Solinas Quality Award and the EVO International Olive Oil Contest in Italy are generally regarded as the most prestigious.

Having attractive presentations

In the past, supermarkets usually displayed a limited number of olive oil brands on shelves in rather drab green and brown bottles. They were often similar in design and sometimes had Italian names, even if they were not produced there. Fortunately, nowadays there are often several shelves dedicated to olive oils, and it's often possible to choose from various producers and to buy oils from different countries (see Figure 13-1).

FIGURE 13-1: Olive oil bottles on store shelves.

Many producers use labels with artwork, traditional motifs, or modern designs that reflect the brand's identity and the product's heritage. There is an increased need to be different especially in the competitive premium market, and producers are becoming more courageous in experimenting with color by using white, gold, or even pink bottles.

Sharing the story of the olive grove, the producers, and the production process can create a connection with consumers. This can be done through packaging, promotional materials, or online platforms.

Mass-produced olive oil also comes with very attractive labels that conjure up idyllic images about olive groves even though the quality of the particular oil may not be the best. It's important not to be deceived by pretty packages or words and focus on the quality indicators mentioned in this chapter.

Special editions or gift packs can attract buyers looking for high-quality, unique gifts, such as packaging in a special box, including a pour spout, or pairing with complementary products like balsamic vinegar. Some producers may market the first day's harvest in a limited-edition format.

Including QR codes on the packaging that lead to recipes, the story behind the product, or virtual tours of the olive groves can engage consumers further and provide pertinent information to the olive oil that they are buying which isn't printed on a label. If you're interested in an extra-virgin olive oil from a particular place, the QR code is a quick way to gain information about them. Collaborating with artists or designers for limited-edition bottles can create a collectible aspect to the olive oil, making it more appealing to consumers interested in design and art.

Maintaining EVOO's Quality

The journey of extra-virgin olive oil from the annual harvest of the olive, through the mill and storage, to a retailer and finally to the kitchen or table of a consumer is a path that can result in the deterioration of the oil. This can potentially result in defective taste and a reduction in health benefits. The factors that most commonly contribute to deterioration include contact with oxygen, heat, and light.

Producers focus on minimizing the exposure of oil to these factors, so that consumers can enjoy extra-virgin olive oil at its best. It's important for you to recognize when the extra-virgin olive oil has been well protected on its journey and to understand how to keep olive oil in the best condition.

Chapters 2 and 3 provide details of the oxidation process, which degrades extra-virgin olive oil. It occurs with exposure to oxygen in the air and is accelerated by heat and light, especially the ultraviolet (UV) light in our environment.

EVOO retail packaging

The numerous ways in which olive oil is packaged after it leaves the sealed storage tanks of a producer depends on several different factors beyond the preservation of the oil, which include

>> Compliance with safety regulations

>> Costs including transportation

>> Convenience

>> Attractiveness

>> Consumer preferences and expectations

>> Market trends

>> Sustainability

Good packaging protects the olive oil from deterioration and ensures it's safely transported. The following packaging forms have advantages and disadvantages and are often aimed at different sectors of the market.

Glass bottles

The most familiar packaging of olive oil is in glass bottles. The shape of bottles, which dates back to the clay *amphorae* (jars used to transport wine and olive oil) used in ancient civilizations, is in part to distribute weight evenly and make them easy to transport. The narrow neck of a bottle not only helps to make it easier to pour, but also minimizes the surface area of the oil exposed to the air at the top. The glass may be dark in color to reduce exposure of the oil to light, though some producers may package their most premium oil in clear glass within a presentation box to show the oil at its best, knowing that consumers are likely to be aware that it should be consumed over a short period of time.

Glass is quite a heavy material to transport, but it's generally able to be recycled. Some retailers offer the opportunity to reuse and refill bottles. The oil used to refill needs to be clearly labeled, so its authenticity can be confirmed. The bottle needs to be clean, free from old oil, to make sure the flavor of the new oil is not adversely affected.

The seals on extra-virgin olive oil packaging can have a limited effect on oxidation. Cork stoppers can leak or absorb oil, and it can oxidize and even become rancid affecting the flavor. This is less likely with a screw top bottle, although oil can build up on pouring spouts. In most cases, if you use the oil quite quickly, as long as it's sealed after each time of opening, the oil is likely to be preserved.

Plastic (PET) containers

PET packaging refers to containers and packaging made from polyethylene terephthalate, a type of plastic. It's cheap to produce, durable, and light to transport. Despite being lightweight, PET is strong and resistant to impact, which helps in protecting the contents during transport and handling.

Recycling rates and infrastructure vary globally, impacting its environmental footprint. Efforts are ongoing to improve PET's sustainability through advances in recycling technologies and the development of bio-based PET alternatives. It's often used for cheaper olive oil, because most consumers associate better oils with glass packaging, or it may be used for oil in larger quantities such as 3- or 5-liter quantities, where glass would be too heavy to be practical for such amounts.

Tin cans

The strength, recyclability, and opacity of tin cans make it a popular choice for many producers. They're slightly heavier and more expensive than plastic yet lighter than glass. Tin cans appeal more to consumers looking for quality particularly in 1-, 3-, or 5-liter packs of extra-virgin olive oil. Currently, this type of packaging is widely used in restaurants. Tin cans provide a protective environment for the oil and are a safe way to store and pour olive oil.

Tetra packs

Tetra packaging is a relatively novel way to present olive oil. It's made from a composite of paperboard, polyethylene, and aluminum and is designed to offer lightweight, space-efficient, durable, and aseptic packaging options. Its many layers offer good protection from light and air, but the complexity of its composition make it less easy to recycle in many regions. The expense can add to the final price of the product.

Bag in box

Bag-in-box packaging is gaining in popularity, particularly for larger volumes of oil, despite some initial concerns that consumers may associate it with low-quality wine. Traditionally, wine has been the main product available in this form. Research has shown that the bag protects high-quality olive oil from light and oxygen, especially when it has a valve dispenser, which reduces air entry when the oil is accessed. The materials are light yet robust. However, because the packaging is usually made from mixed materials — plastics and aluminum foil — some parts are not recyclable. An advantage for the producer is that a large area can be labeled, presenting a greater opportunity to promote and market the oil.

TIP

Your choice of packaging may be most influenced by the quality and quantity of extra-virgin olive oil you are buying/using. It's possible to get all qualities of oil in most of the different packaging previously mentioned, but it's important to make sure that the packaging is fit for purpose and protects your extra-virgin olive oil from oxygen, heat, and light. Always buy the quantity of oil that you and your family will consume in 4 to 6 weeks and the highest quality that you can afford.

REMEMBER

It may not be possible to judge the most sustainable form of packaging. Each of the different packaging materials have pros and cons. Variations in weight, durability, transportation costs, materials used, and recyclability make it difficult to make the case for better environmental credentials of one form over another.

Advances in EVOO packaging

New innovations may change the way in which extra-virgin olive oil is packaged in years to come. These technologies include the use of antioxidant liners in tins or bag-in-box packages, which offer an extra layer of protection against oxidation. The liners are made from materials that actively work to prevent the olive oil from coming into contact with air.

UV protective coatings are being developed to be applied to packaging materials to shield the olive oil from harmful UV light. These coatings can be used on glass bottles, plastic containers, and even labels to provide an additional layer of protection. Some coatings are specifically designed to be transparent to visible light while blocking UV rays, preserving the oil's integrity without compromising the product's aesthetic appeal.

Another option to preserve extra-virgin olive oil is *nitrogen flushing*, which is a process where nitrogen gas is used to displace oxygen in the packaging before sealing. This method significantly reduces oxidation, preserving the freshness, flavor, and nutritional value of the olive oil.

There are novel ways being considered to enhance sustainability with the exploration of more easily biodegradable packaging and other ways to reduce the carbon footprint of packaging and transportation.

Maximizing storage at home

When you get your extra-virgin olive oil home, it's important that you take the appropriate steps to make sure it stays fresh and as delicious as you would expect.

Most extra-virgin olive oil packaging will carry recommended storage instructions. The best advice is to keep your extra-virgin olive oil in a cool and dark environment, away from the heat of cooking appliances and away from sunshine. The best temperature to keep extra-virgin olive oil is around 57 to 64°F (14–18°C), and it's advisable to avoid repeated fluctuations in temperature.

In some places in the Mediterranean, it's unfortunately a common experience in restaurants to see olive oil kept in glass decanters exposed to the heat and light of the midday sun. This oil is very likely to be rancid and demonstrates the need for education even in the regions where extra-virgin olive oil is produced. If this happens in a restaurant with high turnover, the extra-virgin olive oil may be consumed quickly and therefore it may not pose a problem. If it's in a low traffic area, however, we recommend you politely ask the restaurant staff if it's possible to have a new bottle of their best extra-virgin olive oil to try. You'll also be able to see where it originates from.

The best way to make certain your extra-virgin olive oil is in the best possible condition is to enjoy it fresh, over a short period of time. If you use a lot of extra-virgin olive oil, it may be more economic to buy in larger volumes. This is discussed in more detail in Chapter 14. If a large volume container, such as a tin or bag in box, is unwieldy for the table, oil can be poured into a smaller, dark bottle, preferably designed for this purpose and with a good seal.

REMEMBER

Good producers will store their latest season's extra-virgin olive oil in controlled environments away from UV light in stainless steel tanks with a layer of nitrogen gas to keep oxygen at bay. They'll bottle the oil when orders come in. It makes economic sense for retailers to keep stock levels turning over and not to hold on to extra-virgin olive oil for long periods of time. Usually, a good-quality extra-virgin olive oil from the most recent harvest will arrive in your home reasonably fresh with quality maintained.

While it's advisable that extra-virgin olive oil be kept cool, it's not recommended to refrigerate the oil. When extra-virgin olive oil is refrigerated, it begins to solidify and turn cloudy due to the monounsaturated fats and wax crystallizing at lower temperatures. This doesn't harm the oil, and it'll return to its liquid state at room temperature without losing quality. However, the repeated process of solidifying and liquefying can potentially affect the oil's flavor and aroma over time.

WARNING

One of the many myths about extra-virgin olive oil is that the "real" oil will solidify when placed in the fridge. This is certainly true for extra-virgin olive oil; however, the process depends on a number of factors, and it's certainly not a test of authenticity. Adulterated, fake, or rancid olive oil may just as easily cloud and solidify as a high-quality extra-virgin olive oil, so it's not a reliable test.

TIP

If a guest whom you don't see very often brings you a special bottle of extra-virgin olive oil to your home as a gift, make sure you have enjoyed it all by the time they return. It shows that you know to consume extra-virgin olive oil in its freshest, most delicious state.

Chapter **14**

Purchasing, Price, and Affordability

A primarily plant-based diet, which is made even more nutritious and flavorful with good-quality extra-virgin olive oil (EVOO), is sustainable and affordable. And with the growing interest in Mediterranean-style diets, purchasing, price, and affordability are among the first topics to come up in our presentations and interviews about olive oil. These complex topics always take longer than a few sentences to answer. It's our desire to present you with enough information about olive oil to be able to get the most value for your money.

This chapter has all the information you need to make decisions about how to buy the best extra-virgin olive oil to suit your needs, tastes, and budget. While you may have many places to find extra-virgin olive oil locally, you also have options to try new and interesting oils from different parts of the world.

The quality and labeling of olive oil are explored in detail in Part 2 and Chapters 12 and 13. In this chapter, we use that information to guide you through the process of buying extra-virgin olive oil and to show you how to get the best value for your money.

When you're looking for olive oils to buy and enjoy, we recommend that you avoid refined, pure, or blended virgin olive oils. Although these oils contain monounsaturated fats, the industrial process used to make defective olive oil palatable also strips out most of the healthy antioxidant and anti-inflammatory polyphenols.

Prioritizing the Purchase of EVOO

Extra-virgin olive oil has always been a highly valued food in the cultures of the region where olive trees are planted, nurtured, and harvested. The seasons are defined by the work in the olive groves, and the freshly pressed extra-virgin olive oil is awaited with much anticipation — with festivals and celebrations marking the creation of the new oil, especially if the year's production is exceptionally high quality.

Similarly, the freshest colorful fruits and vegetables are prized by followers of the traditional heritage diet in the Mediterranean. People in the region will go to markets where they trust the producer and can smell and feel the produce before they buy.

TECHNICAL STUFF

While the economics of buying extra-virgin olive oil and investing in health are a choice for individuals, there has been research to show the potential financial benefits to the public health of populations with the adoption of a more Mediterranean dietary pattern, which includes the regular consumption of olive oil. A 2019 study modeling potential savings published in the journal *Food & Nutrition Research* estimated that if the US population increased Mediterranean diet adherence by 20 percent, it would generate savings of $8 billion per year in the costs associated with heart disease in the population, with a massive $30 billion per year estimated with an 80 percent shift.

Comparing affordability: Western diet versus Mediterranean-style diets

In the United States and Northern Europe, which have adopted so-called "Western diets," priorities have shifted toward

Citrus-Spice Muffins with Olive Oil (Chapter 18)

Artichoke, Caramelized Onion and Tomato-Basil Frittata (Chapter 18)

Chocolate Banana Bread (Chapter 18)

Bravas-Style Potatoes with Aioli (Chapter 19)

Golden Potato, Pecorino, and Olive Croquettes (Chapter 19)

Sicilian Caponata (Chapter 19)

Barley, Lentil and Chickpea Soup (Chapter 20)

Busiate Pasta with Sicilian Pesto (Chapter 20)

Greek Island-Style White Bean and Feta Puree with Olive Oil-Sautéed Dandelion Greens (Chapter 21)

Milanese-Style Veal Scalloppine with Creamy Polenta and Roasted Brussels Sprouts (Chapter 21)

Seafood Kabobs with Salsa Verde and Grilled Summer Vegetables (Chapter 21)

Fresh Fish Poached in Olive Oil with Sundried Red Pesto and Broccolini (Chapter 21)

Olive Oil-Poached Pears with Dark Chocolate Mousse and Sea Salt (Chapter 22)

Ricotta, Limoncello, Almond, and Olive Oil Cake (Chapter 22)

EVOO and Chili-Infused Chocolate Brownies (Chapter 22)

Olive Oil Gelato with Homemade Chocolate Taggiasca Sauce (Chapter 22)

convenience and highly processed foods with high levels of sugars, salt, unhealthy fats, and artificial flavors and preservatives. "Ready-to eat" meals and fast food are often more expensive compared to healthy homemade meals.

Cooking oils and staple ingredients are generally regarded as items where consumers can cut costs so more money can be spent on the heavily promoted, nutritionally poor products. To make matters worse, large multi-national corporations use this "cheaper is better" mentality to promote their products in the Mediterranean where, even though there is a strong cultural connection with extra-virgin olive oil, economic instability forces consumers to buy less than healthful alternatives.

Yet, there is increasing evidence that shows the Mediterranean diet, with extra-virgin olive oil at its core, is affordable in comparison with the much less healthy "Western diet." While extra-virgin olive oil is one of the more expensive ingredients in Mediterranean-style dishes, it also makes vegetables and salads much more palatable and delicious. Therefore, it's more likely that meals based around the regular use of extra-virgin olive oil will be cooked from scratch, and vegetables will be the main focus of the meal with smaller portions of more expensive meat.

Supporting the cost of EVOO

Research from a study conducted by Miriam Hospital and the Rhode Island Community Food Bank in addition to Australian studies confirmed that at least $30 can be shaved off the costs of a weekly shop with Mediterranean diet ingredients replacing a standard American food profile. With the Mediterranean diet's credentials in improving population and planetary health, the societal, moral, and financial case for adopting a more Mediterranean-style diet becomes even more compelling.

REMEMBER

When considering the cost of an eating pattern, it's important to think about the total dietary plan, not just single components. Switching to a more Mediterranean-style diet and buying more expensive extra-virgin olive oil will be offset by the inclusion of cheaper foods such as legumes, seasonal produce, and whole grains like rice and pasta.

Evaluating purchasing options

There are many ways for consumers to buy extra-virgin olive oil. Although the availability of certain oils through brick-and-mortar stores may depend on where you live, there are other sources. The following sections provide a few options for selecting and buying good-quality extra-virgin olive oil.

Supermarkets

Many supermarkets stock their olive oil section with bottles rather than in other forms of packaging, and it's commonplace to find oils in specific price brackets grouped together. Usually the highest priced, more premium oils are on the top shelves, and the larger volume (and heavier) bottles of less expensive oils are placed on lower shelves.

The following list breaks down how different types of olive oil are placed on supermarket shelves.

>> Lower shelves often contain refined, or pure olive oils, which can be in larger volumes.

>> Directly above the lower shelf is frequently the place to find extra-virgin olive oils that are blended and the product of many countries — likely the lowest quality extra-virgin olive oil.

REMEMBER

An extra-virgin olive oil that is *blended* may be a reference to a blend of oils shipped from different countries to produce a cheap, low polyphenol oil with a mild taste. This should not be confused with a single estate or mill-produced blend of different olive varieties that may well be a high-quality extra-virgin olive oil. The common exquisite and balanced combination of Frantoio, Leccino, and Moraiolo in a Tuscan extra-virgin olive oil is the equivalent of the Merlot, Cabernet Sauvignon and Cabernet Franc grape varieties used together in many Bordeaux wines.

>> In the mid-range of price and height on the shelves, there are usually good-quality extra-virgin olive oils from various regions and countries worthy of consideration. Chapters 12 and 13 explain how to recognize and choose the best

extra-virgin olive oils within this category, depending on your preference for origin, variety, producer, and taste.

>> The topmost shelves are sometimes reserved for the most expensive extra-virgin olive oils. The brands are often single estate and beautifully presented like a fine wine. Producers that have made investments in unique bottles and distinctive branding means that you can choose the most colorful and attractive option among the other olive oils on these shelves. Such premium extra-virgin olive oils may offer a particularly fine taste, or a unique story or origin.

TIP

The quality of top-shelf premium olive oils may be negzatively impacted due to prolonged storage under fluorescent supermarket lights where the turnover is slower. For this reason, it may be best to consider buying these oils at a delicatessen or specialist store.

TIP

While you're shopping in the supermarket, consider the cost of each item and how long it will last. Also, think about how it effects your meals — from prep and cooking times to your enjoyment and health. You may well conclude that, in terms of versatility and value for money, spending more for a good-quality extra-virgin olive oil than for other items is an excellent investment in your lifestyle and health.

Delicatessens and specialty import stores

Delicatessens may have an even larger range of mid and high-end extra-virgin olive oils and even provide customers with the opportunity to taste different ones before purchasing. Educated staff who have a relationship with the producer or importer of the oil should be able to provide more information about the provenance and profile of the oils, giving added value to buying here rather than at a supermarket.

Farmers' markets

A producer who is passionate about their extra-virgin olive oil, especially if it's available in smaller quantities, may be in a position to sell straight to their customers at a market. Not only does this remove the hefty markups required by retailers to run their businesses, but it also will result in returning customers. It also is an opportunity to build trust and to communicate and receive feedback about the story and flavor of the individual oil. Sometimes a relative or friend may act as the representative of a producer abroad, who is taking the extra-virgin olive oil to local markets within the United States.

FROM THE AUTHORS

We definitely recommend chatting to the people who dedicate many weekend hours to standing under a canopy, whatever the weather, with a single estate extra-virgin olive oil. Their stories are likely to be as interesting as the oils they sell. We have known vendors who started their market businesses after passing an olive oil mill while on vacation and became enchanted by the extra-virgin olive oil and the people who produced it.

The Internet

Ordering online, with delivery straight to your home, is an increasingly popular way of buying extra-virgin olive oil. It's a particularly useful way for producers or importers to reduce brick-and-mortar costs. For consumers, online shopping offers convenience and a way to purchase unique oils that aren't available in local stores and to buy in larger quantities as well. For people with larger families, using the equivalent amount of a few tablespoons of extra-virgin olive oil per person per day, it can make sense financially to buy extra-virgin olive oil in bulk.

TIP

Traditionally, the average person in Greece consumes about 20 liters (approximately 5.3 gallons) of olive oil per year. If you live like a Greek, it may be more economic to buy a large tin or bag-in-box volumes that are available online.

WARNING

The Internet is infamous because it's difficult to regulate — scams and sharks everywhere! The limits of permissible health claims are clear and described in Chapter 12, yet many websites will try to sell a "special" extra-virgin olive oil with vague assertions like it will "rejuvenate you" or "make you feel mentally sharper" without an authorized and trading authority-approved health claim. The authors have even seen such claims associated with olive oil being sold by influencers, some even qualified doctors, at a vast premium. Many excellent quality extra-virgin olive oils will have high polyphenol levels, health benefits, and most likely will taste better for a fraction of the price. And remember, those producers are acting with integrity and within the law.

TIP

If you want to determine the quality of an olive oil that you're purchasing online, you can check for factual information that can be provided by a producer, such as harvest and expiration dates, acidity rates, and polyphenol levels. The producer will also list where the extra-virgin olive oil is produced (if it is single estate), as well as any awards or honorable mentions that the producer may have received.

The oleoteca

An *oleoteca* is a specialized shop or tasting room dedicated to extra-virgin olive oil. You can find these shops that are entirely dedicated to extra-virgin olive oil sales, particularly in areas of oil production. Some are even boutique shops in a town or city that act as outlets for a single estate. In an oleoteca, visitors can taste, learn about, and buy different varieties of extra-virgin olive oil. An oleoteca often features a range of high-quality, artisanal olive oils and may include offerings from various regions, each with distinct flavors and characteristics attributed to the olive varieties and terroir (climate and soil conditions where the olives are grown). The staff are usually highly knowledgeable and will educate customers about the way extra-virgin olive oil is produced and can offer tutored tastings.

Mills

If you are passing through olive grove country, be sure to keep a look out for mills that have a visitors' section and a shop. Many offer aspects of an oleoteca experience and *oleo tourism* (combines the tourism experience with olive oil production and tasting), which is discussed in Chapter 23. You may even get a guided tour of the mill and grove — an opportunity not to be missed. You can buy extra-virgin olive oil at a mill with a shop, knowing exactly where it comes from and the story of the people who produce it.

Health food stores

Extra-virgin olive oil is rightly becoming valued for its positive effects on health. Even though there are limits to what can be claimed on the label about the health benefits of extra-virgin olive oil as a food, research into its potential broad benefits is well established and robust. This is explored in more detail in Part 2 of this book.

In fact, some olive oil producers are making "medicinal style" extra-virgin olive oil, through cultivation methods and exceptionally early harvesting that increases polyphenols. These products are sold as *nutraceuticals* (supplements derived from a food source with health benefits) and are marketed as a way to boost the levels of bioactive compounds found in extra-virgin olive oil. Often known as "ultra-high polyphenol" extra-virgin olive oils, the level of polyphenols are in the thousands of mg/kg (milligrams per kilogram), which makes the oil too bitter and pungent for most people to enjoy as a food. The supplements are often sold in health food stores at a high price in very small bottles, sometimes with a small plastic spoon and "dosage" instructions.

WARNING: HIGH POLYPHENOL SUPPLEMENTS

Polyphenol levels that are high enough to have a beneficial effect on health are readily available in a good-quality extra-virgin olive oil. The oil has a great taste, combining fruitiness with a measure of bitterness and pungency that indicates the presence of polyphenols. Extra-virgin olive oil is best consumed in generous amounts over the course of a day and in combination with other ingredients of the Mediterranean diet.

Currently, there is no scientific evidence that suggests taking pill or liquid supplements is particularly healthy. More importantly, there's a lack of evidence about taking very high levels of polyphenols beyond what are consumed in a balanced diet that is rich in extra-virgin olive oil. It's indeed possible that there may be a level above which polyphenols have less of a positive health effect and may even be harmful. At the time of writing this book, we simply don't know.

Examining prices and value

A valued extra-virgin olive oil is one of the more expensive necessary staples of the Mediterranean diet. There's no getting away from the fact that a good extra-virgin olive oil is not a commodity; it's a natural product. Even when farmed intensively, the most flavorsome extra-virgin olive oil is a high-quality, health-giving food that requires investment in technology and human skills to produce. It's very different from refined vegetable oils, which can be produced with identical taste for the mass market.

Choosing the quality of EVOO

The blended extra-virgin olive oils that are the product of many countries are very affordable but are generally low in polyphenols and bland in taste. They represent the largest share of the extra-virgin olive oil market and are often bought by consumers who have heard about the oil's taste and health benefits. These oils certainly have a place in the market as a much better choice when compared with refined vegetable oils. However, when people understand the value of extra-virgin olive oil and its production process, explore the variety of flavors, and discover the importance of high levels of polyphenols, they'll begin to explore different types of extra-virgin olive oils, even if they cost a little more.

Consumers are very fortunate to have thousands of good-quality extra-virgin olive oils to choose from. Although for some people, it's a challenge to know where to begin.

High-quality extra-virgin olive oils from regional mills, local grower cooperatives, and single estates are readily available and can start at prices just a little above the blended extra-virgin olive oils. Brands by specialty olive oil producers are good places to start hunting for excellent value for money. These oils, especially if you buy in larger quantities, are perhaps the best extra-virgin olive oils to cook with and add to finish dishes or drizzle on salads.

Having started with a good extra-virgin olive oil for everyday use, you can start to explore the options in the more premium end of the extra-virgin olive oil market. These oils may offer more complex and balanced flavors, and you can start experimenting with tasting them by themselves, then pairing with food like Amy's recipes in Part 6.

WHY DOES IT COST SO MUCH?

A significant capital investment and years of lead time is required before a newly established grove will reach full production. Harvesting and milling olives is certainly a difficult and expensive process in comparison with seed oil production. As a result, the price of extra-virgin olive oil can vary considerably, depending on supply, which can be affected by global economic conditions including the effects of inflation, climate, and wars.

Depending upon where you live, the supply for olive oil may not be enough to satisfy the demand. This is the case in the United States, for example. Even though California produces wonderful olive oil, it's not enough to fill consumer demand, making imports necessary. Importers in the United States have to pay heavy freight prices (which have increased significantly since the pandemic). They also have to pay brokers, which have become more difficult to find. (Brokers are companies that have a role as intermediaries between olive oil producers and retailers.) In addition, the US government places different taxes on olive oils from different countries.

In recent years, food prices have increased in most countries and extra-virgin olive oil prices have risen at record levels as well due to an olive-oil shortage and food security fears. At the time of writing this book, however, it's still certainly possible to buy a healthy and delicious "mid-range" extra-virgin olive oil and to enjoy 2 tablespoons each day for less than a dollar a day. This is a fraction of the amount the average American spends on coffee. Incidentally, the authors love coffee too!

FROM THE AUTHORS

Knowing how to taste and pair extra-virgin olive oils is a skill that we encourage you to look into. It takes time to build up your experience, just like tasting wines. It's important to recognize fruitiness, bitterness, and pepperiness as well as noting when an oil is defective. However, we believe there is no "right or wrong" way to experience olive oil beyond this. There will be flavors you may experience that are personal to you, and you may not necessarily be able to perceive the tasting notes described by others. Tasting extra-virgin olive oils should be fun and not the exclusive preserve of connoisseurs.

We have tremendous respect for trained and experienced sommeliers, and they can be teachers and guides with tasting notes, who encourage you on your journey to develop your palate even more. If you aren't yet confident, any good-quality extra-virgin olive oil will taste delicious with any food or recipe, so you can use pairing ideas as signposts rather than rules you must follow.

The more expensive extra-virgin olive oils can vary considerably in price, and you may choose to indulge in a premium extra-virgin olive oil for your table or to buy one as a gift. There may be added desirability of these "top end" oils, involving a number of ways a premium extra-virgin olive oil may be distinctive. Whether this adds value depends on your point of view.

Here's a list of qualities you may want to consider when choosing extra-virgin olive oil:

>> A brand that may stand out for taking the most care in its production with lower levels of acidity and high polyphenols. The olive oil may have won numerous gold medals in international taste awards.

>> It may be of a unique or rare variety (cultivar) of olive or olive tree. This may include olives from subspecies regarded as derived from the wild or original olive variety.

>> Limited edition oils may be marketed, perhaps with a specially presented bottle from the first day of harvesting.

>> Secolari trees, which are hundreds of years old, also command higher prices.

>> Traditional pressing methods are used such as a stone mill. This would need to be done very carefully because the older systems of production may increase the risk of oxidation. See Chapter 6 for more information on the oxidation process.

>> There may be a story about the region of origin, having a particular historical or religious significance, such as oils from Galilee, or associated with an ancient site like the foothills of Mount Olympus.

>> The oil may come from a grove with a special philosophy or ethical approach such as regenerative farming or in areas

where people who have been at war come together to produce olive oil as a symbol of peace.

>> An extra-virgin olive oil may be from olives harvested at night. It's claimed that this method reduces fermentation in the olive oil because of the lower atmospheric temperatures. Nighttime harvesting needs to be undertaken responsibly with regard for the safety of workers and roosting birds.

>> Some extra-virgin olive oils are sold with flakes of gold leaf for decoration and to indicate opulence. Gold is biologically inert, meaning it passes through the digestive system without being absorbed. It's nontoxic and should not cause harm when ingested in small quantities. The US Food and Drug Administration (FDA) and European Union Food Safety Authority regard edible gold leaf as safe for consumption, provided it is pure gold. It certainly creates a talking point at dinner.

>> Celebrity endorsements can give extra-virgin olive oil producers more attention for their oils. Some celebrities even produce or import their own oil sourced from estates they've bought or growers they have met.

REMEMBER

Extra-virgin olive oil is a food, and it is best consumed fresh. So if you have a premium bottle of oil, enjoy it over a short period of time. It's not like a bottle of wine — age does not improve its flavor or increase its value. As we say in Italian "*olio nuovo, vino vecchio*" (new oil, old wine).

Understanding the EVOO market

Competition can be fierce in some sectors of the olive oil market. Many producers will describe the challenges they face in bringing extra-virgin olive oil to the market while investing in the latest equipment and sustaining their farms. Growers usually have respect for their neighbors who also produce high-quality extra-virgin olive oil because they understand the passion and dedication necessary to make a success of their business. At farmers' markets, you may see vendors tasting and complimenting their competitors' oil, acknowledging similar ambitions and aspirations to create the best extra-virgin olive oil.

We have taken the opportunity to showcase individual extra-virgin olive oils in the recipes in this book and share stories of some of the groves we have had the privilege to visit. We fully acknowledge there are thousands of equally wonderful extra-virgin olive oils created by passionate, skilled growers we have yet to meet and whose oils we have yet to taste. Even though we chose different oils for each recipe, that does not mean that you cannot enjoy the same recipe with your favorite extra-virgin olive oil.

The market is in fact expanding as customers understand the value of a good-quality extra-virgin olive oil for its health and flavor. With improved communication, within the appropriate constraints of advertising standards, it should be possible to see continued year-over-year expansion of the market.

The average consumption of olive oil (all grades) in the United States and Northern Europe is 1 liter per person per year. Consumption is slightly more in Australia at approximately 2 liters, whereas people who follow a traditional Mediterranean-style diet consume between 10 and 20 liters. So the recommended 2 tablespoons of extra-virgin olive oil per day, which is typically the minimum amount defined by researchers as adherence to a healthy Mediterranean diet, is a little more than 10 liters per year.

Getting the Most Out of Your EVOO

Extra-virgin olive oil is a precious and important food. It's important to know how to maximize its benefits to get the best from the olive oil you buy. Here are a few helpful tips:

>> **Buy in bulk.** You buy in a tin or in a "bag in box," and decant smaller amounts into a suitable dispenser for the table.

>> **Preserve the quality.** Make sure you keep your olive oil away from sunlight and the heat of the oven and stove.

>> **Look out for discounts or special offers.** Always consider the harvest or "best before" date, which should be at least a year ahead to be the freshest oil. Sometimes a reduction in price means it's the oil from the previous harvest — discounted because there is a fresher harvest available. The oil may still retain its qualities and be worth the money, or it may have deteriorated and not be at its best.

It's important to remember that price and quality are relative. If a very high-quality extra-virgin olive oil is from the last year's harvest but still within its expiration date, it will still be a better option than a lower-quality olive oil, just not quite as fresh as it was a year earlier.

>> **Reuse the oil.** It is possible to reuse extra-virgin olive oil within a few days if there is any left over from cooking. This has been practiced in the Mediterranean especially if a lot of oil is left over after frying, there are financial considerations, or local oil supplies are dwindling before the new harvest. Research suggests that extra-virgin olive oil performs well through the first and second cooking, with little degradation, and a reasonable proportion of the antioxidants in the oil are preserved — more than 50 percent, depending on temperature and time of cooking.

Although it is possible to reuse extra-virgin olive oil, we don't advise it other than in occasional situations where deep-frying requires much more oil than usual. To be economical, we suggest using only the amount of extra-virgin olive oil needed in a recipe or to support the cooking process, such as sautéing. We also suggest to pour any leftover oil onto the meal to add texture, nutrition, and flavor. In the Poole household, if there is any leftover oil on your plate, it's considered very acceptable to request a little bread to soak up every last drop. With the exception of deep-frying, it's important to use the proper amount of extra-virgin olive oil, so that you don't have extra on your plate in the first place.

5

Creating Dishes with Extra-Virgin Olive Oil

IN THIS PART . . .

Find ways to cook, fry, and preserve in extra-virgin olive oil.

Discover how to bake and make pastries with extra-virgin olive oil.

Chapter 15

Cooking, Frying, and Preserving with Extra-Virgin Olive Oil

"Can I cook in olive oil"? and "I can't fry in olive oil, can I?" are two of the questions that we get asked most frequently during olive oil tastings, media appearances, and classes. The answer to both questions is an emphatic YES!

Outside of the Mediterranean region, myths about cooking and frying with olive oil have been around for as long as we can both remember. We're not sure if the misconceptions were born out of a lack of knowledge or by marketers trying to promote other oils, but their origins are irrelevant.

The truth is that if good taste, sustainable living, and good health are among your priorities, then you should be cooking with olive oil as much as possible. Extra-virgin olive oil (EVOO), at the heart of the Mediterranean diet, is renowned for its health benefits and unique flavor.

Contrary to common misconceptions about its suitability for cooking, there is a wealth of evidence suggesting that extra-virgin olive oil is not only safe to use at usual cooking temperatures, but also maintains its numerous health benefits during the cooking process. Because it's the only oil used for cooking in the traditional Mediterranean diet, it would be inconceivable if it were anything other than beneficial to use for every aspect of food preparation, cooking, and presentation.

In this chapter, we explain how cooking and frying with extra-virgin olive oil is not only acceptable but preferable to Mediterranean chefs and medical experts alike. You'll also gather great tips for preserving with extra-virgin olive oil whenever the mood strikes.

Cooking with EVOO for Flavor and Nutrition

Cooking with olive oil is a deeply rooted tradition of all Mediterranean countries, and each one expresses their creativity and love for liquid gold in a different way. In fact, the usage of olive oil in cooking is often touted and enjoyed to a greater extent during the Orthodox Christian fasting periods and during Lent for Catholics. During these times, entire groups of dishes are prepared with extra-virgin olive oil in lieu of butter or other oils because it doesn't contain animal fats and is a permissible replacement. From a nutritional standpoint however, these recipes add the healthful fats and flavor compounds that someone abstaining from all animal products and dairy would benefit from greatly.

Understanding the science

From a scientific perspective, the heat tolerance of extra-virgin olive oil is a critical factor that supports its use in cooking. Extra-virgin olive oil is predominantly composed of monounsaturated fats (primarily oleic acid), which are more stable at high temperatures compared to polyunsaturated fats found in most seed oils. This stability is further enhanced by extra-virgin olive oil's high antioxidant content, including phenolic compounds, squalene and tocopherols, which protect the oil from oxidative damage during cooking. Studies have shown that extra-virgin olive oil maintains its integrity and healthful properties for several hours even when used at high cooking temperatures (around 350–400 degrees Fahrenheit), debunking the myth that it becomes harmful when heated.

It's actually very healthy to cook with extra-virgin olive oil. A high proportion of antioxidants present in extra-virgin olive oil, such as hydroxytyrosol and oleocanthal, are not only largely preserved during cooking for usual periods of time, but can also impart beneficial properties to the cooked food with their anti-inflammatory and *cardioprotective* (protects the heart) effects.

Cooking with extra-virgin olive oil can enhance the *bioavailability* (easily absorbed by the body) of fat-soluble vitamins and antioxidants found in other foods, facilitating nutrient exchange and improving the nutritional profile of the overall meal. When extra-virgin olive oil and vegetables are cooked together, polyphenols are exchanged and even new ones created. This synergistic effect contributes to the health-promoting qualities of the Mediterranean diet, which has been linked to the numerous health benefits discussed in Part 2. Numerous research articles provide examples of these protective and beneficial effects of cooking with extra-virgin olive oil.

TECHNICAL STUFF

When meat is cooked and darkens in color, there are chemicals formed called *heterocyclic amines* or *HCAs*. These have been implicated in the formation of cancer and are regarded as being potentially carcinogenic. The use of extra-virgin olive oil in cooking, particularly when marinating meats has a protective effect against the formation of heterocyclic amines. This benefit is attributed to extra-virgin olive oil's high monounsaturated fat content and its rich assortment of antioxidants, which together contribute to its stability under heat and its capacity to inhibit the chemical pathways leading to HCA formation.

FROM THE DOCTOR

Cooking foods that contain fat-soluble vitamins like vitamin D in extra-virgin olive oil enhance the absorption of those vitamins. Cooking mushrooms in extra-virgin olive oil is a particular example of how to get a generous amount of vitamin D, which is important if you're not exposed to enough sunlight. Sun exposure produces vitamin D in the human body.

Exploring the cooking methods

The evidence is clear: Cooking with extra-virgin olive oil is beneficial and a fundamental part of the healthful Mediterranean diet. Even the leftover oil and cooking juices in the pan can be poured over a dish before serving to add flavor, health benefits, and texture.

Adding oil to your diet may seem to contradict the medical advice of the last 50 years to decrease our fat consumption but extra-virgin olive oil, especially when cooking with healthy vegetables, does not, as part of a healthy diet, contribute to weight gain. Reducing your fat consumption isn't necessarily a good thing if it means reducing your use of the healthiest fat in any cuisine — extra-virgin olive oil.

Here are some of our favorite cooking methods to use with extra-virgin olive oil:

>> **Sautéing.** Adding a few tablespoons of extra-virgin olive oil to a hot pan prior to adding your favorite vegetables, flavor base, or sofrito, which we will share recipes for in Chapter 17. Your sauces, soups, and stews will have a boost of flavor and nutrients when vegetables sautéed in olive oil are added.

>> **Marinating and grilling.** Marinating your food in extra-virgin olive, citrus, and herbs prior to grilling will reduce the carcinogenic effects of the grill while adding flavor and bioactive compounds to your dish.

>> **Poaching.** Poaching foods in olive oil enables you to literally bathe them in the nutrients found in extra-virgin

olive oil while coaxing out the maximum health benefits from what you're cooking. It also provides a wonderful, silky texture to your recipe.

» **Pan-frying.** Pan-frying foods in just enough extra-virgin olive oil to coat the bottom of your pan is preferred by many chefs and Mediterranean cooks. The extra-virgin olive oil can stand up to the heat and coat whatever your cooking with its vibrant taste while providing extra nutrients. There's more information on frying with olive oil in the section below.

» **Deep-frying.** If you've had the good fortune of travelling to places like Sicily, Puglia, Spain, Greece, and other olive oil–producing regions, you may have eaten foods fried in olive oil without even knowing it. There are special shops that even specialize in fried food and use only olive oil in the region.

The olive oil can be heated to a higher temperature than what is needed to deep-fry at 365 degrees Fahrenheit, so it's safe to do so, plus it provides much more flavor than frying in other "neutral" oils. The next time you find yourself preparing items like Moussaka, Eggplant Parmigiana, Caponata, and Imam Biyaldi, try frying the vegetables in extra-virgin olive oil. You'll taste the difference for yourself. The same thing is true for frying everything from simple potatoes, fish and chips, or arancini and golden croquettes.

» **Searing.** Searing your meat, seafood, or vegetables in a very hot pan with a few tablespoons of extra-virgin olive oil is a great way to lock in flavor and healthy nutrients and build a golden, crunchy crust that's full of flavor before finishing them off in the oven.

» **Roasting.** Meat, seafood, and vegetables are traditionally roasted in extra-virgin olive oil in the Mediterranean region. Use a bit to coat your roasting pan, then add your ingredients and drizzle on top. Massage the extra-virgin olive oil into the foods to coat, mixing well if necessary, and you'll coax out more flavor, a deeper golden color, and nutrients than you would by using other fats.

There are many chefs and home cooks around the world who have been brainwashed to believe that cooking with extra-virgin olive oil is wrong. They may be following Western media's cues that fat should be avoided or find that other types of mass-produced oils are much cheaper to use. Unfortunately, even traditional Mediterranean dishes are made with lesser quality and less healthful oils for this reason.

In the restaurant world, owners have to pay a lot more money to fry foods in extra-virgin olive oil than with other oils, so using it can be cost prohibitive. In our opinion, if deep-frying with extra-virgin olive oil isn't in your food budget, it's better to skip the deep-frying all together (since it should be enjoyed sparingly) and cook your food by pan-frying or sautéing with extra-virgin olive oil. A little bit goes a long way in promoting your health and the taste of your meal.

Frying in EVOO

While sautéing with EVOO is a common practice preferred by many, frying in extra-virgin olive oil stirs up myths and controversy. For this reason, we have dedicated a section to explaining why frying in EVOO is a good thing. Research suggests that the use of extra-virgin olive oil for frying can help maintain or even increase the content of omega-3 polyunsaturated fatty acids in fish, due to extra-virgin olive oil's higher thermal stability and antioxidant properties, which together minimize the degradation of heat-sensitive omega-3s.

You may hear talk of the "smoke point" of an oil. However, it's not a very useful term because it's much more relevant to consider how an oil changes with heat over a long period of time at common cooking methods and real-world temperatures. There is no single point at which oils are oxidized when heated, undergoing chemical changes and forming potentially harmful and cancer-causing compounds. The breakdown of fats under heat is a process that occurs over time. However, if you are interested in reading more about the smoke point of extra-virgin olive oil, you may wish to visit the North American Olive Oil Association website at www.aboutoliveoil.org/understanding-cooking-oil-smoke-points.

Smoke point does not predict an oil's performance when heated.

The performance of an oil during cooking can be measured in the following forms:

>> **Polar compounds.** When an oil degrades over time with the breakdown of the triglyceride fat molecules, chemicals called polar compounds are produced. Some of these compounds are implicated in causing cancers and neuro-degenerative conditions like Parkinsons disease and Alzheimer's disease.

>> **Trans fats.** Also known as hydrogenated fats, trans fats were once widely used in the food processing industry, until many countries radically restricted their use following evidence of a direct link with heart disease. Trans fats can be formed by oil degradation under heat and can increase in oils particularly when repeatedly used.

>> **Residual oxidative capacity.** The *residual oxidative capacity* is a measure of the capacity left after the heating process. Oils that contain significant concentrations of antioxidant compounds will be protected from oxidation processes of heat that result in oil deterioration during cooking. Antioxidants will give up their capacity as they neutralize free radicals.

Studies show that the performance of extra-virgin olive oil is superior to other common cooking oils including canola oil, sunflower oil, grapeseed oil, peanut oil, coconut oil, and avocado oil. Following heating to around 464 degrees Fahrenheit and then a steady 365 degrees Fahrenheit for 6 hours, the extra-virgin olive oil showed significantly lower levels of polar com-pounds and trans fats and the greatest residual capacity at the end of the experiment, confirming its stability and superior performance under heat.

Table 15-1 can be used as a guide to help determine the oil tem-perature and cook time for some meal favorites.

TABLE 15-1 **Oil Temperatures and Cook Times for Deep-Frying**

Food	Oil Temperature	Time	Internal Temperature
Battered fish	365°F	3-5 minutes	145°F
Risotto, zucchini, potato croquettes	365 °F	3–5 minutes	145°F
Chicken wings	375°F	8–10 minutes	165°F
Chicken strips and tenders	350°F	3–5 minutes	165°F
Loukoumades, churros	375°F	2–4 minutes	
Crispy fried chicken	375°F	12–15 minutes (If need, finish cooking in a 200°F oven)	165°F
Doughnuts	375°F	2–4 minutes	
Spring rolls/egg rolls/samosas/sambousak	350°F	4–6 minutes	
Sigar borek/empanadas	360°F	2–4 minutes	
Falafel	350°F	4–6 minutes	
French fries	325°F then 400°F	Blanch first at 325°F for 3–4 minutes; then fry at 400°F for another 3–4 minutes	
Hush puppies	365°F	2–3 minutes	
Fried mozzarella	350°F	2–3 minutes	
Onion rings	375°F	2–4 minutes	
Oysters	375°F	1–2 minutes	130°F
Potato chips	375°F	8–10 minutes	
Prawns/shrimp	350°F	3–4 minutes	130°F, until the flesh is white, opaque and firm

Preserving Food in EVOO

Preserving food in herbs and olive oil is trendy, but it was an ancient tradition. Cheeses, vegetables, fruits, meat, and fish can all be preserved in extra-virgin olive oil. The Mediterranean region exports many ingredients such as olives, capers, sauces, stuffed vegetables, peppers, stuffed grape leaves, tuna fish, and sardines, as well as many other products that are preserved in olive oil. The natural antioxidants in extra-virgin olive oil, which protect the precious oil from oxidation, also help preserve the foods with which it's combined.

Historically speaking, preserving foods in olive oil was a preferred method because it enabled cooks to capture foods during their harvest period or after a fresh catch or slaughter when food was at its peak. Then the preserved foods were readily available offseason. It's difficult for modern cooks to imagine not having everything at our fingertips all the time, but in the ancient world it simply wasn't that way. Tuna was caught only a few times a year, and produce crops had one specific harvest time. Once the harvest was over, you had to wait until the next year to sample those foods again.

"Putting jars up" in the pantry became a way of reserving foods for another time — especially during winter when there was less food available and before the use of refrigerators and freezers. In addition, when crops were very plentiful, people couldn't eat all the food before spoiling. So preserving enabled the food to be eaten throughout the year.

Some of the popular ingredients to preserve in olive oil are

>> Cheeses, such as mozzarella, feta, and Nabulsi cheese

>> Tomatoes

>> Herbs

>> Peppers

>> Eggplant

>> Fresh tuna fish

If you are preserving foods yourself, it's critical that you follow the exact directions to avoid harmful bacteria from contaminating your food. Everything that you use needs to be completely sterilized and every ingredient needs to be thoroughly washed and dried before preserving. Be sure to use the best-quality extra-virgin olive oil when preserving foods and be sure that the food is completely covered by it. Even if you're storing the preserved food in the refrigerator, it's important that it is always covered with extra-virgin olive oil and contains either 1 tablespoon of salt per 2⅛ cups or lemon juice and vinegar to extend the storing period. For more detailed information on preserving, check out Amelia JeanRoy's book *Canning & Preserving For Dummies*, 3rd edition (Wiley).

Ingredients preserved in extra-virgin olive oil can be combined with other pantry items to make mouthwatering meals in minutes. Toss a bit of preserved tomatoes and fresh tuna or other vegetables with cooked pasta or rice for a quick, tasty, and nutritious dinner. You can also combine several olive oil–preserved vegetables and cheese together to make a quick cooked salad that tastes great with fresh bread or bruschetta.

Chapter **16**

Baking and Pastry-Making with Extra-Virgin Olive Oil

Those who have discovered the joy of baking understand that few activities can be as rewarding and therapeutic as preparing bread and sweet treats. In the Mediterranean region, baking and olive oil have gone hand in hand for millennia, but elsewhere the idea of using olive oil to create baked goods is still relatively new.

If you've never baked with extra-virgin olive oil (EVOO) before, you're missing out on flavor, texture, and health benefits. Adding olive oil into your doughs and batters can actually make them softer, give them a better consistency and help them to be better digested by the body. In baking, extra-virgin olive oil gives off an irresistible aroma.

In this chapter, we explore how extra-virgin olive oil can and should be incorporated into your sweet treats. You'll understand how to swap out butter for extra-virgin olive oil in baking and select a suitable olive oil when making pastries.

Swapping Out Butter for EVOO

By swapping out butter for extra-virgin olive oil in baking, you'll be able to enjoy even more "liquid gold" in your diet. Throughout the Mediterranean region, baked goods were made exclusively with extra-virgin olive oil during the Christian fasting periods when believers abstained from animal products and by the Jewish community who were keeping kosher and could not mix dairy with meat. For this reason, and for the simple fact that olive oil is abundant in the Mediterranean, baking with olive oil became a tradition in many households.

During the 16th and 17th centuries there were many European court baking recipes that used butter. Little by little, they spread in significance and became popular around the world. The popularity of American, British, and Northern European baked goods in the Mediterranean region nowadays has people from Mediterranean countries baking with butter. And in many places, people believe that it's superior to olive oil. It's our hope that you'll experiment with using olive oil instead of butter as often as possible.

Ask yourself the following questions to determine how to make the switch:

>> **What is the desired texture that you're looking for?**
This question is particularly important if you're making scones, pie crust, or croissants, which all call for cold butter. When the cold butter hits the hot air in the oven, it expands and creates the signature texture in those baked items. For scones and pie crusts, you may want to experiment using ½ butter and ½ oil. Try putting the olive oil in the freezer to make it cold before using it so that the olive oil will give a better texture.

>> **Do you want to add color or brown the exterior of your recipe?** Brushing extra-virgin olive oil on the top of breads, cake, and pastries will give them a delicious, golden seal.

>> **Do you need to make a classic recipe in the classic style, or do you prefer to use extra-virgin olive oil regardless of traditional ingredients?** Pound cake, for example, is a recipe made from sugar, eggs, butter, flour, and sugar. If you replace the butter for olive oil, it will give you a slightly different result than the original version. When making muffins, quick breads, and fruit cakes, for example, it's difficult to distinguish (from appearance) when olive oil was used and when butter was used. The extra-virgin olive oil swap out will give moister, slightly denser texture. In pastry, scones, and shortbread-making, however, there will be noticeable differences that are worth noting in recipes. If you need it to be exact, don't deviate from the standard recipe. If you're looking to spice things up with additional flavor and an even moister texture, however, olive oil is a great way to go.

>> **Would you like to adopt a traditional Mediterranean approach to baking?** Mediterranean recipes such as Italian Taralli cookies, Greek holiday cookies and *pites* (sweet and savory pies), Lenten cookies, savory breads, focaccia, breakfast pastries, and olive oil cakes are commonplace in the region and delicious to eat. You may even want to swap out what you normally bake for these types of recipes instead.

REMEMBER

When baking with olive oil, the general rule of thumb for swapping out *other oils for olive oil is a 1 to 1 ratio*. So, for example, if a recipe calls for 1 cup of vegetable oil, you can use 1 cup of extra-virgin olive oil. For swapping out *butter for extra-virgin olive oil, it's better to use a 1 to ¾*, so 1 cup of butter can be replaced by ¾ cup of extra-virgin olive oil.

FROM THE AUTHORS

Baking is one of Chef Amy's favorite activities. Over the years, she has learned to bake almost exclusively (she still makes scones, croissants, and pie crusts with butter) with extra-virgin olive oil. Her students and clients are always surprised when they learn that this is possible, and enjoy the additional flavor and moisture that using extra-virgin olive oil lends to her recipes.

Choosing EVOO for Breads and Sweet Treats

There is a common misconception to not use olive oil in baking because it will "overpower a recipe." Nothing can be further from the truth, especially when you use the right good-quality extra-virgin olive oil for the recipe. In that case, you'll actually be improving the recipes greatly.

That said, there is no reason why you can't use your favorite extra-virgin olive oil as a swap out for your baked goods. You don't *have* to buy different olive oils to bake, just as you probably never bought different butters or olive oils to bake with before. If you do, however, want to pair your baked goods with the proper oil, you will probably enjoy them even more.

How do you know which recipes work the best with extra-virgin olive oil? The following are a few guidelines for recipes that

>> **Call for room temperature or melted butter or vegetable oils.** These recipes fare the best when those ingredients are swapped out for olive oil. They bake and look the same way as they would if you prepared them in the conventional way.

>> **Use baking soda, baking powder, or yeast as leaveners.** If a recipe isn't leavened, but relies on perhaps egg whites for its height, swapping out olive oil may give you too dense of a product. If, on the other hand, the recipe includes a leavener such as baking soda, powder, or yeast, it will still rise properly.

>> **Hail from the Mediterranean region.** Traditionally, Mediterranean recipes have olive oil in their preparations and are easy to reproduce and delicious to eat.

You can use the guidelines above to choose baking recipes to try with olive oil or just use extra-virgin olive for all of your baking. Some good baking options to try are cakes, muffins, cookies, brownies, breads, sweet breads, and tarts, which can all be made with extra-virgin olive oil. In fact, Chapters 18 and 22 have several recipes for breads and desserts that are made with extra-virgin olive oil.

After you choose your recipe, you'll need to select which extra-virgin olive oil to bake with. But first, you have to decide whether you'd like to add a delicate, medium, or robust olive oil flavor to your recipe, using the same guidelines as explained in Chapter 11. Then, you need to understand which olive cultivar will work best for your recipe.

Here are some common olive cultivars from different countries that you can pair with your baking recipes:

>> **If you're looking for a butter substitute:**

In general, when using an oil as a butter substitute, it's a good idea to choose a mild, delicate oil that won't introduce too many additional flavors. Honestly, all baked goods can be done with these types of oils, but they are particularly suited to vanilla-scented sweets, chiffon cakes, cupcakes, and delicate baked goods.

- **Arbequina:** A small, sweet olive that produces a mild and fruity oil, popular for its delicate flavor

- **Leccino:** An olive that produces a delicate and mild oil, also often blended with others

- **Taggiasca:** Tends to result in a mild, fruity oil; mainly found in Liguria

- **Chemlali:** The most widely grown olive in Tunisia, produces a light and fruity oil

- **Nabali:** Produces a mild and sweet oil, with a unique buttery flavor

>> **If you're baking citrusy flavored baked goods:**

Bright citrus flavors in baked goods require oils that have enough of a flavor profile to complement the strong citrus, without overpowering it. Choose medium-intensity oils or oils that have balanced bitter, citrus, and spicy flavors.

- **Hojiblanca:** Characterized by its balanced flavor with hints of bitterness and spiciness

- **Manaki:** Produces a mild and aromatic oil, which is popular in central Greece

- **Memecik:** Known for its balanced and fruity oil, commonly found in western Turkey.

» **If you're making savory breads:**

Savory breads such as pita, focaccia, baguettes, and so on benefit from robust-flavored oils.

- **Picual:** Known for its robust pungent and bitter notes, and high polyphenols; the most widely cultivated olive in the world

- **Koroneiki:** Dominant in Greek olive oil production and known for its high polyphenol content and robust flavor

- **Picholine:** Famous for its robust and peppery oil, popular as a table olive

- **Moraiolo:** Known for its robust and slightly spicy sensations, especially common in central Italy

- **Coratina:** Produces a strong, peppery oil, typically found in regions like Puglia and Calabria in southern Italy

- **Souri:** One of the oldest oil varieties; known for its robust, fruity, and slightly peppery oil

» **If you're baking sweet breads:**

Banana bread, pumpkin bread, apple cakes, and Bundt cakes are best suited to these oils because they are heavier in intensity and offer fruity flavor.

- **Cornicabra:** Recognized for its strong flavor and stability, commonly cultivated in central Spain

- **Manzanillo:** Famous in Spain for its balanced flavor, used as a table olive and for oil

- **Frantoio:** Found in many combined variety olive oils from Tuscany, produces a fruity and slightly bitter oil

» **If you're baking with chocolate:**

Medium- and high-intensity oils with peppery notes, bitterness, fruity, and almond flavors pair well with chocolate.

- **Carolea:** Grown in regions of southern Italy, medium-fruity with balanced bitterness and peppery notes, sometimes accompanied by hints of apple or almond

- **Kalamata:** Famous as a table olive, used to produce a fruity and rich oil (Kalamata is also the name of a region of Greece.)

- **Athinolia:** Creates a balanced oil with slight bitterness, common in the Peloponnese area

- **Chetoui:** Known for its intense and slightly bitter flavor profile

- **Picholine Marocaine:** The dominant variety in Morocco, known for its robust and fruity oil

6

Cooking with Extra-Virgin Olive Oil

Note that the oven temperatures in the recipes are in degrees Fahrenheit. If you need the temperatures in Celsius, use the metric conversions in the Appendix.

Refer to the Tips and Notes at the end of each recipe for cooking and extra-virgin olive oil information as well as wine pairings. The Vary It! sections provide alternative ingredients or instructions to create additional versions of the same recipe.

Prepare flavor-enhancing recipes with extra-virgin olive oil. Use the base recipes to pack powerful flavor bites for your palate.

Check out different ways to start your day with extra-virgin olive oil at breakfast and brunch.

Go beyond the basics with appetizers infused with extra-virgin olive oil.

Enjoy high flavor and nutrition with first courses.

Make olive oil the main event with entrees. Batch-cook the recipes to make a quick meal any time.

Prepare delightful desserts with extra-virgin olive oil.

Chapter **17**

Base Recipes

The secret to mouthwatering meals is to create layers of flavor that start at the beginning of the recipe and finish with the garnish. Since it's healthful and flavor-enhancing to cook with extra-virgin olive oil, we want to share some "formulas" or base recipes that can be incorporated with recipes in Chapters 18 through 22, or with recipes you already have in your repertoire.

Cooking with healthful vegetables, herbs, and spices means that dishes are already full of powerful bioactive compounds and tastiness, so adding extra-virgin olive oil is a wonderful way to enhance the health benefits of the foods.

In this chapter, we provide recipes that add international flair, delicious tastes, or an extra "kick" to your main or side dishes. Becoming familiar with these recipes will enable you to whip up nutritious soups, stews, pastas, and seafood dishes with extra-virgin olive oil in no time.

Italian Soffritto/French Mirepoix

PREP TIME: 10 MIN	COOK TIME: 10 MIN	YIELD: ENOUGH TO USE IN 1 RECIPE

INGREDIENTS

2 tablespoons Anfosso Tumai Extra-Virgin Olive Oil, or other good-quality extra-virgin olive oil

1 yellow onion, finely diced

1 celery stalk, finely diced

1 large carrot, peeled and finely diced

DIRECTIONS

1 Heat the olive oil in a large, wide skillet over medium heat.

2 Add the onion, celery, and carrot and stir to coat.

3 Allow to cook, stirring occasionally until the vegetables are slightly golden and tender, approximately 10 minutes.

TIP: To build on this recipe, add stock, grains, vegetables, and legumes to make a soup. For example, add tomato puree, basil, salt, and pepper to make tomato sauce; add seafood or meat, tomatoes, and stock to begin making a stew; and so on.

NOTE: Sometimes butter is used in place of or along with extra-virgin olive oil in these recipes. I chose Anfosso Tumai, an extra-virgin olive oil with DOP certification (see Chapter 2) from the hills of the Ligurian coast. It has a light and harmonious aroma, sweet with a little spicy touch. The taste is soft and complex, full of delicate fruity tones. The bitter and spicy notes are present and balanced, which enhance the flavors of this classic European "holy trinity."

Cajun Holy Trinity and Spanish Sofrito

PREP TIME: 10 MIN	COOK TIME: 10 MIN	YIELD: ENOUGH TO USE IN 1 RECIPE

INGREDIENTS

3 tablespoons Emblem Extra-Virgin Olive Oil or other good-quality extra-virgin olive oil

1 yellow onion, finely diced

1 celery stalk, finely diced

1 large green bell pepper, peeled and finely diced

½ cup chopped fresh cilantro*

5 garlic cloves, minced*

DIRECTIONS

1 Heat the olive oil in a large, wide skillet over medium heat.

2 Add the onion, celery, and green bell pepper and stir to coat. *If making the Spanish-style sofrito, add in the cilantro and garlic, and stir to coat.

3 Allow to cook, stirring occasionally until the vegetables are slightly golden and tender, approximately 10 minutes.

TIP: To build on this recipe, add in rice or in vegetable and meat dishes for additional flavor and nutritional benefits.

NOTE: The Cajun "Holy Trinity" refers to the combination of onion, celery, and green bell pepper, which is often used in Cajun or Creole cooking. Spanish-style sofrito incorporates cilantro and garlic, which add additional tanginess along with many health benefits. Cilantro is a great detoxifier and garlic has antibiotic and anti-inflammatory properties. When cooked in olive oil, these powerful health-boosting features are compounded. I chose Emblem olive oil for the Cajun Holy Trinity and the Spanish Sofrito because it does a great job of binding the strong flavors together without overpowering them. Since Cajun food is normally spiced, it's important to use an olive oil that won't interfere with the traditional flavor profiles of the cuisine.

Aglione

PREP TIME: 10 MIN	COOK TIME: NONE	YIELD: ENOUGH TO USE IN 1 RECIPE

INGREDIENTS

2 tablespoons Tenute Librandi Organic Carolea Extra-Virgin Olive Oil or other good-quality extra-virgin olive oil

1 rosemary sprig, needles removed and stem discarded

5 sage leaves

1 clove garlic

1 teaspoon juniper berries (optional)

¼ teaspoon unrefined sea salt

Pinch of freshly ground black pepper

DIRECTIONS

1 Place the olive oil in a medium-sized bowl.

2 Combine the rosemary, sage, juniper berries (if using), and garlic on a cutting board and mince. Add to the bowl. Season with the salt and pepper.

TIP: You can make large batches of this mixture and store it in the refrigerator for up to 1 week.

NOTE: If you've ever been to Italy's Emilia-Romagna region in the spring, you may notice the beautiful juniper berries on bushes everywhere. They're used as a flavor enhancer that can be rubbed into roasted chicken, turkey, or meat, or tossed with roasted potatoes a few minutes before serving. I used Tenute Librand Carolea extra-virgin olive oil in this recipe because it's pronounced flavors of olive, almond, and artichoke stand up to the intensity of both the ingredients in this condiment and the meats that they will season.

Toum/Lebanese–Style Garlic Sauce

INGREDIENTS

½ cup garlic cloves, peeled, sliced in half, sprouts removed

1 teaspoon unrefined sea salt

1½ cups Italian Leccino Extra-Virgin Olive Oil or other mild extra-virgin olive oil, divided

¼ cup fresh lemon juice

DIRECTIONS

1 Place the sliced garlic cloves into a food processor and add the salt. Process for a minute until the garlic becomes finely minced. Make sure to scrape down the sides of the food processor as it sticks to the sides.

2 Remove the lid of the spout, and with the food processor running, slowly pour 1 to 2 tablespoons of olive oil, then stop and scrape down the bowl. Continue adding another tablespoon or two until the garlic starts looking creamy.

3 Once the garlic looks emulsified, increase the speed of pouring the oil and alternate with the lemon juice until all the oil and lemon juice is incorporated. This will take up to 15 minutes.

4 Transfer the sauce into a glass container and cover with plastic wrap. Store in the refrigerator overnight. The following day, stir the mixture, and replace plastic wrap with an airtight lid. Store, covered, up to a month in the refrigerator.

TIP: If you've ever eaten at a Lebanese restaurant, you've probably tasted this ubiquitous white sauce on Chicken Shawarma and served with other condiments. Many people like to dip french fries in it.

NOTE: *Toum*, which is the Arabic word for "garlic," is also the name of this sauce because of the heavy dosage of garlic in the recipe. Normally a "neutral" oil, such as safflower, is used in this recipe as traditional Lebanese

(continued)

olive oil is very full-flavored. In order to enhance the health benefits and taste of this dish, I make it with a mild Leccino variety from Italy.

VARY IT! There is a version of this sauce in every Mediterranean culture. Greek Skordalia and Egyptian Toumeya, for example, were also born out of the garlic/oil base recipe. We suggest trying those recipes too!

Salad Dressing/Vinaigrette

PREP TIME: 2 MIN	COOK TIME: NONE	YIELD: 4 SERVINGS

INGREDIENTS

½ cup Arbosano Chilean Extra-Virgin Olive Oil or other good-quality extra-virgin olive oil

3 tablespoons vinegar (red or white wine, balsamic), apple cider, or lemon juice

1 tablespoon Dijon mustard (optional)

⅛ teaspoon unrefined sea salt

Freshly ground black pepper

DIRECTIONS

1 Combine the olive oil, vinegar, Dijon mustard (if desired), salt, and a few twists of pepper in a medium bowl.

2 Whisk well until incorporated and then another few minutes until emulsified. Toss with salad and serve immediately or store, tightly sealed, in the refrigerator, up to a week until needed.

TIP: Using your own, homemade salad dressing with good-quality olive oil and vinegar is one of the best things that you can do for your diet.

VARY IT! Different cultures approach dressings in different ways. To serve your salad Italian style, omit the Dijon mustard; add the Dijon mustard to serve a French-style salad. To make a North African vinaigrette, swap out lime or lemon juice for the vinegar. If you like your dressings with a hint of sweetness, add a touch of maple syrup.

NOTE: I choose the Chilean Arbosano olive oil because of the unique intensity that this Spanish cultivar has when grown in South America. You can substitute your favorite extra-virgin olive oil when making vinaigrettes, if desired.

Aioli

PREP TIME: 5 MIN	COOK TIME: NONE	YIELD: 4 SERVINGS

INGREDIENTS

2 cloves garlic, minced

1 large pasteurized egg yolk (see Note)

½ teaspoon fresh lemon juice

¼ teaspoon unrefined sea salt

½ cup Positively Good For You Extra-Virgin Olive Oil or other good-quality Spanish extra-virgin olive oil

DIRECTIONS

1 Place the garlic in a mortar and pound with the pestle until a paste is formed. Add the egg yolk to the garlic along with the lemon juice and the salt. Use the pestle to combine.

2 Slowly pour the olive oil into the garlic and egg mixture, stirring continuously with the pestle. (It can be helpful to have two hands in the kitchen, or you can do this step in a small food processor.)

3 Continue stirring for 1 minute after all the ingredients are combined until the mixture is a creamy, mayonnaise–like consistency.

TIP: This is a classic Mediterranean topping used for potatoes, omelets, vegetables, rice dishes, and bread. While we tend to associate it most with Spanish cooking, it has been around since antiquity. Remnants of it were recently found in sunken Phoenician trading vessels.

NOTE: If you are pregnant, elderly, or have compromised immunity, you should avoid consuming raw eggs. Substitute your favorite mayonnaise or vegan Aioli for this version if desired. I chose Positively Good For You extra-virgin olive oil because it is made in Spain, from Picual olives, representing a Spanish Alioli version of this sauce. In recipes as simple as this, it's important to choose good-quality and delicious-tasting oil to enhance the flavor.

Tapenade

PREP TIME: 5 MIN	COOK TIME: NONE	YIELD: 1 CUP, APPROXIMATELY 6-8 SERVINGS

INGREDIENTS

¾ cup pitted olives (Castelvetrano, Nocellara, Picholine, or Kalamata work well)

3 teaspoons capers, rinsed and drained well

3 cloves garlic, chopped

⅓ cup Bono Sicilian Val di Mazara PDO Organic Extra-Virgin Olive Oil or other good-quality extra-virgin olive oil, plus more if needed

1 teaspoon lemon zest

Freshly ground black pepper

DIRECTIONS

1 Combine the olives, capers, and garlic in the food processor.

2 Remove the lid of the spout and slowly pour in the olive oil, a little at a time, while pulsing the food processor on and off. The tapenade should have a paste–like consistency but should not be completely smooth.

3 Stir in the lemon zest and season with freshly ground pepper to taste.

TIP: Leftover roasted chicken or fish and raw vegetables taste great dipped into tapenade. I also like to stir it into blanched green beans that I toss with cucumbers, chickpeas, and cherry tomatoes for a fun and flavorful salad.

NOTE: The Romans named Provence *Provincia Romana*, or The Roman Province, in Latin when Nice was their capital in the first century CE. The Romans left vineyards and olive groves as well as the Latin language during their time there. As a result, Provencal cuisine developed strong Italian undertones, as this recipe demonstrates. The word tapenade comes from the ancient Provencal word *tapena*, which means "to cover." I chose the Sicilian Val di Mazara PDO organic extra-virgin olive oil to underline the strong olive flavor of the dish.

VARY IT! Swap out the black olives for green, or use a combination of the two, if desired.

Salsa di pomodoro/Fresh Tomato Sauce

PREP TIME: 5 MIN	COOK TIME: 20 MIN	YIELD: 6 SERVINGS

INGREDIENTS

2 tablespoons Quattrociocchi Olivastro Extra-Virgin Olive Oil or other good-quality extra-virgin olive oil

2 large cloves garlic, peeled and minced

1½ pounds strained (seeded and skinned tomatoes) boxed or jarred tomatoes, such as Pomì brand; or 2½ pounds fresh, ripe tomatoes (see Tip)

Unrefined sea salt, to taste

Freshly ground black pepper, to taste

4–5 leaves of fresh basil, oregano, or parsley

Freshly grated Parmigiano Reggiano or Pecorino Romano cheese, for garnish

DIRECTIONS

1 Heat the olive oil in a medium saucepan over medium heat. Add garlic and reduce heat to low.

2 When garlic begins to release its aroma (before it turns color), add the tomatoes.

3 Stir and allow the mixture to come to a boil to create caramelization on the sides of the pan.

4 Add the salt, pepper, and fresh herbs; stir and cover. Reduce the heat to low, and simmer for 10 to 20 minutes, until the sauce has thickened slightly. Taste and adjust the seasonings. Garnish with grated cheese before serving.

TIP: If you are using fresh tomatoes instead of boxed or jarred tomatoes, place them in boiling water until their skins peel (just a few minutes), strain, and allow to cool to touch. Peel the tomatoes, remove the seeds, and cut them into chunks. Then use the prepared tomatoes in Step 2.

TIP: Most Italians make large batches of this sauce to have one recipe on hand at all times in the refrigerator and a spare or two in the freezer. This sauce keeps in the refrigerator for up to a week or in the freezer for a few months.

NOTE: If you are serving this sauce with pasta as a first course, the second course should not contain tomatoes. Simple grilled or pan-fried chicken, veal, beef, or seafood are natural accompaniments. This simple sauce is the base for Italian tomato soups, as well as the Arrabbiata, Norma, Amatriciana, and Aurora sauces in Italy. The rich, fruity olive taste of the Itrana olives that are used in Quattrociocchi's oil makes it a great complement to tomato sauce.

Pesto/Fresh Basil and Pine Nut "Sauce"

PREP TIME: 5 MIN   COOK TIME: NONE   YIELD: 4 SERVINGS

INGREDIENTS

¼ cup pine nuts

1 clove garlic, peeled

3 cups lightly packed fresh basil leaves, preferably Genovese basil

¼ cup Anfosso Extra-Virgin Olive Oil or other Ligurian extra-virgin olive oil, plus extra for serving

¼ cup Parmigiano-Reggiano cheese, freshly grated

Pinch of unrefined sea salt (optional)

DIRECTIONS

1 Combine the pine nuts, garlic, basil, and olive oil in a large mortar or food processor, and grind or process until a smooth paste forms.

2 Using a spatula, scoop the pesto out of the mortar or food processor and into a bowl. Stir in cheese and the salt, if desired.

3 Transfer the pesto to a plastic container, and cover with a layer of olive oil to store or toss directly into fresh, hot pasta.

TIP: Italians never heat pesto sauce. It's either slathered onto bread or tossed into vegetables or pasta at room temperature. If serving on pizza, spread it on baked pizza dough, after taking the pizza out of the oven.

VARY IT! While traditional pesto is made only in summer when basil is at its peak, variations can be made year-round. In the winter, I substitute the pine nuts for walnuts or almonds and the basil for baby kale or arugula to make a delicious and nutritious sauce that brightens cold days.

THE "OFFICIAL" PESTO RECIPE

In the region of Liguria, on the Italian Riviera where pesto origi-nates, there is a Consortium that dictates whether pesto sauce is authentic enough to boast the DOP label. To qualify, the pesto must be produced within the Liguria region, with specific types of each of the ingredients listed in the pesto recipe above and in a certain manner. The official recipe is mandated to be made with a mortar and pestle, not with a food processor as is done in many modern homes and restaurants. To learn more, visit: https://www.mangiareinliguria.it/pesto-genovese/disciplinare-del-pesto-genovese.

Vegetable Stock

PREP TIME: 5 MIN	COOK TIME: 30 MIN	YIELD: 8 SERVINGS

INGREDIENTS

1 medium yellow onion, halved (not peeled)

1 carrot, trimmed and halved

1 stalk celery, trimmed and halved (can include leaves, if desired)

4 ounces cherry tomatoes

4 sprigs fresh basil, with stems

1 small bunch (approximately ¾ cup) fresh flat-leaf parsley, with stems

½ teaspoon unrefined sea salt

DIRECTIONS

1 Place the onion, carrot, celery, tomatoes, basil, and parsley in a large stockpot. Cover with 16 cups of water. Bring to a boil over high heat. Reduce the heat to medium-low. Add the salt, and simmer, uncovered, for 30 minutes.

2 Drain the stock, reserving the liquid. Discard the rest. If you're not using it right away, allow to cool and then store in the refrigerator for up to a week or freeze it for up to a month.

Chicken Stock

PREP TIME: 5 MIN | COOK TIME: 40 MIN | YIELD: 8 SERVINGS

INGREDIENTS

1 medium yellow onion, halved (not peeled)

1 medium carrot, trimmed and halved

1 medium stalk celery, trimmed and halved

1¼ pounds chicken bones or carcass from cooked chicken

1 teaspoon whole black peppercorns

1 dried bay leaf

½ teaspoon unrefined sea salt

DIRECTIONS

1 Place the onion, carrot, celery, chicken bones, peppercorns, and bay leaf in a large stockpot. Cover with 16 cups water. Bring to a boil over high heat. Reduce the heat to medium–low.

2 Skim off the residue that forms on top of the stock and discard. Add the salt, and simmer, uncovered, for 40 minutes.

3 Drain the stock, reserving the liquid. Discard the rest. If you're not using it right away, allow to cool, and then store in the refrigerator for up to a week or freeze it for up to a month.

Chapter **18**

Breakfast and Brunch

RECIPES IN THIS CHAPTER

☼ Citrus-Spice Muffins with Olive Oil

☼ Almond and Orange Biscotti

☼ Artichoke, Caramelized Onion, and Tomato-Basil Frittata

☼ Avocado Toast with Olive Oil, Sea Salt, and Flaxseeds

☼ Chocolate Banana Bread

There's no better way to start your day than with a healthy dose of extra-virgin olive oil. Olive oil enthusiasts and people in the Mediterranean enjoy consuming olive oil at breakfast.

In this chapter, we show you how to reap the benefits of starting your day with flavorful dishes made with extra-virgin olive oil (EVOO). With these crave-worthy recipes, you can make every morning a celebration.

Starting Your Day with a Shot of EVOO

Extra-virgin olive oil has literally been a food of the champions since ancient times when it was fed to Olympic athletes. Given all of the health benefits that we've discussed in Part 2, plus its fabulous taste, there's no reason not to include it in your morning repertoire.

We promote the consumption of olive oil all day long, but when you enjoy it each morning, you start to boost your nutrient quotient early in the day. This chapter includes perennial breakfast favorites plus some family heirlooms from Chef Amy's repertoire, which can also be enjoyed in the dishes as an afternoon snack, for brunch, or whenever the mood strikes.

Working EVOO into Your Morning Routine

People take their breakfast routines very seriously, having personal preferences about what breakfasts should look like, and often aren't willing to part with them. Some people prefer short and sweet breakfasts, while others languish in long, leisurely breakfasts that feature savory items.

Brunch, which is widely popular in America and Northern Europe, is also becoming trendy in Southern Europe. It's a great way to make the fusion of breakfast and lunch into a grand affair — especially on weekends.

Extra-virgin olive oil can take center stage to make your morning meals more wholesome and mouthwatering. Each recipe in this chapter is paired with the particular olive oil that Chef Amy prefers for it, but feel free to swap out with your favorite type of extra-virgin olive oil.

The Citrus-Spice Muffins recipe was created especially for our friends at Tierra Callada who import superior extra-virgin olive oil from Spain. The Almond and Orange Biscotti recipe originally hails from Chef Amy's ancestral homeland of Calabria, Italy. The Artichoke, Caramelized Onion, and Tomato-Basil Frittata, which is a wonderful brunch option, would traditionally be served with a salad for dinner in Italy. Chef Amy's version of an avocado toast offers a flavorful twist on a nutritious trend, and the Chocolate Banana Bread is moist, sumptuous, and full of powerful polyphenols.

Citrus-Spice Muffins with Olive Oil

PREP TIME: 10 MIN	COOK TIME: 20 MIN	YIELD: 12 SERVINGS

INGREDIENTS

1⅓ cups whole milk ricotta cheese

⅓ cup Tierra Callada Envero or other good-quality extra-virgin olive oil

¼ cup whole milk

1 large egg

1 teaspoon pure vanilla extract

1 teaspoon ground cardamom

1⅔ cups unbleached all-purpose flour

¾ cup turbinado sugar, plus 1 tablespoon

2 teaspoons baking powder

Zest and juice of 1 orange

DIRECTIONS

1 Heat the oven to 400 degrees. Place paper baking cups into a 12-cup muffin pan. Set aside.

2 Combine ricotta cheese, olive oil, milk, egg, vanilla, and cardamom in a large bowl and mix well to combine with a wooden spoon.

3 Stir in flour, ¾ cup sugar, and baking powder and mix well to combine.

4 Carefully stir in orange juice and zest into batter.

5 Spoon the batter evenly into prepared muffin cups. Sprinkle the tops with remaining tablespoon of sugar.

6 Bake 15 to 20 minutes, until a toothpick inserted in center comes out clean.

7 Cool 5 minutes in pan; remove to cooling rack. You can double the amount in this recipe to make 24 muffins, and freeze the ones that you don't want to serve immediately. They last for up to two months stored in an airtight container in the freezer.

TIP: I chose Tierra Callada Envero extra-virgin olive oil because it delivers bright, sweet flavors of ripe fruit. It's a balanced and medium intensity oil that pairs well with sweet baked goods. Envero is made from Spanish Picual olives, which is collected during the *envero* (the period when the olives change the color from green to black).

NOTE: You can pour the batter into a loaf pan to make a sliceable sweet bread instead of muffins. If making bread, the recipe will need to cook for at least 15 minutes longer, or until it is golden and pulls away from the edges.

VARY IT! To make these muffins gluten free, swap out the flour for almond flour and make sure that the baking powder is gluten free. You can also add fresh or dried fruit such as cherries, cranberries, blueberries, or even chocolate chips to this recipe. Swap dairy milk for almond or rice if preferred.

Almond and Orange Biscotti

PREP TIME: 15 MIN	COOK TIME: 35 MIN, PLUS COOLING TIME	YIELD: 14 SERVINGS

INGREDIENTS

2¼ cups almond flour

½ cup granulated sugar

2 teaspoons baking powder

¼ teaspoon unrefined sea salt

2 large eggs

¼ cup Amy Riolo Selections or other good-quality extra-virgin olive oil

2 tablespoons pure honey

2 tablespoons orange juice

2 tablespoons orange zest

1 teaspoon pure vanilla extract

1 teaspoon pure almond extract

½ cup sliced almonds, toasted

DIRECTIONS

1 Preheat the oven to 375 degrees. Line a baking sheet with parchment paper or a silicone baking mat.

2 Place the flour, sugar, baking powder, and salt in a large bowl and combine with a wooden spoon.

3 In another large bowl, combine eggs, olive oil, honey, orange juice and zest, vanilla and almond, and mix well to combine.

4 Pour the egg mixture into the flour mixture. When done mixing, stir in the opposite direction to make sure that all the ingredients have been incorporated.

5 Stir in the almonds. Drop dough onto baking sheet to form 2 (14-x-4-inch logs that are spaced 2 to 3 inches apart.

6 Wet your fingertips, and smooth out the logs into even shapes. Bake for 20 to 25 minutes until the logs are golden and cooked through. Remove from the oven and allow to cool 10 minutes.

7 Reduce oven temperature to 325 degrees. Carefully transfer the logs to a work surface, and using a serrated knife, cut them into ½-inch-thick slices. Re-line the baking sheet and arrange the slices on the sheet.

8 Bake again for 10 minutes, or until crisp. Cool completely and store in an airtight container for a week. Serve with espresso or coffee for dunking.

TIP: I pair this recipe with my own, private label olive oil produced by Tenute Cristiano in Calabria, Italy where Simon has filmed. The estate is known for producing Carolea olives, which are indigenous to Calabria. This extra-virgin olive oil is very low in acidity and high in polyphenols. When tasted alone, its aroma is a mosaic of tomatoes and wild herbs with black pepper. It has a very fluid, harmonious texture while its taste is round and full ending in notes of almonds and citrus that pair perfectly with the main ingredients in this biscotti recipe.

NOTE: The combination of almonds and oranges are very popular in both Calabria and Sicily. They are often eaten together as a snack or after a meal, and these biscotti can also be eaten in those times. Biscotti are always dunked into sweet wine or espresso after a meal, and cappuccino or caffè latte in the morning. Children dunk them into warm milk for breakfast.

VARY IT! You can substitute the oranges and almonds for lemon and almond or lemon and walnuts, if you prefer. Sometimes I use a combination of citrus with pistachios as well.

Artichoke, Caramelized Onion, and Tomato-Basil Frittata

PREP TIME: 10 MIN	COOK TIME: 30 MIN	YIELD: 4 SERVINGS (MAIN COURSE) 6-8 SERVINGS (APPETIZER)

INGREDIENTS

¼ cup Anfosso Tumai Monocultivar Taggiasca or other good-quality extra-virgin olive oil

½ medium yellow onion, thinly sliced

2 cups fresh or frozen, thawed artichoke hearts

1 large tomato, or 2 Roma tomatoes, diced

1 cup basil leaves, hand torn

6 large eggs, beaten until foamy

¼ cup grated Pecorino Romano or Parmigiano-Reggiano cheese

1 teaspoon unrefined sea salt

DIRECTIONS

1   Preheat the oven to 350 degrees. Heat the olive oil in a large, wide, ovenproof skillet over medium-high heat.

2   Add the onion and sauté, stirring occasionally, until softened and golden, about 4 minutes. Add a few tablespoons of water to the pan, stir, and continue cooking, stirring often, until onions get very golden and tender, about 10 more minutes.

3   Add the artichokes, and stir to combine. Sauté, until golden, approximately 5 minutes. Add the tomatoes, stir, and cook for another 4 minutes.

4   Add the basil leaves, beaten eggs, cheese, and salt. Mix well, and reduce heat to medium-low. Cook, undisturbed, for 4 to 5 minutes, until the eggs are cooked through.

5   Finish off the frittata by putting the skillet in the oven and bake until the frittata top is golden and the eggs are set, about 4 to 5 minutes. Cut into 4 pieces, and serve. Store in an airtight container in the refrigerator for up to 2 days. Reheat in a preheated 300-degree oven for 5 minutes, or until warm.

TIP: The Taggiasca olives used in this single variety olive oil have been produced by the Anfosso family in Liguria for generations. This award-winning oil has aromas of vegetables and herbs, while tasting like artichoke and green tomato on the palate, which makes it the perfect combination for this dish. If serving for brunch, it pairs well with a Ligurian Vermentino wine.

NOTE: Serve this dish at brunch or by itself with bread, salad, and a cheese selection for a light dinner, or preceded by a vegetable- or legume-based soup at lunch. In addition to being served as a second course, it can be an appetizer or an item at a buffet.

VARY IT! Frittata should be made with the best seasonal produce, so you can substitute what's in season.

Avocado Toast with Olive Oil, Sea Salt, and Flaxseeds

PREP TIME: 10 MIN	COOK TIME: 2 MIN	YIELD: 2 SERVINGS

INGREDIENTS

2 slices good-quality sourdough, whole-wheat, barley, or oat bread

2 tablespoons Geraci Nocellara del Belice or other good-quality extra-virgin olive oil, divided

1 ripe avocado, halved and pitted

Unrefined sea salt or fleur de sel

1 tablespoon ground flaxseeds, divided

DIRECTIONS

1 Toast the bread in a toaster or under the broiler to desired doneness.

2 Drizzle ½ tablespoon of olive oil over each piece of bread and brush to coat both sides.

3 Scoop the avocado out of the shell and place the flesh from half of each avocado on each of the pieces of bread. Mash the avocado down.

4 Drizzle the remaining olive oil (½ tablespoon each) over the toast.

5 Sprinkle the toast with sea salt and ½ teaspoon flaxseeds each and serve immediately.

TIP: Nocellara olives grow in the Olis Geraci olive groves in the Belice Valley in Sicilia. These olives are also known as Castelvetrano because that's the name of the commune where they are grown. They have an intense aroma of fruitiness with hints of grass, artichoke, and tomato leaves, which pair well with both bread and avocado. On the palate, this extra-virgin olive oil is well-balanced with an intense spiciness and soft bitterness.

NOTE: I like to pair vegetarian dishes with more intense olive oils like Nocellara to help provide a more complete flavor profile. If serving for brunch, I would pair the toasts with a Spritz cocktail made from a Sicilian Amaro.

VARY IT! Mashed beets, tomatoes, chickpeas, or cannellini beans also make great, Mediterranean inspired toast toppings. Add a poached or soft-boiled egg on top for a complete meal.

Chocolate Banana Bread

PREP TIME: 10 MIN	COOK TIME: 50 MIN	YIELD: 10 SERVINGS

INGREDIENTS

½ cup A l'Olivier or your favorite good-quality extra-virgin olive oil, divided

1 cup granulated sugar

2 large eggs

¼ cup unsweetened cocoa

1 teaspoon pure vanilla extract

1 tablespoon espresso coffee

3 ripe bananas, mashed

2 cups unbleached all-purpose flour

Pinch of unrefined sea salt

1 cup semisweet chocolate chips

DIRECTIONS

1 Preheat the oven to 350 degrees. Grease a 9-x-5-inch loaf pan on bottom and sides with a bit of the olive oil.

2 In a large bowl, combine the remaining olive oil and sugar with a wooden spoon and mix until well incorporated.

3 Add in the eggs, cocoa, vanilla, espresso, and bananas and mix well.

4 Add in the flour and salt. Mix well to combine. Stir in the chocolate chips.

5 Pour the mixture into the loaf pan and bake for 50 to 60 minutes, until a toothpick inserted in the center comes out clean and the bread begins to pull away from the side of the pan.

6 Cool completely and serve immediately or store in an airtight container in the refrigerator or freezer until serving. Bread will stay fresh in an airtight container at room temperature for 2 days.

TIP: I chose A l'Olivier extra-virgin olive oil from France for this recipe because it is known for its notes of green apple and artichoke. It also has a touch of bitterness and a slight pungency which both compliment and contrast this sweet bread. Honestly, I have used many varieties of extra-virgin olive oil in this recipe, and they all work well.

NOTE: You can also make 12 muffins by placing it in the holes of a lined muffin tin and baking for 20 to 25 minutes, until firm.

VARY IT! Omit the cocoa and espresso to make traditional banana bread. For a gluten-free version, use almond flour and gluten-free baking powder.

Chapter **19**

Appetizers

D o you love indulging in appetizers in restaurants but tend to overlook them when entertaining at home? For many people, enjoying a few appetizers on their own is a great way to experience different flavors. Within the Mediterranean region, there's the Spanish tradition of Tapas, the Italian Antipasto ritual, the Arabic Mezze table, the Greek Mezedes feast, Turkish Meze spread, and Egyptian Salatat selections — just to name a few.

Starting meals with good-quality extra-virgin olive oil opens up a world of flavor and nutrition for your palate and body. Best of all, it sets the stage for a delicious and healthful meal to come.

Since Mediterranean appetizer recipes revolve around olive oil, Chef Amy specifically chose to focus on some of the heavy hitters in the region for this chapter. These decadent dishes illustrate how well you can roast, deep-fry, pan-fry, and sauté olive oil to make your starters sing.

This small selection is just the tip of the iceberg in terms of appetizers that you can create with extra-virgin olive oil. We hope that preparing them will inspire you to create new and exciting meals of your own.

TIP

When you fry vegetables in extra-virgin olive oil, you don't have to throw the oil away after one use. Instead, allow it to cool completely and strain it into a metal can or glass container. Keep it sealed until you need to fry again. You can reuse the olive oil two to three times if you're not cooking proteins.

DRESSING SALADS AS APPETIZERS

Many people like to eat salads as appetizers, even though the Italian and French cultures eat them at the end of a meal to cleanse the palate prior to dessert. Whenever you choose to eat salads, using extra-virgin olive oil as the base for your dressing will give you an edge of flavor, authenticity, and health properties.

Here are some tips for making great salad dressings at home:

- Skip the mayonnaise and condiment-based varieties that are laden with fat and sodium.

- Taste various olive-oil types on their own so you'll become familiar with the ones that you enjoy the most.

- Store your favorite olive oils and vinegar in the pantry to always have on hand.

- Keep Dijon or honey mustard and Greek yogurt in the refrigerator, if you like thicker dressings.

   To make your own vinaigrette, place the following ingredients in a medium-sized bowl:

- ½ cup extra-virgin olive oil

- ⅓ cup citrus of choice (lemon juice, orange juice, lime juice), balsamic vinegar, red wine vinegar, white wine vinegar, or any combination

- ¼ teaspoon unrefined sea salt and a sprinkle of freshy ground pepper

Whisk the ingredients until emulsified, pour over your salad, toss to coat. This is how most people in the Mediterranean region dress their salads. If you're used to something more substantial, you can add in:

- 1 tablespoon Dijon or honey mustard for creaminess and color

- 2 tablespoons Greek yogurt and 2 tablespoons freshly chopped herbs such as dill, mint, parsley, or basil for creaminess.

- 1 tablespoon maple syrup or honey for sweetness

For more creative salad recipes, check out our book *Diabetes Cookbook For Dummies* as well.

Bravas–Style Potatoes with Aioli

PREP TIME: 15 MIN	COOK TIME: 45 MIN	YIELD: 4 SERVINGS

INGREDIENTS

3 tablespoons Positively Good For You Extra-Virgin Olive Oil or other good-quality Spanish extra-virgin olive oil, divided

2 large Russet potatoes, peeled and cut into 1-inch cubes

1 teaspoon unrefined sea salt

Freshly ground black pepper

2 cloves garlic, finely chopped

1 tablespoon smoked paprika

Flat-leaf parsley leaves, for garnish

1 recipe Aioli (see Chapter 17), for serving

DIRECTIONS

1 Heat the oven to 425 degrees. Grease a baking sheet with 1 tablespoon olive oil.

2 Place the potatoes on a baking sheet, season them with salt and pepper, and place in the oven. Allow to roast for 35 to 40 minutes, or until the potatoes are completely golden, turning halfway through cooking.

3 Heat the remaining 2 tablespoons olive oil in a small frying pan over medium heat. Add the garlic and cook until it releases its aroma, about 3 minutes. Add the paprika and cook for 30 seconds. Let cool slightly.

4 When potatoes have finished cooking pour the paprika mixture over them and gently toss to coat. To serve, place them on a platter, garnish with parsley, and serve with aioli sauce on the side or drizzled on top.

TIP: This is my all-time favorite potato recipe and one that Simon enjoys while spending time at his home in Spain. I recommend using the Positively Good For You Extra-Virgin Olive Oil because it, like the recipe, hails from Spain. It's made from the local Picual olives and contains certified high phenol levels with a demonstrated capacity to improve health and reduce heart disease. It's also the first European extra-virgin olive oil to hold an authority approved and regulated health claim. Because this recipe only has a few ingredients, the rich and intense flavor of the Picual variety will be evidenced in the final dish. If you cannot find Positively Good For You, substitute your favorite olive oil brand. Pair with dry Spanish sherry.

NOTE: While aioli is a trendy item on many restaurant menus, it actually is an ancient recipe that was found in jars in the remnants of ancient Phoenician trading vessels off the coast of the Mediterranean. Make extra portions to serve with Spanish-style omelets and for slathering on sandwiches. Due to the raw egg content, it's important to consume it within a day or two.

VARY IT! You can swap out the potatoes for any root vegetable. Turnips, rutabaga, carrots, and even Brussels sprouts all taste great prepared this way.

Roman Risotto Croquettes

PREP TIME: 15 MIN	COOK TIME: 1 HOUR	YIELD: 8 SERVINGS

INGREDIENTS

2 cups homemade chicken or vegetable stock (see Chapter 17), plus extra, if needed

2 tablespoons unsalted butter

1 small onion, finely diced

1 cup Carnaroli, Vialone Nano, or Arbario rice

1 cup white wine

¼ cup freshly grated Parmesan cheese

Salt, to taste

¼ cup tomato sauce (see Chapter 17) or tomato puree

2 large eggs, beaten

½ cup plain dried breadcrumbs mixed with ¼ cup Parmigiano Reggiano cheese and some pepper

1 (8 ounce) ball fresh mozzarella, cubed

Sabina PDO Extra-Virgin Olive Oil or other good-quality extra-virgin olive oil, for frying

DIRECTIONS

1 Warm the stock in a medium-sized saucepan over medium heat.

2 In a large pot, melt the butter in a large saucepan over medium heat. When it foams, add the onion. Next, add the rice and stir to combine, then add the wine and increase the heat to high.

3 When the wine has evaporated from the rice mixture, begin adding the stock one ladle at a time. Reduce the heat to medium, and stir. After each ladle of broth has evaporated, add another ladle full and stir.

4 Continue cooking, adding stock, and stirring until the rice is done, approximately 15 to 20 minutes.

5 Stir in the Parmesan cheese. Taste, and add salt, if necessary. Stir in the tomato sauce. Allow risotto to cool completely. In the meantime, set up a breading station with the beaten eggs in a bowl and the breadcrumb mixture on a plate.

6 Form the risotto into equal-sized balls, ranging in size from a small to large ice cream scoop. (The balls need to be the same size for frying.) Then shape each ball into an elongated egg-shaped croquette. Stuff a cube of mozzarella into the center of each ball.

7 Dip the croquettes first into egg (lightly shaking off excess), then into breadcrumb mixture and set on a plate. Store in the refrigerator until ready to fry.

8 Heat 2 inches of oil in a large shallow frying pan to 325 degrees. Carefully lower one ball into the oil and monitor the browning process. If it becomes golden right away, proceed. If not, increase the heat before continuing. If it becomes too dark too quickly, lower the heat and proceed. Serve hot.

TIP: Whenever I make risotto, I always make a double batch so that I can make these croquettes, called *Suppl al telefono* in Rome because when you bite into them, the mozzarella stretches and resembles a telephone cord. If you want to use leftover rice or risotto for this recipe, start with Step 4.

NOTE: Sabina PDO comes from the Roman hills and is a blend of Carboncella, Leccino, Raja, Frantoio, Olivastrone, Olivago, Salviana and Rosciola olives. It combines perfectly with Roman dishes and lends a peppery flavor. Pair with Frascati wine, Prosecco, or beer.

Zucchini Fritters with Pesto Sauce

PREP TIME: 20 MIN	COOK TIME: 20 MIN, PLUS 1 HOUR STRAINING TIME	YIELD: 6 SERVINGS

INGREDIENTS

1 pound zucchini, grated

⅔ cup unbleached all-purpose flour

1 large egg yolk

1 tablespoon Emblem Olive Oil or your favorite extra-virgin olive oil, plus enough for frying

2 tablespoons unrefined sea salt, plus extra, if needed

Freshly ground black pepper

Pesto sauce (see Chapter 17)

DIRECTIONS

1 Put the grated zucchini in a colander over a bowl and sprinkle with salt and let stand for 1 hour.

2 In the meantime, combine the flour, egg yolk, and 1 tablespoon of olive oil in a large bowl and slowly stir in ½ cup water. If batter seems too thick, add a tablespoon more at a time. Mix well to incorporate and smooth out lumps by beating with a whisk. Season with the salt and pepper and let stand for 30 minutes.

3 After the zucchini has been in the colander for 1 hour, rinse thoroughly. Drain the zucchini and dry with paper towels. Combine with the batter and stir to coat well.

4 Heat ½ inch of olive oil to 365 degrees in a large wide frying pan over medium-high heat. Spoon in teaspoons of batter and fry approximately 2 minutes per side, or until golden.

5 Drain on paper towels and serve immediately on a large platter with the pesto sauce arranged in the center for dipping.

NOTE: I chose to fry this recipe in Emblem; their 100 percent American extra-virgin olive oil embodies quality and versatility, perfectly complementing African American culinary heritage. It's a mild and buttery oil, ideal for a wide range of dishes, especially when you don't want to add too much additional olive flavor, such as in baking or frying. Pair these with Vermentino or your favorite white wine.

VARY IT! Zucchini fritters come in different guises all over the Mediterranean. I've eaten them stuffed with feta in Greece, with dill in Turkey, and a very similar version, croquettes de courgettes, in Provence. Feel free to add your favorite herbs and swap out the pesto with tzatziki or your favorite dipping sauce as well. This recipe also works well with carrots.

Golden Potato, Pecorino, and Olive Croquettes

| PREP TIME: 15 MIN | COOK TIME: 30 MIN | YIELD: 4 SERVINGS |

INGREDIENTS

2 pounds Yukon Gold potatoes, peeled and cut into medium-sized chunks

1 teaspoon unrefined sea salt, divided

¼ teaspoon freshly ground black pepper

2 large eggs

Cobram Estate Robust Extra-Virgin Olive Oil or another good-quality extra-virgin olive oil, for frying

¼ cup pitted, chopped green olives

¼ cup all-purpose flour, for dredging

¼ cup Pecorino Romano cheese

2 cups plain dried breadcrumbs

DIRECTIONS

1 Place the potatoes in a large pot full of water. Add ¼ teaspoon of salt and bring to a boil over high heat. Reduce the heat to medium, stir, and cook for 15 minutes, until the potatoes are soft and can't be picked up with a fork. Drain in a colander and pass them through a food mill or potato ricer into a bowl. (You can also substitute leftover mashed potatoes for this step.)

2 Stir the remaining salt, pepper, 1 egg, and green olives into the potato mixture.

3 Flour a pastry board or clean work surface and your hands. Using a small ice-cream scoop, shape the croquettes into even-sized balls and place them on the board or clean work surface.

4 Whisk the remaining egg in a small shallow bowl with a few tablespoons of water. Place the remaining flour onto a plate. Place the cheese and breadcrumbs onto a plate and mix to combine. Dredge the potato balls into the flour to coat, then dip it into the egg to coat, and finally, turn them to coat in the cheese/breadcrumb mixture. Allow to chill in the refrigerator until frying. (This step can be done a day ahead of time.)

5 Heat about 1 inch of oil in a large, heavy skillet over medium-high heat. When the oil reaches 385 degrees, carefully add the croquettes into the skillet with a slotted spoon. Be careful not to overcrowd the skillet or the croquettes will be soggy. Fry them for approximately 2 minutes on each side, turning often, until evenly golden. Drain on paper towels and serve hot.

TIP: Potato croquettes can be eaten as an appetizer, snack, or as an accompaniment to roasted meat and chicken. While they are normally eaten plain, you can dip them in Fresh Tomato Sauce or Aioli, if desired (see Chapter 17 for the recipes).

NOTE: We chose Cobram Estate Robust from Australia, which is a blend of the Greek Koroneiki and Italian Coratina olive cultivars. The bold flavor, deep fruity aromas, and notes of freshly cut grass combined with its high phenolic content make it the perfect choice. Pair with Prosecco, beer, or Etna Bianco wine.

Sicilian Caponata

PREP TIME: 15 MIN	COOK TIME 35 MIN, PLUS 1 HOUR STRAINING TIME	YIELD: 8 SERVINGS

INGREDIENTS

3 small eggplants, trimmed and cut into ¼ inch cubes

2 tablespoons Ravida Extra-Virgin Olive Oil (house blend or organic) or another good-quality extra-virgin olive oil, plus enough for frying

2 tablespoons unrefined sea salt

1 celery stick, cubed

1 yellow onion, diced

¼ cup capers, rinsed well and drained

½ cup pitted green olives, chopped

½ cup Amy Riolo Selections White Balsamic or red wine vinegar

2 tablespoons sugar

½ cup tomato sauce (see Chapter 17)

¼ cup finely chopped fresh mint

¼ cup finely chopped fresh basil

¼ cup raisins, black, golden, or a mixture, if desired

Freshly ground black pepper

2 tablespoons toasted pine nuts, for garnish

DIRECTIONS

1 Place the eggplant cubes in a colander and cover with the sea salt. Allow to stand for 1 hour until the moisture comes out of the eggplant. Rinse them well to remove all the salt and pat well to dry.

2 Heat 2 inches of oil in a large, heavy skillet to 385 degrees. Using a slotted spoon, carefully lower in the eggplant and fry one-third of the cubes at a time until light golden, approximately 3 minutes per batch. Drain the eggplant on a baking sheet lined with paper towels.

3 Heat 2 tablespoons olive oil in a very large, wide, deep skillet over medium heat. Add the celery and onions and stir. Sauté until golden and soft, about 7 minutes, stirring occasionally. Add the capers, olives, vinegar, sugar, and reserved eggplant and stir to combine.

4 Add in the tomato sauce, mint, basil, raisins, and pepper, and allow to cook, stirring occasionally, until thickened, approximately 15 minutes. Allow to cool to room temperature, garnish with pine nuts, and serve.

TIP: Caponata is a summertime Sicilian staple that can be served as an appetizer, or as a salad, or alone with bread. There are variations of the dish all over the island of Sicily. I like to eat it cold and the day after it is made. Try it as an accompaniment for grilled meat or fish or tossed into pasta for a twist.

NOTE: I chose Ravida because it's a superior quality extra-virgin olive oil from Sicily. Their multi-award-winning field blend of Biancolilla, Cerasuola and Nocellara del Belice olives, which are native to the island, adds the perfect touch of authentication to this and many other Sicilian dishes. Pair caponata with Nero d'Avola wine.

Chapter **20**

First Courses

First courses (or *primi*) traditional Italian meals are often satisfying and substantial enough to enjoy on their own. The recipes in this chapter range from creamy soups and rich risotto to savory pastas. We also show you how to pair the dishes with the perfect extra-virgin olive oil and wine.

Everyone knows that pasta and extra-virgin olive oil are a match made in heaven. But if you've never tried making risotto (which is traditionally made with butter) and soups with extra-virgin olive oil, you're missing out on its great taste and nutrient quotient.

Over the years, Chef Amy has perfected these recipes, pairing them with the perfect oil that both complements and enhances their ingredients. However, the recipes are just the beginning of a world of delectable dishes that pair beautifully with extra-virgin olive oil to provide the most nutrients and flavor possible.

COOKING WITH POETRY

The aroma of olive oil sautéing in a pan takes Amy straight back to Italy. Images of meals with her family and the many olive-producer estates that she has visited come into her mind as do the words of this poem written by Gabriele D'Annunzio, a 20th century Italian Nobel Prize recipient. The verses of this poem are part of a poetry collection published in 1903 called *Alcyone,* which celebrates the symbolic end of the summer season. Light, sounds, and colors are used to illustrate the poet's experience in words.

L'olio

Olio con sapiente arte spremuto
Dal puro frutto degli annosi olivi,
Che cantan - pace! - in lor linguaggio muto
Degli umbri colli pei solenti clivi,
Chiaro assai più liquido cristallo,
Fragrante quale oriental unguento,
Puro come la fè che nel metallo
Concavo t'arde sull'altar d'argento,
Le tue rare virtù non furo ignote
Alle mense d'Orazio e di Varrone

English translation:

Oil with wise, squeezed art
From the pure fruit of the ancient olive trees,
That sings - peace! - in their silent language
Of the Umbrian hills for the solitary mountains,
Clear much more liquid crystal,
Fragrant as an oriental ointment,
Pure as the iron that in the metal
Concave to you on the silver altar,
Your rare virtues were not unknown
At the tables of Horace and Varrone

Cream of Cauliflower with Chile-Infused Olive Oil

PREP TIME: 15 MIN	COOK TIME: 30 MIN	YIELD: 8 FIRST-COURSE OR 4 MAIN SERVINGS

INGREDIENTS

1 head cauliflower, florets only

2–4 cups homemade vegetable stock (see Chapter 17)

¼ cup Morgenster Estate Extra-Virgin Olive Oil or other good-quality extra-virgin olive oil

1 teaspoon finely ground red chili powder, preferably Calabrian

2 tablespoons unsalted butter

2 tablespoons all-purpose flour

2 cups whole milk, heated to warm

½ teaspoon unrefined sea salt

Pinch of freshly ground black pepper

DIRECTIONS

1 Place the cauliflower in a large saucepan and pour in enough vegetable stock to barely cover. Bring to a boil over high heat. Reduce the heat to medium and boil, approximately 15 minutes, until the cauliflower is very tender.

2 Carefully transfer the cauliflower and stock to a blender. Place the lid on the blender and remove the fill cap (or pour spout). Cover the lid with a folded clean kitchen towel. Puree until creamy and set aside.

3 Pour the olive oil into a small bowl and stir in the chili powder. Set aside.

4 In another medium saucepan, melt the butter over medium heat. Add the flour and stir with a wooden spoon until well incorporated. Allow the mixture to become golden while stirring, approximately 4 minutes.

5 Add the milk and begin to whisk lightly, being sure to incorporate the bits on the bottom and sides of the pan as the sauce thickens. Cook uncovered, whisking lightly, until the béchamel sauce coats the back of a spoon. (If you place a spoon into the mixture and use your index finger to make a line down the middle and it doesn't run, the sauce is finished.) Season with the salt and pepper. Stir the cauliflower puree from Step 2 into the sauce. Taste and season with additional salt and pepper if needed.

(continued)

6 Serve equal amounts in 8 bowls, swirling equal amounts of chili-infused oil on each one.

TIP: This soup can be made in large batches and frozen. If you prefer your soup chunky, you can omit the pureeing step, strain the cooked cauliflower from the stock into a bowl, and add it directly to the béchamel sauce. Slowly whisk in the remaining stock into the béchamel/cauliflower mixture until you've reached the desired thickness.

NOTE: Morgenster Estate's award-winning extra-virgin olive oil is a premium South African blend of up to 14 Italian olive varieties. Vibrant and versatile, its well-balanced, fresh and fruity flavor has been perfected over decades. It offers or produces aromas of grass, artichokes and tomato leaves with notes of basil, mint and rosemary. It has a pleasant bitterness and spicy flavor that adds character to this soup, which combines well with the chili-infused oil. Pair with Pinot Grigio or an off-dry Riesling.

Carrot and Cardamom Risotto with Burrata and Pistachios

PREP TIME: 15 MIN | COOK TIME: 30 MIN | YIELD: 4 SERVINGS

INGREDIENTS

5 tablespoons Olivko Extra-Virgin Olive Oil or other good-quality extra-virgin olive oil, divided

1 medium onion, finely chopped

2 cups Tenuta Margherita or other good-quality Carnaroli rice

Juice and zest of 2 oranges

½ teaspoon ground cardamom

6–8 cups homemade vegetable or chicken stock (see Chapter 17), heated

6 carrots, peeled and sliced into rounds

1 teaspoon unrefined sea salt, divided

Freshly ground black pepper, to taste

¼ cup Parmigiano-Reggiano cheese

2 small burrata cheese balls, cut in half

4 teaspoons ground, unsalted pistachios

DIRECTIONS

1 Heat 3 tablespoons olive oil in a large saucepan over medium-high heat. Once hot, add the onion, and cook on low until soft, approximately 8 to 10 minutes. Stir in the rice and cook until coated with olive oil.

2 Heat the stock in a stockpot over high heat, turn down to low, and keep warm.

3 Add the orange juice, stir, and cook until it evaporates, around 3 to 5 minutes. Stir in the cardamom. Add a ladle full of stock and increase the heat to high. Cook until the stock has evaporated.

4 While the stock is absorbing, heat 1 tablespoon olive oil in a large wide skillet over medium-high heat. Sauté the carrots until golden, approximately 5 minutes. Add ¼ cup of water. Cook uncovered for 5 to 10 minutes, until the carrots are tender.

5 Continue adding stock, cooking, and stirring over medium heat until most of stock is used, and rice is al dente. Resist the urge to add more than a ladle full of stock at a time. It will be worth the wait.

6 Add the salt and pepper to taste.

(continued)

7 Puree the carrots in a blender and stir the Parmigiano-Reggiano into risotto. Transfer one-quarter of the risotto into 4 individual plates. Place one-half of a burrata ball, cut side up, in the middle of the risotto. Garnish with pistachios, orange zest, and a quarter tablespoon each of the remaining olive oil.

NOTE: Olivko produces an extra-virgin oil made from the chetoui cultivar indigenous and only found in Tunisia. Known for its bold and robust flavor profile and aromatic complexity, it offers aromas of green leaf tomatoes, fresh green, grass artichokes, and a blend of herbs that complement the carrots and citrus. Pair with a Gewürztraminer from Alsace because its slight sweetness and full-bodied structure can stand up to the richness of the burrata, while its exotic fruit flavors complement the orange juice.

Barley, Lentil, and Chickpea Soup

PREP TIME: 15 MIN | COOK TIME: 1 HOUR | YIELD: 8 SERVINGS

INGREDIENTS

2 tablespoons LIÁ Koroneiki Extra-Virgin Olive Oil or other good-quality extra-virgin olive oil

1 stalk celery, diced

1 carrot, diced

1 large yellow onion, diced

2 cloves garlic, finely diced

¼ cup dried porcini mushrooms, soaked in water for 20 minutes, drained, and rinsed

2 cups tomato sauce (see Chapter 17), boxed chopped tomatoes, or canned reduced-sodium diced tomatoes

2 cups chopped savoy cabbage

¼ cup brown lentils, rinsed and sorted (see Tip)

½ teaspoon unrefined sea salt

¼ teaspoon freshly ground black pepper

1 cup cooked barley

1 cup cooked chickpeas

4 cups homemade vegetable or chicken stock (see Chapter 17), reduced-sodium stock, or water

½ teaspoon crushed red pepper

DIRECTIONS

1 Place the olive oil in a large, heavy stockpot or Dutch oven over medium heat. Add the celery, carrot, onion, and garlic. Sauté until golden, approximately 5 minutes.

2 Stir in the mushrooms, and sauté for another 2 to 3 minutes. Add the tomato sauce, cabbage, lentils, salt, and pepper. Stir and simmer for 5 minutes.

3 Add the barley and chickpeas to the vegetable mixture along with stock and the crushed red pepper. Bring to a boil over high heat; reduce the heat to medium–low and simmer, covered, for 40 minutes, or until the barley and beans are tender. Serve hot.

TIP: Sort lentils by placing them in a bowl of water with cold water, make sure that no unwanted debris or stones float to the top, and rinse them until the water runs clear. This soup gets better as it sits, which is perfect for a make-ahead dish. You can also freeze it in individual containers to reheat later. Serve larger portions with salad for a healthful and satisfying meal.

NOTE: These types of Mediterranean soups have been nourishing people since antiquity, and their appeal is every bit as satisfying now as it was then. LIÁ is an exemplary representation of 100 percent Koroneiki extra-virgin olive oil from a single estate in Greece. It boasts a medium fruity flavor that masterfully balances between the bitterness of arugula, radish, artichoke, and Mediterranean hartwort. It has aromas of Greek herbs, freshly mown grass, hartwort, green banana, apples, and flowers that enrich this soup. Pair with a Greek Malagouzia or another intense and highly expressive white wine.

Linguine with Olive Tapenade and Pecorino

PREP TIME: 5 MIN   COOK TIME: 10 MIN   YIELD: 4 SERVINGS

INGREDIENTS

½ teaspoon unrefined sea salt

1 pound linguine

½ cup black olives such as Gaeta or Kalamata, pitted

Juice and zest of 1 lemon

¼ teaspoon freshly ground black pepper

¼ cup The Governor Extra-Virgin Olive Oil or other good-quality extra-virgin olive oil

½ cup freshly grated pecorino cheese (Romano, Sardo, Toscano, or Crotonese)

½ cup finely chopped Italian parsley

DIRECTIONS

1 Bring a large pot that is three-fourths full of water to a boil over high heat. Add the salt and pasta, using tongs to twist the pasta to submerge in the water. Reduce the heat to medium-low and continue to cook according to package directions, stirring often, until pasta is al dente.

2 While the pasta is cooking, place the olives, lemon juice, pepper, and olive oil in food processor and mix to combine and form a paste.

3 When pasta is cooked, drain it and reserve ¼ cup of the hot water. Return the linguine to the pan and scoop in the tapenade. Stir in the reserved pasta water. Use tongs to coat the pasta well. Plate on 4 individual plates or a large bowl. Garnish with cheese and parsley, and serve hot.

TIP: Tapenade is an olive paste that originally hails from Roman times. You can serve this tapenade on its own with crudités or on bread or bruschetta as a separate appetizer. It also tastes great slathered over grilled chicken and fish.

NOTE: The Governor is a well-balanced, single variety, robust, intensely bold extra-virgin olive oil produced from the centenarian Lianoli variety of olive from the island of Corfu. It's a robust olive oil with aromas of fruity green olive, freshly cut grass, green bell peppers, almond, and walnuts. A velvety mouthfeel and a long intense peppery finish complement the olive tapenade. Pair with a Grillo from Sicily, an Assyrtiko from Santorini, or another wine with crisp acidity and citrus flavors.

VARY IT! Use other varieties of olives or sun-dried red tomatoes in the tapenade. You can also use the tapenade to coat other varieties of pasta such as penne, farfalle, and fettuccine.

Busiate Pasta with Sicilian Pesto

PREP TIME: 15 MIN	COOK TIME: 12–15 MIN	YIELD: 6 SERVINGS

INGREDIENTS

1 teaspoon unrefined sea salt, divided

1 pound dried busiati pasta

1¼ pounds ripe heirloom cherry or grape tomatoes

⅓ cup blanched almonds, ground

1 cup packed fresh basil leaves, chopped

¼ cup fresh flat-leaf parsley leaves, chopped

2 cloves garlic, minced

¾ cup grated pecorino cheese, plus more for garnish

¼ cup Sicilian Nocellara del Belice or Biancolilla Extra-Virgin Olive Oil or other good-quality extra-virgin olive oil

1 teaspoon finely grated fresh lemon zest

Freshly ground pepper, to taste

DIRECTIONS

1 Bring a large pasta pot of water to a boil over high heat. When the water is boiling, add ½ teaspoon salt and cook the pasta according to package directions, or until al dente.

2 While the pasta is cooking, set a pot of water on high heat and bring to a boil. Add the tomatoes, reduce heat to medium, and cook for 2 to 3 minutes, until the skin begins to split. Using a slotted spoon, remove the tomatoes from the hot water and place in cold water. When the tomatoes are cool enough to handle, remove the skins and seeds. Place the skinless tomatoes in a food processor.

3 Add the almonds, basil, parsley, and garlic to the food processor. Pulse until a smooth paste forms. Stir in the cheese, olive oil, and lemon zest. Season with the salt and pepper to taste. Set the pesto aside.

4 Drain the pasta, reserving one-third cup pasta water. Toss the pasta with the pesto, adding reserved pasta water, if needed, and garnish with the cheese. Serve hot.

TIP: Sicilian pesto, also known as pesto alla Trapanese, hails from the seaside town of Trapani known for its salt production and fishing communities. It features delicious Sicilian specialties, such as tomatoes, almonds, and pecorino (sheep's milk) cheese. Busiate are a traditional, artisan made chain-shaped pasta made in Sicily that holds its shape and delicious sauces well.

NOTE: I specifically choose Sicilian olive oil when making this dish. The Biancolilla variety combines the aroma of orange blossoms with a light, fruity flavor, and a soft, spicy finish. Nocellara del Belice olives hail from an area southwest of the Sicily region and are known for their extremely low acidity which is a characteristic of high quality.

Chapter **21**

Second Courses

While extra-virgin olive oil can do a lot to elevate both the taste and health benefits of main dishes, many people have difficulty choosing which olive oils to use when making entrees. There is a misconception that you don't need to use a "good" olive oil for dishes with stronger flavors, because it won't get noticed.

In this chapter, recipes pair beautifully with different types of extra-virgin olive oils (EVOO), and we show you cooking styles that benefit from using it. Whether you're grilling, poaching, roasting, sautéing, or pan-frying, a properly paired extra-virgin olive oil will make all of the difference in terms of flavor, texture, and nutrition.

We took special care to match each of these recipes with extra-virgin olive oils that we have tasted. For the last decade, the trend in Italy has been to pair different olive oils with each course of elegant meals. This is a practice that we both enjoy because it gives olive oil the important role that it deserves while highlighting various notes and flavors of different oils.

That said, our pairing suggestions are just that — suggestions. Each of the recipes are versatile enough to taste great with the extra-virgin olive oil that you prefer to use.

Pairing dishes together in a meal is a fine balancing act that is sometimes difficult for home cooks to achieve. If you have a heavy, hearty main course, for example, you may want a rich dessert but not necessarily one that's made with a lot of flour. If your main course consists of seafood, a milk-based dessert may clash with it.

Greek-Island Style White Bean and Feta Puree with Olive Oil–Sautéed Dandelion Greens

PREP TIME: 15 MIN	COOK TIME: 5 MIN	YIELD: 4 SERVINGS

INGREDIENTS

For the Puree:

1½ cups (15 ounces) cooked cannellini beans, drained and rinsed if using canned

1 cup Greek feta, cut into small pieces or crumbled

Juice and zest of 1 lemon

¼ cup Darmmess Extra-Virgin Olive Oil, or other good-quality extra-virgin olive oil

¼ cup fresh mint, plus extra for garnish

½ teaspoon unrefined sea salt (optional)

¼ teaspoon freshly ground pepper (optional)

For the Greens:

2 tablespoons Darmmess Extra-Virgin Olive Oil, or other good-quality extra-virgin olive oil

DIRECTIONS

1 To make the puree: Combine cannellini beans, feta, lemon juice and zest, olive oil, and mint in a food processor. Puree, pulsing on and off, until smooth. Taste and season with salt and pepper, if desired. Set aside.

2 To make the greens: Heat the olive oil in a very large skillet over high heat, until the oil is very hot. Add the dandelion greens (working in batches, if needed) and cook, stirring, for about 1 to 2 minutes; the dandelion should turn bright green and wilt slightly.

3 Add the garlic and crushed red pepper and continue to cook, stirring constantly, until the garlic begins to release its aroma, approximately 30 seconds. Remove the greens from the heat, and season with the salt and pepper. Toss well to combine.

4 Spoon the puree onto a large serving platter and use a spatula to spread it around the bottom. Place the greens in the middle and serve with the lemon wedges.

TIP: This dish is a nutritional powerhouse and great example of hearty Mediterranean cuisine. If making in advance, store the puree and greens separately. Reheat the greens before serving.

(continued)

2¼ pounds dandelion greens, chicory, spinach, or kale, trimmed at stems; well-washed, dried, and roughly chopped

3 cloves garlic, minced

Pinch of crushed red pepper

⅛ teaspoon unrefined sea salt

¼ teaspoon freshly ground black pepper

1 medium lemon, quartered

Sweet Olive Oil and Red Wine Taralli Cookies, for dessert (optional; see Chapter 22)

NOTE: I chose Darmmess Extra-Virgin Olive Oil because it's an award-winning monocultivar using the souri olives from Lebanon, creating a complex yet harmonious taste reminiscent of unripe early harvested green olives with bitter spicy notes and a fruit aroma. The olive oil has hints of green tomato, cut grass, banana, and tropical fruits. Pair with an intense red wine such as Primitivo di Manduria.

Milanese-Style Veal Scallopine with Creamy Polenta and Brussels Sprouts

PREP TIME: 15 MIN | COOK TIME: 30 MIN | YIELD: 4 SERVINGS

INGREDIENTS

⅓ cup EYZA Extra-Virgin Olive Oil or other good-quality extra-virgin olive oil, divided

2 cups trimmed Brussels sprouts, halved

⅓ cup Parmigiano-Reggiano cheese, divided

1 cup polenta

½ cup unbleached, all-purpose flour

¼ teaspoon unrefined sea salt, divided

⅓ teaspoon freshly ground black pepper, divided

1 pound (4 pieces between .25 and .30 pound each) veal scaloppini

1 medium lemon, quartered

EVOO and Chili-Infused Chocolate Brownies, for dessert (optional; see Chapter 22)

DIRECTIONS

1 Heat the oven to 425 degrees. Grease a baking sheet and top with 1 tablespoon of olive oil. Drizzle another tablespoon of olive oil over the Brussels sprouts and sprinkle with 2 table-spoons of cheese. Toss to coat and roast for 20 minutes, until tender and golden.

2 While the Brussels sprouts are roasting, cook the polenta by placing 3 cups of water in a large pot over high heat and bring to a boil. Slowly whisk in the polenta. Add 1 more cup of water and turn down to low heat to simmer for approximately 10 to 15 minutes, stirring fre-quently. (If you're use instant polenta, it should be cooked according to package directions). If your polenta is very thick, whisk in an addi-tional ½ cup of water. The polenta should be creamy and have the consistency of grits. Stir in 2 teaspoons of olive oil, 2 tablespoons of cheese, and ⅛ teaspoon of salt and pepper, to taste.

3 Place the flour on a large plate and add 2 table-spoons of cheese, stirring to combine. Dip the veal pieces into the flour mixture, turn over to coat, shake off the excess, and place on a platter.

4 Heat 2 tablespoons of olive oil in a large, wide non-stick skillet. Add the veal to skillet, season with ⅛ teaspoon of salt and ⅛ teaspoon

(continued)

pepper, and cook for 2 to 3 minutes per side, turning only once, until meat is cooked through.

5 Serve the veal on a plate with one-fourth of the cooked polenta and Brussels sprouts. Garnish with 1 lemon quarter on each plate.

NOTE: I chose EYZA Extra Virgin Olive Oil for this recipe because it's made with Turkish Memecik olives, which offer the flavor and aroma of greens, lemon, grass, and almonds. This high-quality and delicious olive oil is produced from early harvested olives and cold pressed at under 75 degrees within a few hours using ancient oil pressing techniques. Pair with Pinot Noir.

VARY IT! Chicken, beef, and fish fillets work equally well in this elegant, yet easy recipe.

Seafood Kabobs with Salsa Verde and Grilled Summer Vegetables

PREP TIME: 15 MIN | COOK TIME: 10 MIN | YIELD: 4 SERVINGS

INGREDIENTS

1¼ pounds skinless swordfish, cut into 1-inch cubes

24 grape tomatoes

2 medium zucchini, trimmed, and sliced into ½-inch circles

Salsa Verde (see the following recipe)

Juice and zest 1 lemon, for garnish

Ricotta, Limoncello, Almond, and Olive Oil Cake, dessert (optional; see Chapter 22)

DIRECTIONS

1 Heat a grill or grill pan to high. Thread the fish onto 8 skewers, alternating with the tomatoes and zucchini.

2 Brush the kabobs with half of the Salsa Verde. Grill until the fish is opaque, 6 to 10 minutes, turning occasionally.

3 With a clean brush, coat the cooked kabobs with the reserved Salsa Verde. Garnish with lemon juice and zest. Serve immediately.

TIP: You can prepare the Salsa Verde in advance to make this easy dish come together even more quickly, or prepare it in large batches, reserving some for later use.

NOTE: This dish reminds me of the fish dishes in the coastal towns of Morocco, so I chose the Moroccan Gold Extra-Virgin Olive Oil because it's made with superior quality Picholine Marocaine olives, selected early in the season, handpicked by a co-op of female harvesters, and cold pressed within 24 hours of picking in Morocco. It's high in polyphenols and lends green fruitiness, hints of sweet almonds and herbs that complement the fish. It has the distinctive pepperiness of a fine extra-virgin olive oil, giving Morocco Gold a clean, well-balanced finish. Pair with Greco di Tufo wine or Moroccan Mint Lemonade.

VARY IT! Chicken cubes and shrimp can also be used instead of the fish.

(continued)

Salsa Verde

½ cup lightly packed fresh Italian parsley

¼ cup capers, drained and rinsed well

4 tablespoons Moroccan Gold Extra-Virgin Olive Oil, or other good-quality extra-virgin olive oil

1 clove garlic

¼ teaspoon unrefined sea salt

¼ teaspoon freshly ground black pepper

Crushed red pepper, to taste

Place the parsley, capers, olive oil, and garlic in a blender, and puree until smooth. Season with the salt, pepper, and crushed red pepper. Reserve half the salsa in a separate container.

Fresh Fish Poached in Olive Oil with Sun-dried Red Pesto and Broccolini

PREP TIME: 15 MIN | COOK TIME: 40 MIN | YIELD: 4 SERVINGS

INGREDIENTS

1 large lemon, sliced into thin rounds, divided

4 (6 ounce) skinless cod or halibut fillets

¾ teaspoon unrefined sea salt, divided

½ teaspoon freshly ground black pepper, plus ⅛ teaspoon, divided

1 pound grape or cherry tomatoes

2 cups Maida Arbequina Extra-Virgin Olive Oil, or other good-quality extra-virgin olive oil, plus 2 tablespoons, divided

5 sprigs fresh rosemary

1 bay leaf

5 black peppercorns

3 cloves garlic

1 pound fresh broccolini or broccoli rabe, trimmed

DIRECTIONS

1 Preheat the oven to 250 degrees. Lay half the lemon slices in a 9-x-13-inch baking dish. Pat the fish dry, sprinkle with ½ teaspoon of salt and ½ teaspoon pepper and place on top of the lemon slices. Top with the tomatoes and remaining lemon slices.

2 Pour 2 cups of olive oil over top. Add rosemary, bay leaf, peppercorns, and garlic, pushing down to submerge in the oil. Bake until the fish is cooked through and flakes easily, approximately 30 to 40 minutes.

3 While fish is baking, heat the remaining 2 tablespoons of olive oil in a large, wide skillet over medium heat. Add the broccolini and season with the remaining ¼ teaspoon of salt and ⅛ teaspoon of pepper. Turn to coat and sauté for 5 to 10 minutes, until it's tender but still slightly crunchy. Reserve the olive oil in the skillet.

4 To serve, use a spatula to lift each fish fillet out of the oil. Place on 4 plates with an equal serving of the broccolini. Slather 1 tablespoon sun-dried red pesto over each fish fillet and drizzle a few tablespoons of the leftover oil from poaching over the broccolini.

(continued)

¼ cup Amy Riolo Selections Sun-dried Red Pesto, or your favorite brand of red pesto

Olive Oil–Poached Pears with Dark Chocolate Mousse and Sea Salt, for dessert (optional; see Chapter 22)

TIP: The combination of fish, greens, and good-quality extra-virgin olive oil make this dish a nutritional power-house. Poaching in extra-virgin olive oil gives it a much more tender consistency than cooking over a gas stovetop or grill.

NOTE: I chose Al Maida Extra-Virgin Olive Oil for this recipe because it comes from a single-family estate and private mill with a sustainable and zero-waste farm. Their unique Arbequina olive oil is grown in the Jordanian desert and has both herbaceous and floral notes with a hint of spice that complement this delicate recipe. Pair with an Albariño from Spain or a dry rosé.

Herb Roasted Chicken with Chestnuts, Shallots, and Fennel

PREP TIME: 15 MIN	COOK TIME: 1 HOUR 30 MIN	YIELD: 6 SERVINGS

INGREDIENTS

1 whole (3½ pound) chicken, giblets removed

¼ cup Šoltansko Organic Extra-Virgin Olive Oil or other good-quality extra-virgin olive oil, divided

1 teaspoon unrefined sea salt

Freshly ground black pepper

1 tablespoon Herbes de Provence

1 head garlic, stem sliced off, left intact

2 lemons, divided, 1 sliced in half, 1 zested and juiced

4 shallots, peeled and quartered

2 cups roasted chestnuts

2 bulbs fennel, trimmed, cored, and sliced into quarters

Olive Oil Gelato with Homemade Chocolate Taggiasca Sauce, for dessert (optional; Chapter 22)

DIRECTIONS

1 Preheat the oven to 425 degrees. Place the chicken breast up in a roasting pan and drizzle the olive oil over the chicken, turning to make sure that both the pan and chicken are coated.

2 Season with the salt, a sprinkle of pepper, and the Herbes de Provence by rubbing them into the top and sides of the chicken. Place the garlic and half of 1 lemon inside the chicken cavity and squeeze the juice from the remaining half lemon over the chicken.

3 Bake, uncovered, for 45 minutes. Carefully (oil tends to splatter), remove the chicken from the oven and scatter the shallots, chestnuts, and fennel around the edges of the pan. Toss to coat in the olive oil and season with lemon zest and additional lemon juice. Turn well to coat.

4 Return the chicken to the oven to bake for another 45 minutes, or until the chicken is done and green beans are tender. (Chicken is done when clear juices run from the thickest part of the thigh after being pierced with a fork and the internal temperature is 165 degrees.)

(continued)

5 Cover the chicken and let it rest for 10 minutes before carving. Discard the garlic and lemon from chicken cavity before serving.

TIP: This recipe is traditionally eaten in fall when chestnuts are plentiful. In the United States, they can usually be found peeled and vacuum-packed in jars or packages during the late fall in winter, or you can special order them online.

NOTE: I chose Šoltansko Organic, which is the "Most Awarded Dalmatian Olive Oil" from the super-variety Šoltanka in Croatia. It has a fruity aroma of green apple, fresh grass, and green olive fruit, which complement the chicken and the fennel. Pair with Spanish Rioja.

Chapter **22**

Desserts

Many people believe that it's hard to bake with olive oil. Years of advertising for "neutral" oils in baking have conditioned the world to believe that "an olive flavor" would ruin your desserts. In fact, just the opposite is true.

As we've outlined in previous chapters and explained in detail in Chapter 11, extra-virgin olive oil can and should be paired with sweets. The secret to success with olive oil–infused dessert recipes is to recognize the flavor profiles of the olive oil and use them to elevate the recipes themselves. In addition to being a healthful butter "swap out," olive oil provides smooth, glossy finishes and aromas ranging from fruity to almondy and peppery. When you pair them properly, they will take the finale of any meal to new heights.

The recipes in this chapter not only have extra-virgin olive oil (EVOO) as an ingredient but are actually enhanced by it. Chef Amy purposely chose these dessert recipes because they aren't very complicated and can be used for a wide range of occasions throughout the year. We encourage you to experiment with extra-virgin olive oil in your favorite dessert recipes.

Sweet Olive Oil and Red Wine Taralli Cookies

PREP TIME: 20 MIN	COOK TIME: 30 MIN	YIELD: 48 COOKIES

INGREDIENTS

¾ cup red wine

¾ cup Peranzana Extra-Virgin Olive Oil (Puglian) or other good-quality extra-virgin olive oil

3¾ cups unbleached all-purpose flour

1¼ cups granulated sugar, divided

1 teaspoon baking powder

1 teaspoon ground cinnamon

Pinch of unrefined sea salt

DIRECTIONS

1 Preheat the oven to 350 degrees. Line 2 large baking sheets with parchment paper.

2 In a large bowl, combine the wine and olive oil and stir to combine. Stir in the flour, 3/4 cup of sugar, baking powder, cinnamon, and salt. Mix well to combine the ingredients. Continue mixing until the dough forms a ball.

3 Pinch off small pieces of the dough to form 48 (1-inch) balls. On a clean surface, roll each ball into a 3-inch cylinder. Bring the 2 ends together and pinch in the center to form a circle.

4 Place the remaining ½ cup of sugar on a plate, and dip the cookies in sugar to coat.

5 Place the cookies ¼-inch apart on the lined baking sheet. Bake for 15 to 20 minutes, or until the cookies are hard and bottoms just begin to turn golden. Remove the cookies from the oven and allow to cool.

TIP: I always save leftover red wine and my private label extra-virgin olive oil to make this recipe. They're perfect for dunking into caffè latte or cappuccino for breakfast and also make a great treat or light dessert anytime.

NOTE: *Taralli dolci* and all types of taralli are a Puglian specialty, but they are made all over Southern Italy. For this reason, I featured a Puglian extra-virgin olive oil. To date, Puglia is the largest olive oil–producing region in Italy, but few people know about it outside of the region because their olives often get blended and sold under labels from other regions. You don't have to look far to discover olive orchards if you ever travel to the beautiful area because they enhance most of its landscape, surrounding visitors with their beauty and age-old grace. Peranzana single varietal oil is low in acidity and high in polypenols with a balanced flavor of delicate fruit and a spicy finish, that enhance the simplicity of this recipe. If you'd like to pair this dessert with wine, look for *a Puglian passito* or similar.

Olive Oil–Poached Pears with Dark Chocolate Mousse and Sea Salt

PREP TIME: 15 MIN PLUS OVERNIGHT CHILLING	COOK TIME: 22 MIN	YIELD: 4 SERVINGS

INGREDIENTS

Chocolate Mousse (see the following recipe)

5 cups Peruvian Hojiblanca or your favorite extra-virgin olive oil

1 cup honey

2 cinnamon sticks

1 tablespoon vanilla bean paste, or 1 vanilla bean, scraped

Half of lemon

4 medium pears, firm yet ripe, stem on and peeled

2 tablespoons granulated sugar

Whipped cream, for garnish

DIRECTIONS

1 Combine the olive oil and honey in a medium pot (roughly 3-quart capacity). Place the pot over medium heat and bring to a simmer, stirring occasionally, until the honey has completely dissolved. Add the cinnamon sticks and vanilla bean paste.

2 Gently rub each pear with the lemon half to prevent the pears from oxidizing. Using a large spoon, lower the pears into the poaching liquid. The poaching liquid should almost completely cover the pears. Return the poaching liquid to a low simmer, cover the surface of the pot with a parchment round, and simmer the pears for about 12 to 15 minutes, or until tender; occasionally flip the pears during the cooking process.

3 Cool the pears to room temperature in the poaching liquid. If not serving immediately, transfer the pears to a large container and refrigerate for up to a week.

4 To serve the dish, place 1 pear on each plate, cut it in half down the middle, remove the seeds. Using a medium-sized ice cream scoop, place 1 scoop of Chocolate Mousse in the middle of the pears. Drizzle with the cooking liquid and garnish with whipped cream.

NOTE: Pears are normally poached in wine or tea, but poaching them in extra-virgin olive oil gives a richness to the recipe that makes it even more decadent. I used Peruvian Hojiblanca Extra-Virgin Olive Oil for this recipe, but you can use your preferred types as well. Hojiblanca's creamy mouthful and sweet taste in the beginning is followed up with notes of almond and fruit that complement the pears. Pair with a Moscato d'Asti wine. Save the excess poaching liquid to drizzle over cakes or ice cream.

Chocolate Mousse

8 ounces good-quality dark chocolate

3 large eggs

1 tablespoon orange liqueur or vanilla or chocolate (optional)

1 cup whipping cream, whipped until stiff

1 Preheat the oven to 200 degrees. Put the chocolate pieces in a small ovenproof bowl or glass pan and place in the oven for a few minutes until chocolate has melted, approximately 8 to 10 minutes. Remove and allow to cool.

2 Beat the eggs until foamy. Whisk the eggs slowly into cooled chocolate until incorporated. Stir in the liqueur, if using. Fold in the whipped cream. Spoon the mousse into a large bowl. Allow to chill overnight.

Ricotta, Limoncello, Almond, and Olive Oil Cake

PREP TIME: 10 MIN	COOK TIME: 45 MIN	YIELD: 9 SERVINGS

INGREDIENTS

½ cup plus 1 teaspoon LEYA Ismailia Extra-Virgin Olive Oil or other good-quality extra-virgin olive oil, divided

½ cup sliced blanched almonds

2 large eggs, separated

⅓ cup limoncello or orange juice (optional)

2 teaspoons grated lemon zest or orange zest (optional)

1 cup granulated sugar

2 teaspoons pure vanilla extract

1 teaspoon pure almond extract

2⅓ cups almond flour

1 teaspoon baking powder

½ teaspoon unrefined sea salt

½ cup whole milk ricotta

2 tablespoons confectioners' sugar, to serve

DIRECTIONS

1 Preheat the oven to 350 degrees. Grease (with 1 teaspoon olive oil) and flour a 9-inch spring-form pan. Line with parchment paper. Brush the parchment paper with olive oil and sprinkle with sliced almonds.

2 In the bowl of a standing mixer or in a large metal bowl using a hand mixer, beat the egg whites until stiff peaks form. Set aside.

3 In a separate bowl, combine the limoncello, lemon zest, remaining olive oil, egg yolks, sugar, vanilla extract, and almond extract.

4 In a large bowl, sift together the flour, baking powder, salt, and almond flour. Stir in the limoncello mixture, and fold in the ricotta. Fold in the egg whites. Pour the batter into the prepared pan, and smooth out the top with a spatula.

5 Bake 40 to 45 minutes, until a toothpick inserted into the middle comes out clean and the cake begins to pull away from the sides of the pan. Cool completely.

6 Invert the cake onto a platter and release the sides of the pan. Remove the parchment paper, sprinkle with confectioners' sugar, and serve.

NOTE: LEYA Extra-Virgin Olive Oil is pressed from olives harvested from the fertile soil of Ismailia alongside Egypt's Mediterranean coast, where olive oil has been produced for 8,000 years. The olive oil derived from the koroneiki olives is full-bodied, aromatic, and intensely flavored. If you substitute another olive oil, make sure you like the taste before adding it to the recipe. If you'd like to pair this dessert with wine, look for *Greco di Bianco passito* or similar.

EVOO and Chili-Infused Chocolate Brownies

PREP TIME: 10 MIN   COOK TIME: 35 MIN   YIELD: 16 BROWNIES

INGREDIENTS

½ cup Olearia San Giorgio's Altanum Extra-Virgin Olive Oil or any good-quality extra-virgin olive oil

½ cup red wine

2 teaspoons pure vanilla extract

¾ cup granulated sugar

½ cup brown sugar, packed

3 large eggs

½ cup Fair Trade cocoa powder, sifted

¼ teaspoon ground red pepper (optional)

1 cup unbleached all-purpose flour

½ cup Fair Trade chocolate chips

Raspberries and confectioners' sugar, for serving

DIRECTIONS

1 Preheat the oven to 350 degrees. Line an 8-inch square pan with parchment paper.

2 In a large mixing bowl, add the olive oil, wine, vanilla extract, and sugars and mix briefly.

3 Add the eggs to sugar mixture, along with cocoa powder, ground red pepper (if desired), flour, and chocolate chips. Gently mix with a spoon or spatula to combine. Pour into the prepared pan.

4 Bake for 25 minutes, until a knife inserted in the middle comes out clean. Leave to cool slightly before removing from the pan.

5 Lift the paper out of pan and place the brownies on a cutting board. With a sharp knife cut into 16 squares.

6 Garnish with raspberries and confectioners' sugar and serve.

TIP: My ancestral homeland of Calabria is famous for its pepperoncino. This is a recipe that I created for the annual Peperoncino Festival in Diamante, Calabria in 2023. I wanted to combine the flavors of Calabria (ground red peppers, Gaglioppo wine, and Carolea olive oil) with an American recipe to highlight my heritage. It was a success there, and I get rave reviews when serving it in America too.

NOTE: Olearia San Giorgio produces many high-quality Calabrian extra-virgin olive oils. Altanum is the name of an ancient Calabrian city, which was inhabited by indigenous Italic tribes who gave their name to the nation of Italy. The IGP oil is made with millenia-old traditions and has a very complex yet harmonious flavor that marries well with the chocolate, wine, and hot pepper in this recipe.

VARY IT! If you want to omit the wine, you can add cold, brewed coffee in its place.

Olive Oil Gelato with Homemade Chocolate Taggiasca Sauce

PREP TIME: 15 MIN, PLUS CHURN TIME	COOK TIME: 10 MIN	YIELD: 8 SERVINGS (MAKES 3½ QUARTS)

INGREDIENTS

3½ cups whole milk

1 cup heavy cream

1 cup granulated sugar, divided

10 large egg yolks

1 teaspoon unrefined sea salt

1½ teaspoons pure vanilla extract (optional)

¼ cup Taggiasca or other good-quality extra-virgin olive oil, plus extra for drizzling

Ravida Sea Salt or other flaky sea salt

Chocolate Taggiasca Sauce (see the following recipe)

DIRECTIONS

1 Combine the milk and cream in a large heavy bottom saucepan and bring just to a simmer over medium heat. Remove from the heat. Add ¾ cup of the sugar to the milk and bring just to a simmer over medium heat, stirring to dissolve the sugar.

2 Meanwhile, whisk the egg yolks, the remaining ¼ cup sugar, and the salt together in a medium heatproof bowl. Gradually whisk in about 1 cup of the hot milk mixture, then return the mixture to the saucepan and cook, stirring constantly with a heatproof spatula or a wooden spoon, until the custard registers 185 degrees on an instant-read thermometer.

3 Immediately strain the custard through a fine-mesh strainer into a heatproof bowl. Stir in the vanilla extract, if using, and chill over an ice bath, stirring occasionally, until cold. Cover and refrigerate for at least 6 hours, preferably, overnight.

4 Freeze the gelato in an ice cream maker according to the manufacturer's instructions, stopping to add the olive oil about halfway through the freezing process. Pack into a freezer container and freeze for at least 1 hour before serving. (*The gelato is best served the day it is made.*) Sprinkle a few flakes of sea salt and drizzle with EVOO.

5 Serve the Chocolate Taggiasca Sauce hot over the gelato.

Chocolate Taggiasca Sauce

1 (14 ounce) can sweetened condensed milk

1 cup dark chocolate chips

2 tablespoons Taggiasca, or other good-quality extra-virgin olive oil

1 teaspoon pure vanilla extract

Place the sweetened condensed milk and chocolate chips in a saucepan over medium heat. Stir constantly until the chocolate chips are melted. Remove from the heat and stir in the olive oil and vanilla until the sauce is glossy.

7

Diving Deeper and the Future for Olive Oil

IN THIS PART . . .

Find out how to enroll in tasting and sommelier courses and understand how oleo tourism works.

Navigate the future of olive oil.

Chapter **23**

Enrolling in Tasting/Sommelier Classes and Oleo Tourism

I n this chapter, we present you with various opportunities to dive deeper into the world of extra-virgin olive oil (EVOO) aromas and flavors. Decide for yourself how far you want to go on the journey to discover the different ways to enjoy the subtle and nuanced taste profiles of extra-virgin olive oils from around the world.

You can start by attending a course on olive oil tasting, or maybe you prefer to host a tasting dinner at your home. Ultimately, you may want to experience the freshest oils with visits to the lands where olive oil is produced, meeting the farmers and millers and touching the ancient trees revered and nurtured by so many generations of local people.

But first, try to imagine the amount of work that goes into promoting and sustaining an olive oil producing business year-round. Although the months around harvest time are the most hectic, farmers may have to split their time between traveling the world to promote their products in trade shows and running the day-to-day operations. They may even have another way for consumers to experience their olive oil — through oleo tourism.

Oleo tourism combines a visit to an olive-growing region with in-depth information about local olive oil production, which is quite a new travel concept. It's an option specifically geared toward tourists who are looking for a more meaningful and memorable experience, immersing themselves in local culture and cuisine. Many travelers are choosing to visit olive oil producing countries specifically to tour the groves and sample different varieties of olive oils. Some travelers even choose to base their tours around the olive harvest in order to participate in the millennia old ritual. This chapter provides many options for exploring olive oil from around the world. Welcome to the journey!

Tasting at a Whole New Level

For most people, the first step in finding more information about extra-virgin olive oil is to understand the flavors of olive oil. A beautiful olive oil that is fruity, bitter, and pungent can be deliciously paired and harmonize on the palate in combination with foods. It must be a fresh experience, and most certainly it has to be free of defects such as a rancid, vinegary, or musty sensation in aroma or taste.

The details of aromas and flavors are explored in Chapters 9 and 10, and explanations on how to recognize defects in olive oil are in Chapter 2. Because flavors that indicate poor quality or degraded oil are important to distinguish, you'll need the skills to know how to find the oils that make the extra-virgin grade and those that fall short.

Sampling olive oil in an informal setting

It's great fun to experience the flavors of extra-virgin olive oil informally with guests for lunch or dinner, reading about their provenance and the regions of origin while comparing everyone's impressions of the oil flavors. If you are in the company of friends, you'll discover new things about the oils. And if you've invited guests who are less familiar to you, olive oil tasting will serve as a great ice breaker.

TIP

Experimenting tastings at home allows for a more comfortable and relaxed setting. It's good to choose perhaps three extra-virgin olive oils from diverse regions and with distinctive tasting notes. You can make your selections by looking at producers' websites before you go to a local olive oil shop or ask for advice during your visit to the store. Refer to Chapter 9 about the best ways to taste the oils before you sit down for lunch or dinner with your guests. After everyone has decided on their preferences, you can use the oils with different foods on the table.

In a more structured setting, you can take the experience of extra-virgin olive oil tasting to another level by signing up for a course on olive oil tasting. There are various tutored tastings available including one-day introductory seminars. You may regard this as a tasting taster!

More formal courses may last up to a week at a time and aim to not only provide a sommelier experience and qualification, but also a broader insight into the health and production of olive oil.

Approaching EVOO like a pro: sommelier training

Professional extra-virgin olive oil tasters are called *sommeliers*, just as they are in the world of wine. There are some amazing people who have trained to become professional sommeliers, working for organizations that regulate standards in extra-virgin olive oil, or employed by mill companies or cooperatives to describe this season's oils for their customers.

They may also support the producer in understanding the best time to harvest and to identify distinctions among the different qualities of oils harvested in the fall, be commissioned to be judges in competitions, or employed as educators for consumers at workshops or masterclasses. Some sommeliers work with retailers or restaurants to select extra-virgin olive oils for sale and recommend the pairing of oils with foods.

The art, science, language, and rituals of the professional sommelier may seem mysterious and daunting to many people. But with an understanding of the basics of taste and an open mind, anyone can begin to discern the distinct flavors of extra-virgin olive oils that denote high quality and health benefits.

REMEMBER

At the time of writing this book, there's no specific qualification that defines terms you may come across such as "oleologist" or "master of olive oil." But for an individual to describe themselves as an *olive oil sommelier*, it would be expected that they have completed a recognized, reputable, and certificated olive oil sommelier course, which was delivered by an instructor who is among the most experienced in the field.

Some institutions deliver sommelier training with advancing levels of achievement, and the qualifications will be recognized by authorities involved in regulation of olive oil production.

FROM THE AUTHORS

Simon teaches the health modules on the New York and London Olive Oil Times five-day sommelier courses. Meeting the extraordinary people who complete the course and witnessing their transformation under the tutelage of some of the world's greatest experts in olive oil is an extraordinary privilege.

The language of aroma and flavor

As you become more experienced and confident in tasting different extra-virgin olive oils, you'll begin to compare your impressions with any tasting notes or descriptions on bottle labels or producers' websites.

REMEMBER

Professional tasters will bring years of experience and expertise to any commentary, but it's important to allow yourself the freedom to form your own views. Perceptions will depend on many of your personal experiences as well as the foods you have grown up with. As you develop your interest in exploring various oils, you'll begin to refine your palate and opinions.

THE AUTHORS' EVOO FAVORITES

Simon has particular favorite extra-virgin olive oils because their smell or taste recall happy childhood memories in Wales. There is a Picual variety extra-virgin olive oil from Spain with a particularly beautiful aroma, combining cut grass and meadow flowers that evokes a summer's day in the garden. A Sicilian Nocellara del Belice oil has strong notes of tomato on the vine, reminding him of his first experience of growing tomatoes from seed in a greenhouse.

While Amy appreciates every olive oil cultivar she has tasted and enjoys pairing them with various foods, it's the varieties from places that she loves, which evoke the best memories for her. Carolea olives from Calabria and Intosso from Abruzzo in Southern Italy, Koroneiki from Greece, Biancolilla from Sicily, Arbequina from Spain, and Picholine from Morocco are some of her favorites.

Discovering Oleo Tourism

There is a promising future for oleo tourism in most producing areas, not just confined to those regions long established as vacation destinations, such as Southern Italy. The Olive Oil Times reported in 2024 on the increasing potential for educational and recreational oleo tourism in places like the Central Coast of California where social media posts and informal recommendations are resulting in a dramatic increase of visitors to olive oil mills in that region.

Considering that there are olive groves in many parts of the world, why not visit a region where olive oil is produced? Some regions are just begging to be explored, particularly where the climate or history is attractive to visitors from other countries.

Locals involved in olive oil production are passionate about what they do and are usually keen to show others the skill and hard work that goes into creating a fine extra-virgin olive oil. In olive oil producing regions, there are initiatives — sometime sponsored by local authorities — to encourage educational trips for local schoolchildren to engage them in their important heritage.

For travelers from afar, a visit to an olive grove can be seen advertised as part of tour packages and cruise ship shore days.

Planning your visit to a grove

For most olive farmers, their land is also their home, and it's courteous to call or e-mail ahead of time if you want to visit. Unplanned visits may work out fine in a serendipitous way, but it's also possible that you'll find no one at home. Alternatively, you may be greeted by a frustrated owner who could misinterpret your intentions. Therefore, we don't recommend showing up at an olive grove, or any other farm unexpected.

It's often possible to visit a farm and mill that are located in close proximity to each other. Most guided tours will include a visit to see the olive trees in their natural environment, especially if they grow in a place of historical or cultural significance or are particularly ancient trees. The size of olive groves and mills vary considerably. Sometimes the mill is small and services a single estate, and others may be a large commercial venture that buys the olives from farmers and then labels and sells the oil to consumers abroad. In Spain specifically, mills may be owned by a cooperative of farmers.

A tour may progress from the grove where you'll be introduced to the way in which the farm is managed, and end at the mill where you will see firsthand the equipment used for the processing of the oil from the fruit. If you plan your trip properly, or go as a part of a tour, you'll probably also enjoy a tasting, some locally made products, and perhaps even a meal. Amy's tours also include visits to ancient mills and ruins where it's possible to show the contrast between how olive oil was once produced in the same region in antiquity and how it's currently produced.

Preplanning a visit to an olive mill during harvest time may even offer the experience of picking olives, seeing them pressed, and buying the olive oil. Make sure you ask for advice on the most appropriate clothes and footwear before your visit. And observe all the health and safety protocols provided by your guide.

Combining travel experiences

Exploring an olive oil producing region can begin at home by searching online for information about mills, museums, and specialist shops. Once you arrive at your destination, you can go to local tourist information offices for assistance.

Here are a few ways you can make the most of a trip:

TIP

>> **Olive oil grove and wine tours.** In many countries, olive trees thrive with grape vines, and some producers offer the opportunity to combine a visit to their winery with a visit to an olive oil mill. For example, if you are visiting South Africa's wine route in Stellenbosch, you can download a helpful map of olive oil producers called *The Guide to Extra Virgin Olive Oil in South Africa (EVOOSA)*.

>> **All-inclusive tours.** Some tourist boards combine oleo tourism with experiences that relate to the production of olive oil. Tours include boutique accommodations and restaurants featuring local oil that is integrated into regional cuisine, creating a comprehensive oleo tourism experience. See the next section for information about tour packages sponsored by olive oil mills (see Figure 23-1).

FROM THE
AUTHORS

>> **Virtual reality tours.** A memorable experience for Simon at the Picualia mill in Andalusia, Spain included being given the opportunity to play in their virtual reality studio. Visitors can engage in many aspects of olive oil production by using a headset and imagined instruments such as a pole for harvesting.

>> **Olive oil museums.** Olive oil museums, especially in towns that rely on olive oil production, may be part of an olive oil trail (for visiting different groves) in order to provide another boost to the local economy. Museums provide fascinating insights into the history of olive oil production, with reference to the land and the generations of people who had a relationship with olive oil. You may see reconstructions of ancient equipment such as donkey driven stones for milling, mats for pressing the juice from the crushed oil, and old *amphorae* (vases) for storage.

>> **Festivals.** Time your travel to coincide with an olive oil festival and enjoy a variety of events that celebrate olive oil.

Festivals often occur after the harvest has been completed. The origins may go back many hundreds of years and be linked with giving thanks for another year's gift of nature successfully gathered in.

TIP

If you're passing through Edirne in Turkey in June, you'll definitely want to stop to witness the longest running sports competition in the world — *kirkpinar*. This "modern" olive oil wrestling event has run since 1346 with pugilists squaring up to each other entirely covered in olive oil. It follows a tradition of oil wrestling that can be dated back to 2500 BCE in ancient Babylon, Egypt, Iran, and Assyria. It's said that Atilla the Hun settled a dispute by olive oil wrestling. The defeated foe relinquished substantial lands and financial tributes. This would surely be one of the most fascinating oleo tourism events to write home about. And it's perhaps not a bad way to settle a dispute with a neighbor!

FIGURE 23-1: Tasting Room at the Olive Oil House, Corfu Town

Courtesy of The Governor

Tasting at the mill

Some mill owners will offer visitors the opportunity to taste and buy their oil at their mills. This experience is very special, particularly when fresh olive oil is available soon after harvest time.

At larger mills, staff may be on hand to help you taste the oil. The area may produce different varietal oils, and some mills may have shops that stock other products made from their oil, including olive oil preserves, pastes, chocolate, and even beauty products.

REMEMBER

To get the most from a mill visit, it's best to do your research beforehand. There are some amazing places to visit. You may have an even richer experience than you expected. For example, the LA Organic mill near the historic city of Ronda in Spain hosts tasting and tours of their estate in golf carts. You can also view some exquisite artwork designs created in collaboration with the internationally acclaimed architect Philippe Starck.

TIP

Where a mill is owned by an estate, there's sometimes a complete package offered of accommodations, olive oil tasting, a guided tour of the grove, and a dinner combining local cuisine with the oil. For example, the Villa Campestri, run by the Pasquali family, is one of the first and most innovative olive oil resorts. It's set in the beautiful and historic region of Mugello, Tuscany where you can plant an olive tree, paint the landscape, meet the hens that peck beneath the olive leaf canopy, or celebrate a wedding in the grove. You can find more information on their website www.villacampestri.com/en.

For people who want to enjoy a vacation that is focused on olive oil and other culinary experiences from a region, there's the possibility of joining a group hosted by an expert. Oldways, the Boston-based nonprofit organization that promotes tradition diets including the Mediterranean lifestyle, offers escorted tours in Europe. The Master Chef UK winner, writer, and qualified olive oil sommelier Irini Tzortzoglou is at the vanguard of experts to host retreats experiencing olive oil and Greek island life.

FROM THE AUTHORS

With her extensive experiences of cultures of the Mediterranean, Amy has for several years led cuisine, culture, and wellness tours to numerous places, including Italy, Egypt, Greece, Turkey, and Morocco. Visiting olive groves, explaining the culinary heritage and health benefits, and sharing the joy of preparing and cooking meals together, Amy has taught guests about olive oil at the source, which provides them with knowledge that they can use for life. Touring the olive groves allow tourists the opportunity to truly experience the blessings of the land and the role of the olive fruit in the local culture.

IN THIS CHAPTER

» **Discovering the latest production and quality standards**

» **Understanding the opportunities for education**

» **Appreciating discussions about extra-virgin olive**

Chapter **24**

The Future of Olive Oil

The olive tree is continuing its historical journey of expansion to new regions. Olive oil production is modernizing, and as its value for health and nutrition is becoming more widely understood and recognized, it's being incorporated into the diets of people far from the Mediterranean. Yet, it also clings to its ancient pedigree as a symbol of peace and hope. With changing climates and increasing interest in olive oil, the story of the olive tree and its oil will continue to evolve.

As more consumers recognize the benefits of regularly enjoying extra-virgin olive oil (EVOO), there's no doubt that it has a bright future. Despite the challenges of rising production costs, changing climate conditions, and devastating conflicts in some parts of the world, the enduring relationship between humans and the ancient olive tree and its fruit continues to flourish.

Recent discoveries about the extraordinary health benefits of extra-virgin olive oil and the increasing recognition of its range of exquisite flavors have resulted in an exponential rise in interest measured by Internet search analytics and other parameters.

In this chapter, we discuss the latest developments and innovations in olive oil.

Cultivating Better Production and Quality

As the awareness of the importance of high-quality extra-virgin olive oil rises, people who are involved in its production and sales are exploring new ways to maximize efficiency and sustainability. The planting of new groves, and the introduction of modern technology and innovation to the ancient traditions of olive oil production should help to meet increased demand. These advances are able to support methods of farming that have a positive effect on the environment, while producing extra-virgin olive oil that has the potential to increase the health and well-being of many populations.

Identifying new innovations

The global olive oil market was valued at approximately $22.3 billion in 2022 and is projected to reach $33.12 billion by 2030. Therefore, improving quality and output from existing groves and milling processes is key to meeting future expectations of olive oil production. Large new intensive groves are also being established in regions such as Australia and New Zealand and the Middle East as well as expansion of existing farms in locations where there is a strong tradition of olive cultivation. This may involve expansion into land defined as having desert conditions.

Olive trees are one of the hardiest plants on Earth, but sometimes need the addition of water in areas with very low rainfall. This problem can be solved by installing new irrigation systems to maximize the efficiency of water usage.

Breeding and selecting olive varieties that show greater resistance to disease and improved yield are among collaborations with agricultural research facilities and universities. The objectives of the research are to find ways to reduce the need for pesticides and accelerate the move to more sustainable production systems.

Improving sustainability by combining new and traditional methods of recycling in all aspects of olive oil production contributes to the *circular economy* of olive oil — using all the by-products including those for fertilization or biofuels. Regenerative farming is also using new technology to create more biodiverse and *carbon-sequestering* groves (the trees capture and store carbon from the atmosphere).

The use of drones, satellite imaging, and AI are helping to bring precision farming to large olive groves. For example, measuring the leaf density from aerial analysis can help farmers make decisions about the timing and degree of tree pruning required. Smart sensors can measure soil temperatures and moisture in real time to indicate when to provide irrigation.

There are opportunities for further automation of pruning and harvesting with robotic machinery to decrease costs and waste, and to improve quality through increased efficiency. Milling and storage technology have improved over the years and continue to be refined to decrease the risks of damage to the olives and to minimize exposure to heat, light, and oxidation during oil production and storage.

Researchers are also beginning to address environmental changes using advanced climate modeling to predict, adapt, and mitigate the impact of climate change on olive production. The International Olive Council (IOC) has committed to investing in further exploration of how olive oil production can improve our environment and the health of our planet.

Improving standards and traceability

Olive oil contains healthy unsaturated fats, but the greatest benefits come from the combination of those healthy fats with polyphenols in extra-virgin olive oil. (See Chapter 6 for more information on polyphenols.) Many olive oil producers are changing strategy to focus on harvesting earlier in the season and using technology to improve quality and polyphenol levels to make even finer olive oils. The end result is usually premium tasting oils that are better for health. The yield may be lower for a higher-quality extra-virgin olive oil, but this is usually balanced by the additional price educated consumers are willing to pay.

Meanwhile, agencies involved in regulating the market have more sophisticated tests to make sure that extra-virgin olive oil is genuine, unadulterated, and meets the minimum standards. It's interesting to note that scientific studies suggest that professional sommeliers are still more likely to be able to recognize defects in olive oil better than laboratory analysis, which shows the extraordinary sensitivity and accuracy of a trained human taster.

Traceability is important to ensure that extra-virgin olive oil is authentic, and new authentication programs in blockchain technology are supporting the process. *Blockchain technology* is a decentralized digital ledger that records transactions across multiple computers in such a way that the registered transactions cannot be altered. It can be used to ensure the traceability and authenticity of olive oil. Producers can record each step of the production process on the blockchain, from the harvesting of olives to the bottling of the oil. Consumers and retailers can verify the authenticity and quality of the olive oil by accessing the blockchain, for example, from a QR code, ensuring that they are purchasing genuine and high-quality extra-virgin olive oil. These systems are already in use by some producers in Argentina, Tunisia, and Spain.

Spreading the Great News of EVOO

Unfortunately, extra-virgin olive oil is still a niche food in many countries. The Mediterranean diet, widely accepted as one of the healthiest dietary patterns, is still only embraced and fully understood by a small segment of the world's population. Most people regularly make processed food choices based on convenience and often morally dubious marketing strategies of food manufacturers.

However, research suggests that more people are turning to extra-virgin olive oil, and surveys reveal that new consumers of olive oil are especially focused on its health benefits. This is good for society and sustainability.

For those who are involved in promoting the benefits, it's important to be informed, truthful, passionate and to declare any conflict of interest. For producers, there's a need to comply with trading and advertising standards. At the heart of any communication should be integrity and respect for the audience.

Promoting the health benefits of EVOO

In Part 2, the established and evolving research on the health benefits of extra-virgin olive oil and the Mediterranean diet is described in detail. Future studies are likely to consolidate and expand the existing scientific database, exploring even more aspects of the polyphenols in extra-virgin olive oil and their effects on oxidative stress, inflammation, hormone regulation, and the gut microbiome. It's important that this evidence will be made available for the public and communicated in a way that faithfully translates the science into understandable concepts.

Even though many people have heard of the benefits of the Mediterranean diet and olive oil, surveys show that most only have a very superficial understanding. They may not know the difference between refined olive oil and extra-virgin olive oil and certainly don't know the significance of polyphenols for health and flavor. Even people who appear to know the principles of the Mediterranean diet are unlikely to be enjoying enough of the right type of extra-virgin olive oil.

There's also widespread misinformation about olive oil. It certainly cannot be replaced by other fats, including seed or vegetable oils, even if those oils are promoted as being healthy or given unregulated status such as "cold pressed" or "virgin." As a fat, olive oil adds calories, but as part of a Mediterranean diet, it doesn't add pounds to weight or inches to waistline. The extraordinary fruit juice of the olive tree possesses qualities from its varied polyphenols, which are unique and respond to its environment. Cooking with olive oils is not only desirable but is actually desirable and integral to the Mediterranean diet.

Its comparative cost must be considered in the context of the value it brings to one's health.

Many educated health professionals recommend the regular consumption of extra-virgin olive oil. Organizations involved in medical care are realizing that the current model of attempting to reverse illnesses with drugs and surgery is not as effective as making lifestyle changes that can prevent disease in the first place. The Mediterranean diet is recommended in the current US Dietary guidelines and in the future it's likely that more public health institutions around the world will acknowledge the incontrovertible evidence that already exists and encourage the adoption of a diet which has extra-virgin olive oil at its core.

There's increasing interest in extra-virgin olive oil beyond Europe and America, in regions such as the Middle East, India, and China. Extra-virgin olive oil is much loved in Japan, after its introduction in experimental agriculture in the late 19th century, followed by increased public health awareness and chefs successfully exploring its versatile inclusion in traditional cuisine. Other countries in Asia are following this example.

Extra-virgin olive oil is even traveling beyond the limits of our world, with support from NASA, the European Space Agency, and the Italy Space Agency. It has provided important nutrition for astronauts on the International Space Station, in anticipation that it will help mitigate the physical and psychological stresses of life away from Earth.

With rising awareness of the extraordinary qualities of extra-virgin olive oil, it's important that people know how to get the most from the best oils, appreciate why olive oil is so healthy and delicious, and understand how to enjoy it. Education and communication are key to a future where people can see and realize the benefits of extra-virgin olive oil every day.

Creating opportunities for further education

There are different ways to access credible information about olive oil, but everyone must be wary of unreliable and false claims that often circulate on the Internet and social media channels.

Producers are finding more ways of reaching out to existing and potential new consumers with information about their oils. And customers want to be assured that they are buying oils based on trustworthy, accurate, and validated descriptions. Mill owners also have a role in education by welcoming the public to see how extra-virgin olive oil is produced. Olive grove and mill tours are popular travel experiences known as *oleo tourism*, which is discussed in more detail in Chapter 23.

Organizations that represent producers clearly have an interest in publishing positive news about olive oil. However, producers must comply with regulations and laws that govern what they can say in order to ensure high standards and an outstanding reputation are maintained.

There are online publications that are reviewed by editors with expertise in olive oil or are written by health professionals, which are available to consumers. In particular, websites such as the Harvard University's T.H. Chan School of Public Health's Nutrition Source (https://nutritionsource.hsph.harvard.edu) can be very helpful in ensuring people have access to up-to-date information.

The Olive Wellness Institute is a science repository on the nutrition, health and wellness benefits of olives and olive products, subject to extensive peer review and informed by an independent scientific advisory panel. It's a social responsibility venture sponsored by industry, the Australian government, and the not-for-profit research and development corporation for Australian horticulture. It has very useful resources for health professionals and the public.

The Olive Oil Times is an independent industry online publication that provides comprehensive news and opinions on all aspects of olive oil, as well as organizing the New York competition and sommelier courses.

The UC Davis Olive Center is a world-renowned center bringing together nearly 60 UC faculty members, research specialists, and farm advisors who address the research and education needs of California olive growers and processors. The center also collaborates with institutions worldwide.

Efforts have been underway to establish an entity at the Yale School of Public Health with the vision to advance research and scholarship, education, and preservation, focusing on the olive tree and its products. The concept is to provide a centralized hub to facilitate and oversee various research initiatives focused on understanding the health benefits associated with olive oil consumption and playing a pivotal role in fostering collaboration among researchers, institutions, and experts in the field.

The physical health and psychological well-being of populations is not just of interest to public health organizations. Simon had the privilege of Chairing the first *Food Values* conference at the Pontifical Academy of Sciences, which brought nutrition scientists, food technologists, chefs, culinary institutes, and public health specialists together at the Vatican to discuss the future advancement of healthy and sustainable dietary patterns including the Mediterranean diet with extra-virgin olive oil.

Some governments and educational institutions are recognizing that the study of nutrition should be incorporated into school curricula, including at universities. Schools can equip individual students with the skills to keep them healthy, and perhaps begin to reverse the rise in chronic illnesses in populations. There is certainly an opportunity to teach younger generations about basic nutrition and the advantages of traditional dietary patterns such as the Mediterranean diet rich in bioactive compounds like those in extra-virgin olive oil. A program at Yale University has shown that dramatic increases in adherence to the Mediterranean diet and consumption of extra-virgin olive oil among students can be achieved through the communication of its benefits.

Culinary schools, like the Culinary Institute of America, are reversing past shortcomings in chef training about nutrition by including an appreciation of extra-virgin olive oil in their courses.

Medical schools, lifestyle medicine institutions, and nutrition courses are beginning to incorporate the Mediterranean diet with extra-virgin olive oil into their programs. As a member of the International Academy of Nutrition Educators and the Global Institute for Food, Nutrition and Health in Cambridge, United Kingdom, Simon has the pleasure of regularly teaching students about the health properties of extra-virgin olive oil.

There are even more opportunities to educate and inspire people further about extra-virgin olive oil through health and well-being events in communities or in a workplace setting, collaborating with healthcare providers, companies, and other interested organizations. There's evidence that this improves performance and can be made into fun, team-building exercises. Tutored extra-virgin olive oil tastings, seminars (perhaps in collaboration with producers), or cooking classes and demonstrations with a chef who is knowledgeable about extra-virgin olive oil can provide audiences with interactive and enjoyable educational events.

FROM THE AUTHORS

When Amy and Simon host an event on the history, traditions, health, taste, and culinary applications of extra-virgin olive oil, it's extraordinarily rewarding to witness the changes in people's understanding and appreciation of this "liquid gold." Oftentimes, participants in their events report a noted change in overall health after using good-quality olive oil as a gateway to the Mediterranean lifestyle.

For the regions that produce olive oil, cultural festivals and programs that celebrate extra-virgin olive oil along with Mediterranean cuisine can attract diverse audiences from the locality or further afield. These events provide the opportunity for disseminating information and foster a grassroots recognition of the importance of extra-virgin olive oil. People who are passionate about furthering olive oil education are valuable ambassadors.

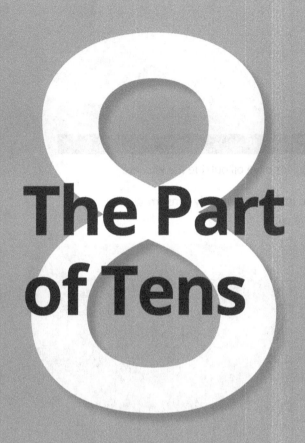

The Part of Tens

IN THIS PART . . .

Explore the uses for olive oil outside the kitchen.

Identify ways to increase your daily consumption of extra-virgin olive oil.

Chapter **25**

Ten Other Uses for Olive Oil

O live oil has been used to make soaps, creams, cosmetics, and many other beauty products for millennia. Stores across the Mediterranean region (and in upscale boutiques around the world) sell olive oil–infused soaps, skin care products, and conditioners for the hair.

In this chapter, we share how extra-virgin olive oil (EVOO) can be used outside of the kitchen. We also provide historical references to cultural practices to help you understand the benefits of using olive oil in skin care as well as discover its healing properties.

Note: The application of olive oil to the skin is a very ancient use as a natural beauty product. However, it should be used with caution — under medical advice and supervision if you have any underlying skin conditions, allergies or other relevant medical conditions. It has been traditionally used to shield skin from sun damage, but it cannot be relied upon on its own to give adequate protection as a sunscreen if you have concerns about ultraviolet (UV) exposure and risk of sunburn.

EVOO IN BEAUTY PRODUCTS

Researchers are studying possible effects of olive oil on skin moisture levels, protection from UV radiation, and the potential for vitamin E, squalene, and polyphenols to have local anti-inflammatory, antioxidant, antibacterial, and even anticancer effects on the skin. Polyphenols like Oleocanthal and Oleacein found exclusively in extra virgin olive oil have been shown to reduce wrinkles and other signs of aging, positioning extra virgin olive oil as a key focus in anti-aging research.

Just like the concerns about processed foods, there are some disturbing suggestions of possible harmful physical and environmental effects of industrial chemicals added to many commercial skin care products. Olive oil–based skin products are often formulated with entirely natural ingredients.

In ancient times, olive oil was used for everyday bathing rituals but was also available in attractive cosmetics and made to use delicate, scented perfumes. Today, it's possible to enjoy the effects of olive oil with simple homemade recipes or to find good quality soaps and creams online or in stores. Skin care companies like Furtuna Skin, a US-based company that sources its ingredients from a family-owned estate in Sicily, are leading the way in creating exquisite new premium cosmetic products with sustainability and environmental credentials, redefining the relationship between skin care and nature.

FROM THE AUTHORS

As a cookbook author interested in helping her readers eat the best foods possible, culinary recipes are invaluable to Amy. As a woman on a constant quest to look her best, however, she prizes beauty "recipes" just as much. They were every bit as important in her childhood as preparing food was. She remembers leafing through her maternal great-grandmother's recipe cards with her mother as a preteen. Mixed in with the Easter bread, Christmas cookie, and spicy tomato sauce recipes were other cards with ingredients that promised clearer, smoother skin, and shinier hair when applied properly. When they saw the first beauty recipe card, Amy's mother looked at her and exclaimed, "Look, she did just what you do!"

Years of traveling and working in Morocco, Italy, Greece, Turkey, Egypt, the Middle East, and so on — through spice markets and into the herbalists and food markets — have confirmed Amy's theory that what does well for the insides of our body can be a safe, multipurpose beauty product. While researching her second book *Nile Style: Egyptian Cuisine and Culture* (Hippocrene Books) with Egyptian doctors, historians, and Egyptologists, Amy learned of Cleopatra's usage of olive oil as a beauty ingredient.

Amy also shares in this chapter her own tried-and-true beauty recipes with olive oil and other natural products, which can save you time and money.

Bathing in olive oil

Homer described the use of olive oil in bathing rituals. In the *Odyssey*, the princess Nausicaa and her maidens bathe and anoint themselves with olive oil. Olive oil, sometimes infused with aromatic herbs and essences, was also used during massage treatments following bathing and left on the skin.

For your own royal bath, pour a few capfuls of olive oil into your bathtub as you run the bath water. Stir to combine and enjoy. Soak for as long as desired. Be sure to clean the bathtub after each treatment to prevent it from being slippery.

Removing Makeup

In ancient Greece and Rome, olive oil was applied to the skin for cleansing and removed with a special instrument called a *strigil*. However, to remove your makeup, you don't need to buy a special tool or a beauty brand's makeup remover.

Place 1 tablespoon of olive oil in a small bowl. Dip a clean washcloth into the oil and wipe over your face to remove the makeup. Rinse and follow with your regular cleanser.

Glossing and Nourishing Your Hair

Olive oil was used to condition hair, prevent split ends, and promote hair growth in antiquity. The Greeks and Romans applied olive oil to the hair and scalp, then massaged gently to promote blood flow and stimulate the hair follicles. It was believed that olive oil prevented premature graying of the hair. Nowadays, olive oil is said to prevent hair loss by blocking the action of hormones often responsible for causing it in the first place.

For glossy hair, place a few drops of extra-virgin olive oil into a small bowl or container. Dip your fingers into the olive oil. Rub onto fly-aways or dry areas of your hair. This practice can be done at night for extremely dry hair.

Shaving Oil

The Roman physician Galen wrote extensively on the use of olive oil in skin care. He described how olive oil mixed with other ingredients was used to create creams and ointments for both cosmetic and medicinal purposes. "Olive oil is a soothing agent, suitable for softening the skin and relieving irritations."

Because olive oil can soothe the skin, it can replace your regular shaving cream. Use ¼ cup of extra-virgin olive oil to slather a few tablespoons of oil on each leg (or your face) and shave. Remember to wash the oil residue from shower or bathtub after using to prevent slipping.

Making Facial Masks

Cleopatra is said to have used facial masks (to avoid wrinkles and improve complexion; the recipes are below), and hair treatments made out of olive oil. Nowadays many fashion models and stars of screen and stage use olive oil both internally and externally to enhance their looks.

In addition to consuming olive oil daily, Sophia Loren, for example, said she rubs a small amount into her skin to kept her complexion glossy and moisturized. She even added a few capfuls into a hot bath for a nourishing skin soak. (Amy's great grandmother passed down a skin care routine of using olive oil for skin care.)

Cleopatra's Facial Mask

Ingredients:

2 tablespoons white clay (I use Moroccan ghassoul)
2 tablespoons milk
1 tablespoon honey
1 tablespoon of extra-virgin olive oil

Directions:

Place all the ingredients in a medium bowl. Mix well to combine. Apply this mask on your face. Allow to dry for 10 to 15 minutes and when dry, rinse with lukewarm water.

Pliny the Elder described how olive oil was used both as a cosmetic and medicinal treatment, emphasizing its role in maintaining healthy skin, saying "Olive oil prevents wrinkles and heals all chaps and roughness of the skin, provided it is applied before the time of taking a bath."

Cleopatra's Wrinkle-Prevention Mask

Ingredients:

2 tablespoons whipping cream
2 tablespoons extra-virgin olive oil
1 tablespoon honey
4–6 cucumber slices

Directions:

Mix the first three ingredients together in a small bowl. Add the cucumber slices and allow to soak for 15 to 30 minutes. Wrap a towel around your neck just in case the mask ingredients drip. Then lie down on a comfortable surface and apply the cucumbers to the affected areas on your face. Gently message cucumbers into the skin and allow to sit for 10 to 15 minutes. Remove and rinse skin. Repeat weekly.

Treating Your Hair

While we don't know whether Cleopatra used the following hair treatment, you can use it on your entire head of hair or just the ends of your hair.

Warm Oil Hair Treatment

Ingredients:

2 tablespoons extra-virgin olive oil
2 tablespoons castor or almond oil

Directions:

Combine the oils in a small pot and warm over low heat. When the mixture is cool enough to touch, massage into your scalp, spreading on the length of your hair. Cover with a shower cap and towel and allow to sit for 30 minutes. Wash and condition your hair as normal.

Exfoliating Your Skin

The ancient Greek playwright Aristophanes made references to the use of olive oil highlighting its role in daily life and personal care rituals, writing; "You must anoint yourself with oil and make your skin shine like the goddess Aphrodite." The Roman poet Ovid observed of his characters; "With olive oil, they anoint their limbs, making their bodies gleam like polished marble."

You can use the following recipe to exfoliate or "polish" your skin or lips.

Exfoliating Lip and Body Scrub

Ingredients:

2 tablespoons extra-virgin olive oil
2 tablespoons sugar or coffee grounds

Directions:

Mix the olive oil and coffee grounds well in a small bowl. Slather the mixture over the body and message gently into skin or lips to exfoliate. Rinse off well. Be sure to clean the bathtub or shower after exfoliating to prevent slipping.

Conditioning Your Hands

The ancient Greek physician Hippocrates mentions the use of olive oil in his medical texts, noting its benefits for skin conditions and wound healing and recommending olive oil as a treatment for skin abrasions and as a base for ointments.

Amy uses this skin treatment when she rubs leftover olive oil from cooking into her hands because it helps combat dryness from washing dishes. It can also be used to condition cuticles during a manicure. Just rub a few drops onto cuticles and massage in for a minute or two before using the cuticle stick for shaping.

Moisturizing Your Skin

Storing extra-virgin olive oil in our kitchen cabinets is commonplace, but it's every bit as useful in bathrooms as well. The ancient Egyptians used scented oils, olive oil, and ointments to clean and soften their skin and to protect it from the sun and wind.

While there are many high-quality beauty products containing olive oil on the market, making them yourself can be easy and fun. Olive oil, when applied topically, increases collagen in the skin, leading to greater elasticity and reducing the appearance of dark under-eye circles. The same antioxidants that work to influence age-associated changes inside the body, may affect appearance and smooth the skin overall, which can help prevent wrinkles from forming. Here are a couple of moisturizing applications.

All-over skin remedy. Try extra-virgin olive oil as a moisturizer for extra dry skin, eczema, diaper-rash, and cradle cap by applying a few drops to the affected area and rubbing it in.

Cracked heel repair. Use a pumice stone to gently exfoliate the heels and wipe the excess skin off with a cloth. Massage 1 teaspoon of extra-virgin olive oil into your feet and heels, put on clean socks and allow treatment to work while you sleep.

Cleansing Makeup Brushes

Adding olive oil to your makeup brush cleaning ritual is a won-derful way to keep the bristles of the brushes soft. Many people clean with soap alone, but most soaps have a drying effect. The addition of olive oil helps to moisturize the brushes.

Makeup Brush Cleaner

Ingredients:

2 tablespoons antibacterial liquid soap
1 tablespoon extra-virgin olive oil

Directions:

In a tall glass or cylindrical-shaped container, mix the soap and olive oil with a cup of water. Mix well to combine. Add the cosmetic brushes and allow to soak for 15 minutes. Drain the liquid, rinse the brushes well, and towel dry. Allow the brushes to dry completely before use.

EVOO IN HEALING

If you've ever seen the movie *My Big Fat Greek Wedding,* you may recall the father's comical usage of Windex as a cure-all solution. In Amy's family, and in many families around the Mediterranean region, it's actually olive oil that is used with the same enthusiasm in folk medicine. Olive oil and wild thyme are consumed together in order to help respiratory issues in the Eastern Mediterranean. Olive oil and fried onions and/or garlic are used to help cure bronchial issues in Southern Italy. Olive oil is often commonly applied to baby's gums when teething and as a remedy for ear wax.

Chapter 26

Ten Easy Ways to Consume More Extra-Virgin Olive Oil

The average consumption of extra-virgin olive oil (EVOO) in most parts of the world, including the United States and Northern Europe, is less than 1 liter per person per year. Between 2 and 5 tablespoons of olive oil are consumed each day in the traditional diets of people in Spain, Italy, and Greece, which is recommended by scientists and validated in the Mediterranean Diet Adherence scores (see Chapter 7). This daily amount equates to between 14 and 20 liters per person per year.

In this chapter, we provide ten strategies to help you increase your daily consumption of extra-virgin olive oil. Increasing your understanding and enjoyment of the oil adds pleasure and health to your life in remarkable and unprecedented ways. When you start to incorporate these strategies into the meals you prepare, you can also share the beautiful flavors and textures of foods rich in extra-virgin olive oil with family and friends.

Cooking with EVOO

Earlier chapters address the well-established evidence for the safety and desirability of cooking with extra-virgin olive oil. We hope we have convinced you beyond any doubt that it's perfect for every aspect of preparing foods. Using liberal amounts of extra-virgin olive oil as a cooking medium or for adding texture and flavor to meals are only a few benefits. Extra-virgin olive oil's health benefits include protective properties that increase when combined with the nutrients in other ingredients.

To get the most out of vegetables, cook them with extra-virgin olive oil whenever possible rather than boiling or steaming them, which results in many of the nutrients being lost.

You may cook whatever you have in refrigerator — choosing to fry or roast a combination of colorful vegetables with some meat, fish, lentils or beans with your everyday extra-virgin olive oil. Alternatively, you can reach for something previously batch-cooked and frozen, create a dish using a base recipe from Chapter 17, or prepare one of Amy's other delicious recipes in Part 6.

Drizzling for Added Flavor

After a meal is on the plate, adding a final drizzle of extra-virgin olive oil for a burst of freshness and taste is a great way to enhance and lift the ingredients to another level. It can refine the texture and appearance of the foods, garnishing and seasoning the dish. It also delivers those extraordinary polyphenols.

It's also great to have the option to choose between a delicate or more robust oil, depending on your preferences and food choices through the day.

Prioritizing Your Health

A good extra-virgin olive oil is a delicious foundation ingredient and flavor-enriching food. It's the cornerstone of the Mediterranean diet and has extraordinary health benefits, which are explored in detail in Part 2.

FROM THE DOCTOR

Increasing your intake of extra-virgin olive oils rich in polyphenols, which impart some pleasant pungency and spiciness to the flavor, is an investment in your physical and mental health and well-being. Simon's experience in his medical practice is that his patients who have increased their consumption of extra-virgin olive oil return within weeks with improved blood pressure and cholesterol levels, saying they felt better in body and mind.

Numerous studies discussed in earlier chapters point to the role of extra-virgin olive oil and the Mediterranean diet in providing protection from heart disease, stroke, diabetes, and many types of cancers. A study published in the journal *Experimental Gerontology* focused on the flip side of disease prevention, concluding that the diet improved quality of life, enhanced health, and improved cognition and mental health. In studies of younger populations, evidence shows reduced levels of anxiety and depression, translating to better psychological and emotional well-being.

Eating More Vegetables and Salads

Antonia Trichopoulou, the renowned professor and leading researcher in the Mediterranean diet, observes that Greeks eat three times the quantity of vegetables compared with Northern Europeans. This can be because vegetables and salads taste so much better when prepared and eaten cooked or raw with their beloved extra-virgin olive oil.

It's easy to increase the recommended amount and variety of vegetables if the flavors are combined with extra-virgin olive oil. The level of fiber, nutrients, and bioactive compounds like polyphenols found in vegetables also combine with the similar compounds in extra-virgin olive oil for an added health benefit.

Consuming EVOO throughout the Day

Research has shown that the silently powerful anti-inflammatory and antioxidant properties of a meal rich in extra-virgin olive oil can be measured with a significant reduction in biomarkers of inflammation. This occurs within a period of just a few hours and is maintained as long as the healthy diet is sustained.

Through every hour of the day and night, our bodies are vulnerable to *oxidative stress* (an imbalance of free radicals and antioxidants in the body) and pro-inflammatory factors associated with many chronic diseases in our internal and external environment. Studies have shown the risks of chronic "low-level" inflammation may be decreased by regularly consuming healthy nutrients and polyphenols from a diet rich in extra-virgin olive oil. This provides another incentive to eat it with every meal.

In the Mediterranean, it's usual to have extra-virgin olive oil with each meal, and the recipes in this book will help you do the same. If making olive oil–enriched meals every day is difficult, drizzle it over fruit, yogurt, oatmeal, ice cream, or dark chocolate. Some people may choose to start the day with a spoonful of olive oil for the health benefit.

Substituting with EVOO

A way to use more extra-virgin olive oil is to substitute it for another, perhaps more familiar food. An obvious choice is to use extra-virgin olive oil in place of butter or margarine. As an unprocessed healthy monounsaturated fat from a fruit, it's not solid at room temperature, but it can still be a much healthier option when it comes to drizzling on your toast or using it for breadmaking or baking. Chapter 16 provides guidance on how you can make the switch.

Extra-virgin olive oil in a dressing can be used instead of mayonnaise, or it can substitute for cream or cream cheese in dips or garnishes. Most importantly, use extra-virgin olive oil for all cooking and salad dressing when you may otherwise have used a vegetable or seed oil.

Introducing Children to EVOO

Children in Mediterranean countries are introduced to extra-virgin olive oil at an early age. It's considered the most natural thing in the world to encourage a young person to recognize and cherish the flavors of extra-virgin olive oil including developing a love of different taste experiences.

FROM THE AUTHORS

Simon and Amy have had some of the most rewarding experiences teaching young people about extra-virgin olive oil in schools. They embrace the new flavors and are keen to take their enthusiasm home to enhance their skills in preparing and cooking food and even teaching their elders a thing or two.

If a parent or guardian has time to prepare one of Amy's simple recipes with their child, it can create wonderful and precious moments, and hopefully inspire a lifetime of enjoying healthy food together.

Exploring New Tastes and Varieties

New varieties of extra-virgin olive oil from different parts of the world provide an opportunity to explore and consume more extra-virgin olive oil. The healthy pleasure of extra-virgin olive oil can be experienced even more if you are able to detect the varied sensations offered by the diverse range of extra-virgin olive oils.

From home tastings to reflecting on which oils may pair with particular recipes will make you more likely to find more ways to incorporate extra-virgin olive oil into your life.

Redefining the Value of EVOO

The unique nature of extra-virgin olive oil as an ancient, natural, and extraordinarily healthy pressed juice of the olive fruit makes it uniquely different from industrially produced and processed food. It's certainly not just another cooking oil.

When consumers understand more about extra-virgin olive oil, there is a natural progression to value it more highly. There's evidence that people are more likely to consider spending more money on extra-virgin olive oil than other food items.

In countries like the United States, Canada, and much of North Western Europe, the average percentage spent on food eaten at home is between 5 and 15 percent of disposable household income. Health-aware consumers are more likely to choose to spend more on better quality foods.

Continuing Your Journey through Travel

It's no exaggeration to say that for many people, bringing high-quality extra-virgin olive oil into their lives is the beginning of a lifelong journey. The connection may be confined to meals at home, using extra-virgin olive oil every day. Eventually, it may turn into travel adventures visiting the beautiful lands where olive trees grow, touring mills, or enrolling in tutored tastings and sommelier classes around the world.

Appendix

Metric Conversion Guide

Note: The recipes in this book weren't developed or tested using metric measurements. There may be some variation in quality when converting to metric units.

Volume

U.S. Units	Canadian Metric	Australian Metric
¼ teaspoon	1 milliliter	1 milliliter
½ teaspoon	2 milliliters	2 milliliters
1 teaspoon	5 milliliters	5 milliliters
1 tablespoon	15 milliliters	20 milliliters
¼ cup	50 milliliters	60 milliliters
⅓ cup	75 milliliters	80 milliliters
½ cup	125 milliliters	125 milliliters
⅔ cup	150 milliliters	170 milliliters
¾ cup	175 milliliters	190 milliliters
1 cup	250 milliliters	250 milliliters
1 quart	1 liter	1 liter
1½ quarts	1.5 liters	1.5 liters
2 quarts	2 liters	2 liters
2½ quarts	2.5 liters	2.5 liters
3 quarts	3 liters	3 liters
4 quarts (1 gallon)	4 liters	4 liters

Weight

U.S. Units	Canadian Metric	Australian Metric
1 ounce	30 grams	30 grams
2 ounces	55 grams	60 grams
3 ounces	85 grams	90 grams
4 ounces (¼ pound)	115 grams	125 grams
8 ounces (½ pound)	225 grams	225 grams
16 ounces (1 pound)	455 grams	500 grams (½ kilogram)

Length

Inches	Centimeters
0.5	1.5
1	2.5
2	5.0
3	7.5
4	10.0
5	12.5
6	15.0
7	17.5
8	20.5
9	23.0
10	25.5
11	28.0
12	30.5

Temperature (Degrees)

Fahrenheit	Celsius
32	0
212	100
250	120
275	140
300	150
325	160
350	180
375	190
400	200
425	220
450	230
475	240
500	260

Index

About the Authors

Simon B Poole, MD, is an internationally acclaimed motivational speaker, communicator, and consultant in health promotion and wellness with a focus on the Mediterranean diet and lifestyle; and the nutrition of extra-virgin olive oil. With more than 30 years' experience as a medical doctor and teacher in Cambridge, United Kingdom, Simon is widely published in the media, radio, TV and journals. He is the author of award-winning books and is a Senior International Collaborator with the Global Centre for Nutrition and Health in Cambridge and a member of the International Academy of Nutrition Educators. In 2018, he was honored with Fellowship of the British Medical Association and is a founding member of the Scientific Advisory Committee of the Olive Wellness Institute and the Mediterranean Lifestyle Medicine Institute, Simon teaches sommelier courses at the Olive Oil Times. He has given event, conference, masterclass, and seminar presentations across numerous platforms and venues to a variety of audiences in the United Kingdom, United States, the Middle East, Africa, and Australia, including the Pontifical Academy of Sciences in the Vatican, the Academy of Medical Royal Colleges, Ivy League universities, international food and beverage shows, and cultural exhibitions.

Dame Amy Riolo is a best-selling author, award-winning chef, television host, and Mediterranean lifestyle ambassador. The author of 18 books was named Knight of the Order of the Star of Italy by the President of the Italian Republic. She has also been dubbed "The Ambassador of Italian Cuisine in the US" by The Italian International Agency for Foreign Press, "Ambassador of the Italian Mediterranean Diet 2022–2024" by the International Academy of the Italian Mediterranean Diet in her ancestral homeland of Calabria, Italy, and "Ambassador of Mediterranean Cuisine in the World" by the Rome-based media agency *We The Italians*. In 2019, she launched her own private label collection of premium Italian imported culinary ingredients called **Amy Riolo Selections** including extra-virgin olive oil, balsamic vinegar, organic pasta, and pesto sauce from award-winning artisan companies.

Dedication

This book is dedicated to all those who devote their lives to working in partnership with the land to create genuine extra-virgin olive oil. It's hard work. It's challenging. It's a vocation. It's a passion. Amy and Simon salute you!

Authors' Acknowledgments

The authors are deeply indebted to Acquisitions Editor Tracy Boggier for her wisdom, support, and for sharing our passion for this very special project. We would like also to thank Donna Wright for editing the work with great care and understanding, and the illustrations team at Wiley for creating beautiful graphics. A special thanks goes out to Rachel Nix for her meticulous job of recipe editing and to Wendy Jo Peterson and Geri Goodale for their fantastic photography and styling. We truly appreciate the expert and efficient editorial support and guidance of Charlotte Kughen and thank Kristie Pyles for all of her support as well. We are uniquely privileged to have the vast experience and exceptional knowledge of Leandro Ravetti, Sian Armstrong, Dr. Claudia Guillaume, and the team of the Olive Wellness Institute all of whom provided the technical edit of the book. We are also very thankful to all of the wonderful producers who share their stories and olive oil with us.

From Simon: I will always be grateful to my family and friends for extra-virgin olive oil, and for their encouragement; and the author and sommelier Judy Ridgway who helped enormously with guidance and support during the writing of our co-authored book *The Olive Oil Diet* nearly 10 years ago.

Friends and professional colleagues throughout my medical career have provided invaluable insights, especially when we've discussed and debated the more nuanced aspects of nutrition research, teaching me the importance of challenging and scrutinizing evidence in search of truths.

I am indebted to fellow members of the Scientific Advisory Panel of the Olive Wellness Institute for their wisdom and common commitment to improving education and awareness about olive oil; and to Curtis Cord, editor in chief of the Olive Oil Times for inviting me to join his team of educators on the Olive Oil Sommelier courses. There is much to learn from the students who attend and from the world-renown experts who teach the course including Carola Dummer, Antonio Lauro, Kostas Liris, and Pablo Voitzuk.

Amy has, of course, been my constant companion and inspirational support during the writing of our books as well as our collaboration in educational masterclasses about the Mediterranean lifestyle and olive oil.

From Amy: The first person I think of to thank with this particular book is my dear friend Mirella Mengilde of the Italian Trade Agency in New York. If it hadn't been for her invitations to attend olive oil conferences and trade shows in Italy, I would have never been able to convert my passion for olive oil into a beloved portion of my career. I am also very thankful to my dear friends and collaborators Francesco Giovannelli and Antonio Iuliano for helping me to create my private label olive oil.

My earliest memories of cooking were with my mother, Faith Riolo, who taught me that food was not just something we eat to nourish ourselves but an edible gift that could be given to express love. I owe much of my professional culinary success to my father, Rick Riolo, for always believing in my talent and supporting my career goals. To my beloved little brother, Jeremy, you are my why, and I am grateful to be able to pass our family's knowledge down to you.

My nonna, Angela Magnone Foti, taught me to cook and bake, as well as valuable lessons that served me outside of the kitchen. My Yia Yia, Mary Michos Riolo, shared her beloved Greek traditions with me as well. I would probably never have published a cookbook if it weren't for my mentor, Sheilah Kaufman, who patiently taught me much more than I ever planned on learning. I am proud to pass her knowledge on to others. Without the assistance and guidance of my late friend, spirit sister, and healer Kathleen Ammalee Rogers, I would never have been able to realize my professional writing goals. I am very thankful to Chef Luigi Diotaiuti for always believing in me and for encouraging me to foster my dreams and goals. Even though I cannot mention everyone individually due to space constraints, know that if I have thanked you in a previous book, I would have liked to mention you here as well.

Many thanks to Melissa's Produce for their generous donation of produce for recipe development. And finally, I would like to thank my co-author, Dr. Simon Poole, for his tremendous knowledge and commitment to the cause of promoting health and happiness, for always inspiring me, and for valuing my voice. It is a pleasure and an honor to collaborate with you.

Publisher's Acknowledgments

Senior Managing Editor:
Kristie Pyles

Senior Acquisitions Editor:
Tracy Boggier

Project Editor: Donna Wright

Recipe Tester: Rachel Nix, RD

Technical Editor: Leandro Ravetti,
Sian Armstong,
Dr. Claudia Guillaume

Production Editor:
Saikarthick Kumarasamy

Color Insert Photographers:
Wendy Jo Peterson and
Grace Geri Goodale

Cover Image: © fcafotodigital/
Getty Images